LIFE BEYOND P

Part Two

THE INFINITE JOURNEY

Author's Note

In this book certain key words are capitalised because I'm using them in a specific way. Words mean different things to different people; the effectiveness of language depends on a consensus of meaning between speaker and listener. To communicate this material effectively I have had to be clear on exactly what I mean by the use of these key words in the context of this Enquiry.

*In **The Story of 'You'**, the first book in this series, I explained and defined these capitalised words as they arose. If you haven't read **The Story of 'You'**, please refer to the Glossary where they have been summarised, along with a few further definitions that appear in this book.*

Conversations have been edited for clarity and simplicity. Other people's personal details have generally been changed for privacy reasons.

Jez Alborough
London, March 2019

LIFE BEYOND PERSONALITY

Part Two

THE INFINITE JOURNEY

Jez Alborough

In discussion with Matthew Wherry

Still Point Press

First Edition

Published by Still Point Press 2019

ISBN: 978-1-9993541-3-8

www.lifebeyondpersonality.com

facebook.com/lifebeyondpersonality

For Seekers everywhere:
May this book be a mirror
in which you See
life beyond Personality.

A frog in a well cannot discuss the ocean,
Because he is limited by the size of his well.

A summer insect cannot discuss ice,
Because it knows only its own season.

A narrow-minded scholar cannot discuss the Tao,
Because he is constrained by his teachings.

Now you have come out of your banks
And seen the Great Ocean,
You know your own inferiority,
So it is now possible to discuss great principles with you.

Chuang Tzu (370 – 287 BC)

CONTENTS

*

WAKING UP

*

BEING

*

ADAPTATION

*

TEACHING

AWAKENING TEACHINGS

*

SHARING

*

Introduction

In my younger years I experienced a series of what I call 'Openings'. These took me beyond the perspective of a teenage boy into a place of Stillness, peace and heightened awareness and set me on a search to understand what they meant: What was the implication of that perspective to the Personality who seemed to be living this life when the Openings were not there?

Unlocking the secret of these Openings seemed to be the most important endeavour I could undertake in this life, much more important than anything I could learn at school or university. This questioning has sometimes set me apart from those around me. Socrates said: 'An unexamined life is not worth living.' It seems to me that many people would disagree because they find asking deep questions about who we think we are and how we live to be too confronting. The fact that you are reading this book could mean that you're not one of these people. Perhaps you have experienced an Opening, or maybe you just have the sense that there is something more to life, something the society you live in does not acknowledge.

In this book and its prequel, I share the answers I have found to the questions posed by the Openings. *The Story of 'You'* focusses on our Natural State of Being, how we lose it and start to live the Dream of Personality. *The Infinite Journey* examines what it means to Wake Up from that Dream, how this differs from the image of enlightenment that has been passed down to us and how life beyond Personality relates to the sometimes-confusing world of Spiritual Seeking and teaching.

Jez

A Message from Matthew

When Jez and I were having the discussions that formed the basis of The Story of 'You', *we were very clear that my role consisted of two parts: First, I was there to interview Jez about what he calls 'Life beyond Personality'. He says:*

> The Personality is the key to understanding the whole mystery of Non-Duality; once Personality is seen through, all becomes clear. But how do we see beyond Personality? First we have to understand what Personality is.

This is where I came in: My interviews were motivated by my own desire to understand what Jez means by Personality, and also to help him explain this elusive subject to others who are interested. To this end, my questions were designed to draw out a comprehensive description of his understanding of the formation and functioning of Personality. Jez felt it was a huge bonus that I came to this project without a deep understanding of the teachings of Non-Duality. He said this allowed me to approach the subjects we discussed without being burdened with preconceptions and 'too much knowledge'. (I think this was a compliment!)

The second part of my role in this project was to be an interrogator. Jez encouraged me to ask all the 'difficult, nitty-gritty' questions that he believes are sometimes glossed over when big statements are made about Spiritual issues. The idea was that, as well as having my own probing questions answered, I might at the same time answer some of the questions a reader might have. In this way I was acting as an intermediary between Jez and you.

During the interviews I was at times confused, elated, uncomfortable and even furious at what Jez said, but I always felt like I was being pulled beyond my usual worldview into a different perspective – a perspective that, I've come to realise, is beyond Personality.

Since The Story of 'You' *was published, several readers have asked how doing all those interviews with Jez has affected me, and whether I have Awakened as a result of this process. The short answer is: "Not yet," but there have been several notable effects that I've observed in my daily life.*

The most noticeable of these is Stillness. It started when Jez helped me gain insight into the busyness of my mind; that glimmer of Choice-less Awareness grew into a deeper understanding that this mind – which I usually took to be 'me' – is not who I am at all. This has given me an ongoing distance from the mind and its patterns and thought loops.

I've also experienced a lot more Joy in my life: I still worry about things, but when I do, I'm less identified with the worry. On the rare occasion that I'm really upset, I notice the inclination to Contract and shut down feeling. It seems the awareness of this inclination actually then stops that Contraction happening.

So my engagement with this Enquiry has given me a new perspective on life, and a new language with which to describe and understand it. I'm much more aware of my own Personality and better at realising when other people are acting from theirs.

Finally, there's one other big thing to share with you: Although I didn't Wake Up, since we finished The Story of 'You' *I've had an Opening. It didn't last long but it's had an important effect in my life: It's allowed me to go much further and deeper into this Enquiry. A lot of what we discussed in* The Story of 'You' *has opened up to me; it's no longer just a conceptual understanding. I know there's further to go on the Infinite Journey, but after everything I learned from those first interviews and my Opening, I feel like I'm ready for it.*

Matthew

REMEMBERING

1

OPENINGS

Glimpses beyond Personality

'If the doors of perception were cleansed,
Everything would appear to man as it is, Infinite.
For man has closed himself up,
Till he sees all things thro' narrow chinks of his cavern.'
— William Blake

Jez: Since we finished our first series of discussions, you've told me that you experienced an Opening. What was it about the experience that made you describe it as an Opening?

Matthew: Suddenly everything we've been talking about opened up to me... It became less conceptual and more real because I had a taste of it...

Jez: Try to describe what happened.

Matthew: I was walking past the village green... It was a beautiful day and I sat down in the shade of an oak tree for a moment. I remember seeing birds swooping in the sky and hearing music playing from an ice-cream van. I was also aware of the feeling of the grass underneath my hand... It's difficult to put this into words...

Jez: Keep going, see what comes...

Matthew: I experienced what you might call 'a different perception of life'... It felt like the part of me that was experiencing this perception hadn't really changed that much since I was a baby. I don't mean it was a child's consciousness that was looking up at the sky, but it didn't seem related to the forty-five-year-old man that I am. It seemed to be a point of view that was somehow beyond time. (Pause.) I remember thinking how wonderful, perfect and absurd this world is. I just sat there, looking at the birds, the grass... the people buying ice creams. I felt detached from it all and yet... connected too.

Jez: Did you feel anything else?

Matthew: I was going to say 'happy', but that's not quite right. I just felt... very still. My problems didn't all disappear, but I had a different perspective... Somehow, everything was all right just as it was.

Jez: You mean your problems didn't need to go away for it to be all right?

Matthew: Yes, that's it: Everything was already all right.

Jez: An Opening is a glimpse beyond Personality, a taste of your original state of Being. It arises within the field of Personality (I mean in the middle of your life in which you're identified as Personality) but where it comes from, its source, is beyond it.

When life is observed from the viewpoint of the Opening, even momentarily, the spell of Personality is broken and the attributes of Being are experienced. In normal consciousness we're identified as Personality, but in an Opening the Absolute Level, in which the Relative Level arises, comes to the foreground. Openings can bring a feeling of objectivity, openheartedness, Joy, Stillness, an increase in physical energy, even bliss. But they can also come with thoughts.

Matthew: I didn't have any particular thoughts; my mind was unusually quiet! What sort of thoughts do you mean?

Jez: There are different kinds of thought: practical thought – such as 'I must buy some bread' – and then all the various thoughts that spring from the workings of Personality. This is the internal dialogue that's continually commenting on and judging what we do, such as 'If I do this I will be liked', 'I'm a bad person', 'I'm a good person' or 'When I get my promotion I'll be happy...' etcetera.

The kind of thoughts I'm talking about in these Openings fall into a third, totally different category. I call them 'Original Thoughts'. They're not original in the sense that no one else has ever had them before; they're original in the sense that *you've* never had them. They're not learnt. You don't pick up these thoughts from parents, teachers or from the Group Personality around you... They just appear in your head, in the same way that talents arise spontaneously in your Character. As a friend of mine put it:

> *You don't know how you know,*
> *But you know that you know.*

Original thoughts express spontaneous Understandings of how life works beyond the viewpoint of Personality. So I'm capitalising this use of the word 'Understanding' to distinguish it from understandings about, say, a mathematical problem or a political situation. These Understandings are spontaneous insights into our fundamental nature.

Matthew: Can you give me an example of one?

Jez: Every one of these talks is built on Understandings beyond Personality. None of these were learnt from a book; they're spontaneous perceptions that arose in my life.

Matthew: So they're uncaused?

Jez: Yes, but you could say there's an environment in which they're more likely to happen. There has to be, on some level, openness to this Mystery, a willingness to see beyond the prevailing view of the Group Personality. In my experience, that Openness seems to attract these Original Thoughts.

Throughout my life, because I've always sought the answer to the question of 'Who am I beyond Personality?', I've been blessed with many Original Thoughts. The earliest I remember came to me when I was about ten.

Matthew: What was it?

Jez: 'The same sun shines on everyone.' It might sound banal but it really meant something to me as a ten-year-old. I didn't know it then, but it was a very primal Understanding of Oneness.

I also remember being on a sightseeing boat in Amsterdam and suddenly having an Understanding about the nature of belief: I realised that if you believe something to be true, then it's true for you, in your worldview. This really helped me understand the way a lot of Personalities around me behaved.

Original Thoughts are like flowers of Understanding, spontaneously opening inside you. They're one possible manifestation of an Opening.

Matthew: The Opening I had was definitely spontaneous. I don't remember being in a particularly peaceful mood that day; looking back I can't see anything that triggered it. I was just doing what I'd done hundreds of times: walking up to the shops and back.

Jez: It's like the Openings I experienced when I was cycling as a boy; the activity didn't cause them, it just happened to be what I was doing when the Opening came. But some Openings *can* be triggered by events or circumstances.

Matthew: What sort of things can trigger them?

Jez: Lots of things: Once it happened to me after hearing the tone of an Indian woman's gentle, relaxing voice; sometimes they were a response to something I'd read. I used to browse in the spiritual book section of an Oriental store in Covent Garden; occasionally a quote from Rumi or Lao Tzu would hit me like a blow to the heart. Something in me recognised the truth encapsulated in the words, even if I didn't fully understand it; there was an energetic response to it in my body and mind.

Quotes from teachers, philosophers, poets or artists are often distillations of Original Thoughts. Being original, the thought behind the quotation has a certain power – that's why they survive. Anyone reading them, who has some openness, can feel that power and the thought can ignite some Understanding inside them.

Stories can be triggers too – that's why there's a tradition in Spiritual Seeking of teaching stories. When I was at college I read about Buddha for the first time. Something about the story of this prince, who one day encountered the Suffering of the people outside the walls of the palace and resolved to find a way beyond it, resonated with me. I was so inspired and fired up about it, I remember writing to my Christian parents and telling them the story of his life.

Matthew: Were they interested?

Jez: Not really, they were probably worried that I was going to run away and become a monk in Thailand! But it wasn't a religious thing, something in me just recognised the truth in the story. There's a great quote from the poet W.H. Auden (a good example of an Original Thought) that points to the power of books and storytelling:

A real book is not one that we read, but one that reads us.

I think that book about Buddha 'read' something about me; though I was young, I knew what Buddha meant when he talked about Suffering. My Mother's unhappiness and occasional depressions were a strong presence in my life, like a great sadness that seeped into our family. It wasn't always active, but it was there, waiting in the background like a threatening rain cloud. I was affected by it because I couldn't escape it.

Sometimes Suffering itself can trigger an Opening: It's as if its intensity pushes us beyond our normal perception to a place beyond Personality. I remember my parents having a really bad argument when I was a young boy. They tried to keep their occasional disagreements private so that my brother, sister and I wouldn't hear them, but it didn't work. When shouts and screams filled the house we *did* hear them and we *did* feel them. When this raw Emotion was released it was very frightening to us. I remember going to my room, covering my ears with a cushion trying to block out the sounds, but there was no escape.

Usually at times like that I just felt really scared and lost, but this one time that feeling that you described in your Opening came; everything was all right, despite what was happening. Logically it didn't make sense: I didn't know why or how it was all right, I just knew that, in that moment, I felt it was.

So thanks to my sporadic Openings throughout the years, I knew there was something beyond that Suffering. This was not a conceptual Understanding; I knew it because I'd experienced it, but I didn't know why or how it was true. I didn't have any overall Understanding yet of what the Openings were pointing to, what they meant.

Matthew: You're reminding me of a feeling I sometimes had when I was a boy: the word that comes to mind is objectivity. Now I come to think of it, it links up with my experience on the village green.

Jez: Tell me about it...

Matthew: It was like I was sitting on the side of the stage watching everyone else rushing around, wrapped up in who they were and what they were doing. I often wondered if anyone else felt like that. As a boy I always felt like there was something else to this life, something the adults weren't telling me, but I didn't know what it was.

Jez: It seems like talking about your experience on the village green has disturbed some deep memories of earlier Openings from your subconscious.

Matthew: Yes, I'm only just remembering them... It's a bit like when something happens in your day that jogs the memory of a dream you had the previous night. Actually... I feel a bit wary of talking about it...

Jez: Why is that?

Matthew: The memory is so fragile, I'm worried that if I catch hold of it, I'll lose it. I don't know why I feel like that.

Jez: In this society we're trained to bury these Openings. Did you tell anyone about those feelings you had of there being something more to life?

Matthew: I remember telling my parents; I think I was trying to understand what those feelings meant...

Jez: That's what parents are for, isn't it? To help you better understand the world from their own, larger experience of it. What did they say?

Matthew: Usually they'd be very supportive and answer my questions about life, but when I told them about those feelings they said things like: 'We all have those thoughts sometimes but don't talk about it, people will think it's strange.' It was as if they tried to play it down and steer me off the subject.

Jez: We've talked about how the Group Personality doesn't want this[*] – that's why your parents weren't interested in hearing about your Opening. This is Personality saying it doesn't want to be aware that there's something other than itself. The Personality wants to go around doing its thing, keeping its viewpoint intact. Your parents' Personalities chose not to become aware of what was, to them, a threatening account of an experience beyond Personality. It's a classic example of Personality Awareness, i.e. the Personality choosing what it becomes aware of.

You said you had the feeling there was something else to this life, something the adults weren't telling you. I'd suggest they weren't telling you because they didn't know about it. Or, to be precise, they'd forgotten what they'd once known about it. Once we've lost that viewpoint of the Natural State, curiosity and wonder can turn into wariness and fear. Then wonderful stories of Openings are ignored or met with ridicule.

---

[*] *The Story of 'You'* – Chapter 7

Matthew: I soon learned not to bring those feelings up again.

Jez: What about your friends? Did you tell them?

Matthew: I did. They were dismissive; they ridiculed me. They seemed to take it as if I was making out I was somehow better than them, because they'd never had those feelings. So I kept quiet about it.

Jez: And, it seems, forgot about it – until now. When the Group Personality refuses to acknowledge a side of you, there's a huge pressure to do the same, to reject in yourself what they reject.

Matthew: Why do you think that is?

Jez: Because you need the acceptance of the Group Personality, so there's an unconscious desire to fit in, to be like them in order to win their approval. You can see how the Group Personality, in this case through family and friends, trains this out of us. It's a crazy situation; in this society we're taught to walk away from what we are, from who we are.

With me you get the opposite. I'm not telling you to ignore that Opening. I'm encouraging you to remember it, to drag it out of your subconscious, to bring it into the light of consciousness and use it as a signpost pointing the way to this Understanding. This is what I did by writing about what was revealed to me.

Recently I found a folder full of these descriptions; here's an example of one. I was visiting my parents and had taken a walk at the back of their house to get some space. Sitting on the earth I suddenly had this Understanding about non-Doing:

> *Horses in the field.*
> *I am the earth and the grass.*
> *I stand at the gate and realise... know*
> *That all 'going in' to sort it out is not 'It.'*
> *All reading to understand is not 'It.'*
> *All waiting to receive it from the guru is not 'It.'*
> *All Yoga to cure illness is not 'It.'*
> *All thinking to work it out is not 'It.'*

All non-thinking to work it out is not 'It.'
All indulging in suffering is not 'It.'
All dramatizing your problems is not 'It.'
All nice thoughts and cute aphorisms are not 'It.'
All trying to project order on the way is not 'It.'
All self-consolations are not 'It.'
All your dreams, hopes, desires are not 'It.'
Only Truth is 'It.'
And that is beyond all your restless doing.

Matthew: What do you think of it when you read it now?

Jez: I can feel the intensity I had; it's a pretty uncompromising look at all the Distractions that Personality can use. It's all true, but just because I saw it in that moment doesn't mean I maintained that clarity continuously after that. Openings are not the deliverance into the Shift, but they are important signposts pointing towards it.

2

CONSCIOUSNESS

The difference between universal
Consciousness and personal consciousness

*"The consciousness in you and the consciousness in me,
apparently two, really one, seek unity and that is love.'
– Nisargadatta Maharaj*

Jez: Before we continue, we need to pin down a definition of the word 'consciousness'. It came up in the last talk and it's going to help shine light on what I mean by Openings – that is, glimpses beyond Personality.

The word has two distinct uses: the more common use relates to the state of *being* conscious, of having awareness of one's own existence, one's thoughts and sensations. The fact that you hear and understand what I'm saying, that you taste the tea in that cup and see steam rising from it, confirms that you are conscious, that you have consciousness.

Philosophical enquiry poses the question: 'What is real?' We think we know things, but knowledge could be just a figment of our imagination. So is there anything we can know for sure?' When this question is asked, consciousness provides the only satisfying answer. If there is thinking – if there is someone asking the question: 'What is real?' – then one thing we can say for sure is that there is consciousness, because without it there would be no question; there would be no capacity for thought.

Matthew: I presume this is what the French philosopher Descartes meant when he said: 'I think therefore I am.'

Jez: Yes, I presume so too. So this consciousness, this ability to think, feel and perceive becomes overlaid with the idea of identity. This begins in childhood as we become aware (through those sensorial attributes of consciousness) that we are in a body, that we're separate from objects and other people that we see in the world. To be more specific, you could call this kind of consciousness 'personal consciousness' because it becomes linked to the idea of separation and identity.

The first level of this identity is purely fact based; it's the basis for what we call 'the self'.

Matthew: You mean: I'm called Matthew, I'm male, in my forties, I have two siblings...etcetera.

Jez: Yes, that's the foundation layer, but identity isn't just based on cold facts that consciousness observes. As you grow up it also becomes informed by psychology: by feelings, Emotions, memories, thoughts and beliefs. We'll go into more detail about how this happens later, but all you need to know for now is that as we grow up, this consciousness takes on a form, and that form is our Personality.

This consciousness constantly shifts from perception to perception, from sensation to sensation. One moment it's perceiving the warmth of the tea cup in your hand, then it's engaged in a thought about what you're going to eat for lunch, then it focuses on a bird outside the window and so on and so on. You'll notice that this consciousness is relative to its content.

Matthew: What does that mean?

Jez: If you think of consciousness as a light, it illuminates whatever it falls upon. There's a subject/object relationship going on: consciousness falls upon the bird outside the window, or on the thought you had about it. This means it's inherently dualistic. It can't be any other way, because this sort of consciousness is part of the Relative Level.

Matthew: It's part of the waking state, isn't it?

Jez: Yes, exactly. That means it can be turned off, like a switch, as happens when we sleep. So, in this world of duality, consciousness has two opposite states: conscious and un-conscious.

Matthew: What about the other use of the word 'consciousness'?

Jez: This is going to be more difficult to talk about because it relates to the Absolute Level. The other use of the word 'consciousness' has a more spiritual application: It relates to Consciousness that originates beyond the human domain. (Let's give it a capital 'C' to differentiate it.) You could call it the universal intelligence that's behind all things. In some eastern religions they call it the 'Self' or 'Atman'.

Matthew: In western religions they'd call it 'God'. We're getting into religious territory now, and the area of belief; how can you be sure it exists?

Jez: You don't have to be religious to see order in the universe: in the way the planets move, the way a heart is built perfectly to do its job of pumping blood around the body, the way life evolves to fulfil certain functions...

Matthew: Isn't that just what we call nature?

Jez: You could call it nature – then at least we won't need to debate whether it exists! But that wouldn't be quite accurate. Although Consciousness includes nature, it's more than that... Nature can be scientifically analysed and recorded, whereas Consciousness can't be. So it's the underlying matrix that's behind the mouse that's being observed in a laboratory, the scientist who's observing it, the air that's being breathed and the bricks that make up the room. If Consciousness is the canvas, nature is a picture that appears on it, and human beings are part of that picture.

Matthew: My brain's starting to hurt!

Jez: We're on the very edge of what language can express and our brains can conceive now... Let me try to make it clearer with an example. Last night I saw a wildlife documentary that featured the Arctic hare. To protect itself from predators, its black pelt miraculously turns white every winter so it can camouflage itself in the snow. This is a good example of what I'm talking about: Consciousness is this beautiful system which has its own undeniable logic and intelligence behind its functioning; the Chinese call it the Tao. When we apply our consciousness (with a small 'c') to it, we can perceive its beautiful order and have a response to it in the form of feelings of wonder and awe. As we've discussed we can also perceive it, in human feeling terms, as Love.[*]

Matthew: 'Consciousness' is a very dry, unemotional word for it.

Jez: Yes, and in some ways this can be an advantage; it's more accurate because, unlike consciousness, Consciousness is free of human attributes. Like I said, it originates beyond the human domain, therefore it's beyond the reach of human characteristics such as feeling. So if, despite its camouflage, the Arctic hare is caught, torn apart and eaten by a wolf... Consciousness doesn't care. It doesn't feel bad for the hare.

Matthew: Really? That grates with me a bit...

Jez: Why?

* *The Story of 'You'* – Chapter 1

Matthew: I suppose I have an idea that a superior Consciousness would be loving and compassionate.

Jez: Compassion and Love are human constructs. They don't exist outside of human life, for example in the animal kingdom.

Matthew: What about when an animal dies? I've seen films of elephants appearing to grieve over the loss of their young...

Jez: Yes, there's connection, care and probably some level of feeling, but that's an evolutionary function; to ascribe Love to it is a human interpretation. Without humans, there's no such thing as Love.

Matthew: I find that a really shocking statement!

Jez: Why?

Matthew: It makes me feel uncomfortable because I don't want it to be true... It seems strange that we humans have compassion and Love and yet a higher Consciousness doesn't.

Jez: You're anthropomorphising Consciousness, giving it human attributes. When I was very young I remember seeing a news report on television about a landslide in a coal-mining community in Aberfan in Wales. It sent tons of rock and shale slurry down onto the village school, killing over a hundred children as they sat in their lessons. There's no compassion, no Love in that. It's just nature, gravity, science. Let me ask you a question: Before humans appeared on the planet, was there any Love?

Matthew: I want to say yes...

Jez: How could there be if there was no brain or heart existing that could feel it? It's only the religiously minded who project the idea of a benign creator that has human-like feelings and motivations. Outside of that belief, there's just Consciousness, or the Tao, doing its thing. Animals are just living out their nature – to protect their young, to survive – and part of that survival is killing other animals. That's also nature; that's also the Tao. So from the point of view beyond human consciousness, when the wolf kills the hare, it's just energy moving round, changing form. It's no longer in the form of a hare; it transforms into energy in the muscles of the wolf. In the end, the hare becomes the wolf. You could say that, in the Relative Level, they become the 'One' that in the Absolute Level, they already were..

Matthew: This is challenging a belief in some cosmic force for good (you could call it Love) that I didn't even realise I have. I feel almost angry with you, because you're kind of threatening it.

Jez: That's because that belief served you in some way; it upheld your worldview and perhaps helped make you feel safe. Then I come along and threaten to dismantle that belief. But remember, I'm not asking you to believe what I've said; you could say I'm just telling you a story. It's up to you to find out if it has any truth in it.

Matthew: But you're not denying the existence of Love, are you? I mean, even though Consciousness is impersonal, you ascribe human attributes to it: You see it as Love.

Jez: Yes, because I'm human, and within human consciousness, where we have feelings of Love, this is how Consciousness can appear when it's perceived. But the point is, Consciousness exists prior to humans and human feelings. It can manifest as humans, and consciousness, but it's prior to that manifestation. Remember, Consciousness refers to the canvas rather than the painting which appears on it. It's the background, whereas manifestation is the foreground. It's the One from which Duality appears.

Unlike 'personal' consciousness, Consciousness can't be turned off. When you wake up in the morning, personal consciousness is turned on, but universal Consciousness is always 'on' – if it weren't, there'd be no 'you' to wake up. It is life itself. Therefore personal consciousness (sentience and the experience of life) arises as a part of universal Consciousness. It's another way of saying the Relative Level appears as a manifestation of the Absolute Level.

Matthew: Our definition of consciousness ('the state of being conscious, of having awareness of one's own existence') suggests that awareness is the same as consciousness. Do you agree?

Jez: Yes, awareness is part and parcel of personal consciousness. You sip the tea, you're aware of the taste, the heat transmitted to your fingers and the weight of the cup. As you taste, see, hear or think about something you usually become aware of it. I say 'usually' because this isn't always the case: You can do something and not be aware of doing it. You might be so engrossed in our talk that, although you have the facility to be conscious of the heat or weight of the cup, you're not experiencing that consciously. You're not aware of it. You can also have thoughts and not be aware you're thinking them. So this is the particular kind of awareness – I call it Personality Awareness* – which can be turned on or off.

Having said that, there's usually some level of awareness applied to the state of being conscious, applied to experiencing this life through our senses. This is why the word 'awareness' is often used interchangeably with the word 'consciousness'.

Matthew: How does awareness relate to Consciousness with a capital 'C'?

Jez: When it comes to Consciousness, awareness is a totally different thing. Let me ask you a question: Can we attribute awareness, which we think of as a human characteristic arising from the functioning of sense organs, to universal Consciousness?

Matthew: You can if you believe in God.

Jez: That's right, the religiously inclined assign human characteristics to Consciousness, or God. They have the belief that a 'cosmic' being loves us, is watching over and taking care of us. But, without holding that belief, can we say Consciousness has awareness?

Matthew: No, because, according to you, Consciousness, with a capital 'C', originates beyond the human domain.

Jez: Right. Consciousness, that universal intelligence, originates beyond the human domain but, having said that, it is expressed in the form of consciousness in humans. The canvas exists before the painting, but it includes the painting.

Matthew: So you're saying that the awareness humans have as part of personal consciousness, is also part of Consciousness?

Jez: Yes, that's true, in as much as everything is an expression of, and

---

* *The Story of 'You'* – Chapter 21

so part of, life. It's all part of Consciousness. But, and this is the point I've been leading to, there is an awareness which appears in human life that's not personal. What I mean is an awareness that doesn't pass through the human Personality, so it's not limited by it.

Matthew: Limited in what way?

Jez: Earlier I said the awareness that's part of personal consciousness is not constant; it can be turned on and off. This is a factor of it being personal. The Personality has a say in what it falls on; it can choose what it becomes aware of.

   The Awareness I'm talking about is different; it's not personal. There's no Personality involved, choosing what it falls on or whether it's turned on or off. This is Choice-less Awareness. Personal Awareness comes and goes; Choice-less Awareness is always latent in us. It exists at the very core of who we are, but that doesn't mean it's always experienced. Most adults usually only experience Personality Awareness – unless they're in extreme situations such as near-death experiences, moments of trauma or danger.

Matthew: Is it the kind of Awareness that's experienced in an Opening?

Jez: Yes. An Opening is a glimpse of the Absolute Level, an experience of Choice-less Awareness. You described it perfectly in the account of your Opening. The whole of spiritual enquiry is about the return to the living and knowledge of this 'universal Consciousness' that sees beyond the personal, beyond Personality.

Matthew: At the same time as having personal consciousness?

Jez: Yes, there is the awareness of being an apparent person. It can't be any other way; if there was no personal consciousness, you'd be dead.

3

CHOICE-LESS AWARENESS

Awareness that comes from beyond Personality

'Without self-knowledge, without understanding the working
and functions of his machine, man cannot be free, he cannot
govern himself and he will always remain a slave.'
– G.I. Gurdjieff

Jez: There are two kinds of awareness, differentiated by the source from which they arise. Personality Awareness is so called because it comes from Personality and is characterised by the fact that it chooses what it becomes aware of. It's what stops people seeing their own psychological patterns, their own limiting beliefs. This lack of awareness of the Personality's functioning is the Personality's key tool to keep you identified with it. Personality only lets you see what it wants you to see.

In your Opening on the village green, you experienced the other kind of Awareness: Choice-less Awareness. It's not the first time you've had it, because we all start out with it as children in the original state of Being, but most people have limited experience of it as an adult. On the green, Choice-less Awareness observed life going on around you: the birds swooping in the sky, the music from the ice cream van.

Matthew: But anyone sitting there could have seen that.

Jez: They could have, but would they have? Most people are so caught up in the concerns of their Personality – in Distraction, worries, goals and compulsive thinking – there's little awareness left to fall on life going on around them. You illustrated this in an earlier talk by your story of walking into a lamppost while looking at your phone.

Matthew: It makes me think of that John Lennon quote: 'Life is what happens while you're busy making other plans.'

Jez: Yes, in the Opening, you temporarily dropped those 'other plans' and became aware of life happening around you. Your awareness took in the birds, the people buying ice creams, and the feeling of grass beneath your hand. But of course, it went far beyond that. Choice-less Awareness spans two directions: outwards towards the world and inwards, towards your inner landscape, to feelings, to whatever is going on in you.

Matthew: Doesn't Personality Awareness do that as well?

Jez: Yes, they both look outwards and inwards, but there's a vital difference: When Personality Awareness looks, in either direction, it only sees what it wants to see. Choice-less Awareness doesn't discriminate over what it sees; it's absolutely impartial. This means it can fall on Personality itself, and all of its workings.

Matthew: When I told you about my Opening I called it 'objectivity'.
Now I think about it, there was nothing arising in me that wanted
anything to be different from how it was.

Jez: That's a good description of Choice-less Awareness. If you
think of a baby before the Wound, all is seen and experienced
without judgement. There's no filter, no rejection of anything
arising in its world. Whatever comes into the baby's life – a new
toy, the sound of a police siren, distress from having a wet nappy
– is experienced fully.

   The source of Choice-less Awareness is not the Personality. In
a baby this is obvious because they haven't even developed one yet,
but how does this work in an adult? What I mean is that Choice-less
Awareness doesn't belong to the Personality's history, its patterns,
its mind; it operates outside of Personality's jurisdiction, beyond its
control. This means it has no past, no agenda, no intent to edit what
it sees. It's totally free of all that.

Matthew: Does that mean it comes from the Absolute Level?

Jez: Yes, Choice-less Awareness is the Absolute Level penetrating
the Relative Level; the impersonal appearing within the personal.
Choice-less Awareness is Consciousness falling on the manifestation
of life around and inside a human being. What's seen is then
translated into cognition and then thoughts in the mind.

   To put it another way, when Choice-less Awareness arises,
something outside of what you take to be yourself – i.e. the Personality
– steps in and sees things from another, totally impartial perspective.

Matthew: Some people might think it sounds creepy, like being possessed.

Jez: That's a projection from the mind. A possession would involve
being taken over by a foreign entity, whereas this is simply returning
to a pure experience of yourself as a human Being. It's not foreign,
it's being in contact with the source of who you are – that's why
when you experience it, you feel like you've come home. It's what
you had as a baby; it's part of the original state of Being.

   Calling it 'Choice-less Awareness' makes it sound a bit grand:

Once you see through Personality, Awareness is mostly no longer divided in two. There's simply Awareness, and it is Choice-less, because there's no identification with a Personality that would be doing the choosing. Once you've seen through Personality, adding the prefix 'Choice-less' pretty much becomes superfluous. It's like talking about the sea and calling it the 'wet-sea'.

Matthew: But you have to use that term because not everyone knows this, right?

Jez: Yes, I'm trying to describe Choice-less Awareness to people whose awareness is mostly not Choice-less, it's Personality based.

Matthew: I've heard some spiritual teachers say Awareness can't help you become free of your Personality, because it's just another part of the Personality's story, a part of the Dream.

Jez: What they're referring to is Personality Awareness, which certainly can't help you because, as I've said, what it falls upon is governed by Personality itself. Therefore Personality Awareness won't become conscious of anything that challenges the Personality.

Choice-less Awareness, like an Opening which can trigger it, arises in the middle of Personality but its source is outside of Personality. It can look outward, towards the world and bring clarity, but when it shines inwards to the dark unconscious of the life of Personality, the power of this Choice-less Awareness is enormous.

Matthew: What do you mean when you say it has power?

Jez: OK, let's look at the context. Unconscious patterns and beliefs have a phenomenal power: They create the Dream of the Personality and they're almost impossible to break through. Personal development courses won't do it, for the reasons I've outlined in my first book.* Positive thinking, will power, all of that is powerless in the face of these patterns.

In *The Story of 'You'* I invented a character called Lucy to illustrate how Personalities form and develop. Lucy has anorexia; no matter how much love and care her parents, friends or therapists give her it's extremely difficult to break the spell of her belief that

---

* *The Story of 'You'* – Chapter 34

she's fat. Why? Because it's so deeply embedded in her Personality's belief system.

Choice-less Awareness is the only thing that could break through the hold that belief has on a person, because it comes from outside the domain in which the belief is arising, i.e. from beyond Personality. Only Choice-less Awareness could reveal to Lucy the fact that, in reality, she's not fat. That's why I say it's powerful, because it can penetrate the stranglehold of beliefs embedded in the Personality.

Personality Awareness is like wearing blinkers: Your vision is severely restricted. An experience of Choice-less Awareness is like taking the blinkers off. Your vision becomes wide and full. Everything can be seen, including all aspects of the Dream of the Personality.

Matthew: I experienced Choice-less Awareness on the village green but it didn't help me much – by the time I got home that objectivity had gone.

Jez: You've demonstrated that it's possible to experience Choice-less Awareness in the middle of the Dream. It could come in the form of just a moment of clarity, or longer periods during an Opening. In those experiences, the Personality can be seen clearly, and then, as you found, that clear vision can disappear again.

Matthew: Why is that? Why doesn't it continue?

Jez: The answer to that is karma or, for a more western phrase, 'cause and effect'. When we talked about feelings* I described them as systems of energy that want to be felt. If they're not felt, they don't disappear, they just get stronger and eventually become Emotions. The more they're repressed, and the longer they're ignored, the stronger and more embedded they become.

Matthew: We're back to that Einstein quote: 'Energy cannot be created or destroyed.'

Jez: Exactly, and that law also applies to the Personality: It has momentum, it wants to continue playing itself out.

Matthew: So... You see the Personality as energy?

Jez: Absolutely, an enormous configuration of energy in constant

---

* *The Story of 'You'* – Chapter 17

motion. That energy is repressing feelings, expressing Emotions, chasing happiness, desires, addictions and Distractions. It's holding onto and defending beliefs and constantly working to protect itself. A Personality is a whole world unto itself, and to run all those parts takes an enormous amount of energy.

Matthew: But there seems to be a contradiction here: If Einstein is correct when he says: 'Energy cannot be destroyed' then how can all that energy of the Personality system be stopped instantaneously in an Opening?

Jez: It's not stopped in an Opening.

Matthew: But isn't that what you said?

Jez: No. In an Opening the Personality doesn't stop; you're simply taken to another viewpoint, to the Absolute viewpoint. Imagine Lucy goes to a party and takes a mind-altering drug. When she takes it, she starts experiencing a different reality: She glimpses the Absolute Level and this gives her a break from her Personality. For a while she has no issues of lack of self-worth, no anorexia and no money worries. She's blissfully free of all that; but when the trip ends, guess what's waiting for her?

Matthew: Reality, everyday life.

Jez: Yes, the body has to be fed, the shopping has to be done, the rent has to be paid; all of that practical stuff that has to be dealt with in the Relative Level. But more than that, Lucy returns to the operating system which is living that 'everyday life' and running the whole 'show' of Lucy. She returns to the world of her Personality and all the issues, patterns and problems that it comes with. During the trip all that seemed to go away, but it didn't. The Personality didn't dissolve; it wasn't destroyed. Lucy was just distracted from it for a short time.

Matthew: And, the same goes for an Opening?

Jez: Yes, the Opening is a space that opens up within Personality. When that space closes again, what you return to is the viewpoint of Personality. However, sometimes the protective system of the Personality has been so deeply infiltrated by an Opening that it leaves behind a yearning to return to what has been glimpsed.

4

THE YEARNING

A longing to return to Being

'I desire you more than food and drink.
My body, my senses, my mind hunger for your taste.
I can sense your presence in my heart
Although you belong to all the world.
I wait with silent passion for one gesture,
One glance from you.'
– Rumi

Jez: If you think about the Opening you had, what do you feel?

Matthew: Happiness, Joy, contentment... But it's one step removed, because it's the memory of those feelings, rather than having them now. So it's bittersweet, because the memory is beautiful, but it's tempered by the fact that it went and I don't know how to get it back. Is there any way you can make Choice-less Awareness appear? How do you get it?

Jez: And so the game goes on...

Matthew: What do you mean?

Jez: Your Personality thinks it's found a new toy to play with, a new practice, a new goal to Distract you with. It wants to be able to say to you: 'When I learn how to get Choice-less Awareness I can be happy.' It's totally understandable – that's what happened after my teenage Openings: I tried to force that clarity of vision to stay. But ironically, that intention is a sure-fire way for the Personality to stay in control, and to *not* experience Choice-less-Awareness.

Matthew: This is confusing: It's obviously really beneficial so of course I want to try and get it.

Jez: The point is, 'you' *can't* get it. Was it 'you' who 'got it' on the village green? No, it would be more accurate to say it appeared when 'you' (i.e. the Personality) was not there in the driving seat. Choice-less Awareness can't be possessed by Personality because it comes from beyond it.

We've ended up in the same Catch-22 situation as when we discussed trying to find liberation through practice.* That's because Choice-less Awareness is a central attribute of Being. You can't 'get' Choice-less Awareness, you can't make it appear; it happens through grace when you're in contact with Being.

Matthew: What do you mean by 'grace' in this context?

Jez: I mean life has a way of reaching us in the form of experiences that push us beyond our usual limits, like your Opening. The Personality is upheld by our belief in it; transcendent experiences

---

* *The Story of 'You'* – Chapter 35

momentarily take us to a perspective beyond that belief, beyond Personality. These are gifts from life; we don't earn them. It has nothing to do with being good, spiritual or having put in years of dedicated practice.

Grace descends in all sorts of ways and situations, not just happy, blissful ones like Openings. As I've mentioned, Choice-less Awareness can appear when the Suffering of Personality creates a kind of pressure, a sharpening of focus that pushes you beyond your normal operating mode. What this means practically is that you're no longer able to deny or look away from Suffering (as happens in Personality Awareness).

Matthew: This reminds me of a documentary about suicidal people who jumped from the Golden Gate Bridge in San Francisco and survived. Apparently very few do survive but, of those who live to tell the tale, most said that, as soon as they jumped, the problems that had driven them to suicide seemed irrelevant.

Jez: That's a pretty radical way to experience a taste of life beyond Personality! The Suffering doesn't have to be quite so dramatic to invoke an experience of Choice-less Awareness; for example, it plays a part in the recovery process of alcoholics. Usually, Personality Awareness means that the drinking problem is not acknowledged, and so it continues. Twelve-Step meetings start with introductions such as: 'I am John and I'm an alcoholic.' John is affirming he's aware of the problem; there's no denial of it any more.

Moments of Choice-less Awareness can be a huge step forward, but they're just the beginning, because the problem that's been acknowledged (such as John's alcoholism) has roots deep within his psychology. This means that, as you move forward and go deeper into what's been repressed, more resistance can come into play. You can get stuck and then lose that original experience of Choice-less Awareness.

Taking the example of John, it's been uncomfortable for him to admit to himself that he's an alcoholic; that has taken Choice-less Awareness and willingness. To pluck up the courage to go to the Alcoholics Anonymous meeting and come out publicly with his problem by declaring: 'I'm an alcoholic' is another huge hurdle. But having done that, he feels like resting; he's wounded and vulnerable, but able to get by with the support of the group.

So there's a danger here of getting too comfortable and becoming stuck after grace has given you the gift of the Opening. What happens then is John ends up with a new identity: the alcoholic Personality. Everywhere John goes, he announces 'I don't drink alcohol, I'm a recovering alcoholic.' So the very act of stopping the denial of his alcoholism turns into an affirmation of a new identity that his Personality has adopted.

So these steps forward, which happen through grace, can falter and disappear: Your childhood Openings were also neutralised when your parents showed no interest and your friends ridiculed you. You were taught to hide them away, ignore them, and then you lost touch with them. They were like flowers starved of sunlight. All Openings and breakthroughs can be 'swallowed up' by Personality, which is infinitely adaptable in neutralising threats to its dominance.

Matthew: That's what happened after your Openings too?

Jez: Yes. After each Opening passed I'd do anything to bring them back.

Matthew: How?

Jez: By writing about them. I wrote pages and pages, wringing the experience of them from my memory, trying to bring them into my everyday reality. I wanted to follow them and find out where they led; it was a yearning to return to Being. To differentiate this Yearning (to Wake Up from the Dream) from other kinds of yearning, let's give it a capital 'Y'.

Matthew: Where do you think Yearning comes from?

Jez: That's a good question. I've never thought about it before. It's certainly not the Personality. Following that call back home is the last thing that Personality wants to do, because that path leads to its dissolution.

Matthew: So how do you explain the existence of this Yearning?

Jez: I don't, because I don't need to. You don't have to understand something for it to exist; most people don't really understand how electricity works but we know that if we switch on a lamp the bulb will light up.

Matthew: But if I pushed you to try to answer where that Yearning comes from...?

Jez: I'd say there's a pattern in human life which I've outlined in the first collection of these discussions: We're born in the original state of Being, then gradually the Personality takes over, that state is forgotten and then we live in the Dream that the Personality creates. But it seems that, in some people, that original state of Being is not totally forgotten. There's a distant, primal memory of it that survives. It's from this memory that the Yearning to Wake Up from the Dream arises.

Matthew: Up until now, you've mostly used the phrase 'the Natural State' to refer to life beyond Personality. Now you're talking about 'Waking Up from the Dream of Personality'...

Jez: Yes, up until now that phrase, 'the Natural State', has been appropriate. It's natural, because we're born with it, and it's a state because, when we become identified with Personality, it passes. But now we're starting to talk about the possibility of returning to that viewpoint as an adult, after the Dream of Personality has become established. So now the approach is different: Rather than the Natural State being a gift that's just part of who we are in our innocence as children, it's returned to from the point of view of experience. So it becomes appropriate to use the phrase 'Waking Up from the Dream of Personality' because it refers to the approach to the Natural State from experience.

Matthew: If Choice-less Awareness is needed to Wake Up from the Dream of Personality, yet there's nothing you can do to make it appear, how does anyone Wake Up?

Jez: 'You' can't make Choice-less Awareness appear, but it can appear, through grace, just as it did in your Opening. It can happen that a faint taste of Choice-less Awareness comes with you, back into your everyday life. It's as if the experience has been so strong that it lingers; there's an imprint of it in your normal daily consciousness.

Matthew: So this isn't just a memory of Choice-less Awareness (from the Opening) that you're talking about?

Jez: No, it's the actual experience of it. It may not be very strong, but it can give you a distance, a perspective on your life that wasn't there before.

Matthew: Without there being an actual Opening you mean?

Jez: Yes, an Opening momentarily stops you in your tracks because its viewpoint is so strong and different from your everyday consciousness. What I'm talking about isn't so dramatic; at first you may hardly even notice it's there.

Matthew: I'm not totally clear on what you mean.

Jez: OK, the Personality creates a Dream; you are unconscious of that fact – you're metaphorically 'in the dark'. Let's symbolise that as the dark of night. What I'm talking about is having a tiny light, which glows in the night and illuminates the objects immediately around it.

Matthew: A glow in the night! That's a pretty small light!

Jez: Yes, it can start small, its reach is limited but even a small light can help you see what's around you; at least you're less likely to bump into things. It's a start. If life has implanted in that person the Yearning to return home, then that Choice-less Awareness – that glow of light – can be picked up like an ember, blown on and nurtured so it gets a bit brighter. Then it can show you the way forward.

Matthew: But I thought 'I' could do nothing to help bring this about?

Jez: You can't. This has nothing to do with Seeking, having a practice or trying to avoid the Suffering of Personality. It's an impulse to see through Personality; a Yearning to return home. Either that impulse is there or not. If it is there, a whole new world beyond the Dream of Personality starts opening up to you.

5

SEEING

When Choice-less Awareness leads to Understanding

'One does not become enlightened by imagining figures of light, but by making the darkness conscious.'
– C.G. Jung

Matthew: You say that Choice-less Awareness can start appearing not just in Openings but in normal daily life. Can you expand on that? What does it mean in practice?

Jez: It means a different viewpoint starts showing up in your life. In Personality Awareness we see the world from the viewpoint of Personality. That means it edits what we see; we see only what it allows us to see. In Choice-less Awareness you start 'Seeing' with a capital S, meaning you See beyond what Personality wants you to see. So 'Seeing' refers to Choice-less Awareness actively falling on aspects of your life and revealing the truth of them to you.

Matthew: How is it different from an Opening?

Jez: It's much more low key than an Opening. It's not dramatic at all; it just becomes a function that arises in your everyday life. Imagine an Opening as being suddenly planted on top of a hill. You can See all of life going on both above and beneath you; if you look down you can See your village, your house, your friends. It's as if you're looking at your life from outside of it, and because you have a distance to it, you See it very clearly, with a certain amount of detachment.

Matthew: When I had my Opening on the village green I wasn't really outside of my life, I was shopping so I'd say that I was in the middle of it.

Jez: In the physical sense you were inside it, but metaphorically you were outside of it. You weren't engaged in that life; it had temporarily stopped and you were watching it, with a degree of distance.

Matthew: That's true; I see what you mean.

Jez: When the Opening passed, you lost that distance. You were back at the bottom of that metaphorical hill. You were down in the valley, in middle of your life and you re-engaged with all its practicalities.

Matthew: I went home, put away the shopping and cooked a meal.

Jez: That's the physical side of it, but what about your emotional life? That returned too, didn't it?

Matthew: Yes, I remember that night I had to make a difficult phone call that I'd been putting off for a long time. A situation with my friend Theo had come to a head and I could feel some resentment I had towards him rising up in me.

Jez: So you re-entered the Dream of your Personality, you 'became' Matthew again, with his Emotional history, his identity built on his past, his beliefs and Distractions. The whole 'Matthew show' was restarted and picked up again. As we know, the attachment to that Dream is not broken by just a couple of Openings.

Matthew: So all the bad habits just flood back in again.

Jez: Those habits and thought patterns are neither good nor bad, they're simply the outcome of identifying as Personality. This isn't about demonising the Dream of the Personality – that's just creating more division and trouble. It's a projection arising from the 'When I get this I'll be happy' syndrome, which just creates more Suffering.

Matthew: But you are talking about Waking up from the Personality's Dream.

Jez: Yes, absolutely, but how does that happen? That's the point. It doesn't come about by making it into an enemy and fighting it; that is all Doing. When this small spark of Choice-less Awareness survives, the Dream is occasionally approached without projections, Emotion or reaction. It's approached from a neutral place, then you start Seeing through these Personality reactions, which means you start to become conscious of them. It's like having access to some of that viewpoint from the hill; it gives you an overview and a detachment. You can See your life going on with more clarity, but the difference is, now you're Seeing it from right in the middle of that life as it's unfolding, rather than being temporarily derailed from it in an Opening.

Matthew: And that's available all the time?

Jez: No, not all the time. Most of the time you may still be caught up in the Dream of your Personality; what we're talking about here are occasional moments of clarity within the Dream.

Matthew: Would it be analogous with lucid dreaming, in that you occasionally become aware that you're dreaming and that you can influence the Dream?

Jez: In a way, yes. What this means practically is that you might start Seeing patterns going on in your life, and this brings Understanding of them. When you're no longer unconscious of patterns going on, once you have Understanding, then you have the perspective to stop those patterns. Seeing leads to Understanding, which leads to changes being made in your life.

Matthew: I think I know what you mean: Since my Opening on the village green I've become more aware of a pattern going on with my friend Theo and it's led to me pulling back from our relationship. Before the Opening I'd gotten into a situation where I'd become his confidant, the person he went to when he needed to unburden himself. I used to think it was fine, that's what friends do: Help each other with their problems.

Jez: So, after your Opening, how did you See this differently?

Matthew: I feel a bit guilty talking about Theo like this; I don't want to complain about him behind him back. It feels like... I'm bitching, for want of a better word.

Jez: I don't think you're bitching about him.

Matthew: But I am talking about him to you, and he's not here.

Jez: Yes, but that doesn't necessarily mean you're bitching about him – it's a question of intent. If you were bitching about him that would just be your Personality firing off some of your resentment, but it's obvious that's not the case. You're trying to understand what happened with him. This is not really about Theo; we may be talking about your experience with him but only as a mirror to focus on you. So, what was it that you understood about the situation after the Opening?

Matthew: I realised he doesn't really want to change – he's had so many opportunities to, and he's never taken them... He just unconsciously creates situations in which he can complain about others and how unfair life is, and I'd become the main recipient of those complaints.

Jez: So, having had that Understanding, what changed?

Matthew: I told him I didn't want to play that role with him any more.

Jez: This is a good example of a moment of Choice-less Awareness shining a light into your life and showing you something in a way that you haven't seen before. The Choice-less Awareness brought Understanding, and that in turn led to a change. How did Theo react when you told him?

Matthew: He was angry: He accused me of being uncaring, of not being a good friend. It's sad in a way, because it's soured our relationship.

Jez: Discord can be one of the consequences of acting on what Choice-less Awareness shows you; some people around you won't like what it leads you to do. Just because *you* have Seen the nature of that side of your relationship, doesn't mean that Theo wants to. I'm sure his Personality was quite happy to continue as it was, in that complaining mode. Obviously at some point in your relationship you must have given him the message that you *would* support this pattern in him. I don't mean explicitly, by telling him, but implicitly, simply by the fact that you did listen to him and didn't pull away or say anything about it.

All relationships have contracts, rules of engagement that both parties agree to. They're not verbal, they just appear through your actions: how you engage with each other and the messages you give out. You had a contract with Theo, and pointing out this side of his Personality wasn't in the contract; you were supposed to support that side of him. That's what you must have tacitly agreed to at some point in the past.

Matthew: I see: I broke the contract.

Jez: Remember we talked about how Group Personalities make their members feel safe because they are hanging out with others just like them, which means their beliefs are supported and not challenged? By breaking the contract with Theo you became someone who made his Personality feel unsafe, because you challenged it. So this is what came between you; you no longer supported that pattern of his Personality.

As your story illustrates, when it comes to relationships Choice-less Awareness can put you in a difficult position. You may have to make a choice; either to honour what Choice-less Awareness has shown you and put your relationship in jeopardy, or ignore what it has revealed to you and save your relationship.

Matthew: So even when you have a moment of Choice-less Awareness, you can still ignore it and look the other way?

Jez: Absolutely. Remember, we're talking about a small light that's brought into the Dream of Personality; it's an ember, not a raging fire. Your Personality is not interested in that light because it exposes the Dream, and that would mean the Personality starting to lose control. So the stakes are high, because that ember of Choice-less Awareness can so easily be blown out.

Matthew: It was difficult for me; my mind tried to convince me not speak up to Theo. It said: 'He's not so bad, just put up with his negativity. You don't want to lose his friendship after all these years.'

Jez: Yes, but you did tell him in the end. Why was that? Why did you break the contract?

Matthew: If I had to sum it up I'd say I didn't feel like I was honouring myself by being in that role.

Jez: Choice-less Awareness has outcomes in the life it falls into. Remember, along with full-feeling engagement with life, Stillness and Joy – Choice-less Awareness is one of the four pillars of Being. It comes from a place of Love. By withdrawing from any relationships that don't honour you, you are honouring yourself. You are honouring the Love that you are, but also the Love that your friend Theo is, because you are being honest with him. (Not that he would see it like that).

As more Awareness comes into your life, any patterns of lack of self-love start to loosen their grip because, outside of the Dream of Personality, they're absurd. Let me ask you, did you feel any lack of self-esteem in your Opening on the village green?

Matthew: No, I was absolutely at peace with myself. I'm not saying I suddenly became an idealised version of Matthew; I felt that whatever version of myself I was, was OK, just as it was. There was no self-criticism of any part of me.

Jez: And when it passed, that came back?

Matthew: Yes, as you said, the whole 'Matthew show' with all the familiar thought patterns returned.

Jez: And yet, somewhere within that appeared this little light of Choice-less Awareness which allowed you to See your behaviour, Understand it and then make a change in your life. That change wasn't about self-development, it didn't come from willpower; it arose from the Understanding brought about through Choice-less Awareness. This is the power of Seeing.

6

READINESS

When an apple is ripe, nothing can stop it
falling from the tree

'Let come what comes. Let go what goes. See what remains.'
– Ramana Maharshi

Jez: We've talked about a small light of Choice-less Awareness falling into this life, illuminating a few patterns of behaviour in others and yourself. As you've shown in the example of your friend Theo, following the Understanding it brings can be challenging. It initiates changes in your life that your Personality would rather not have. Therefore in many cases, Personality will reject this light; it will be extinguished and forgotten about.

Matthew: So, as you said in our last discussion, even if Choice-less Awareness does arise, it can still be rejected?

Jez: Yes, insights can be packed away to the subconscious so that Personality can get on with its business without being challenged – like the alcoholic who admits he has a problem, then adopts a 'recovering alcoholic' identity. Therapeutically this is a huge step forward, there's no doubt about that, but here we're concerned with Seeing beyond Personality. The Choice-less Awareness has taken him so far: It's revealed that he has a drink problem, but it doesn't then show him that his Personality has regained control. It's also what happened to you with your Openings as a boy: Your parents and friends wouldn't listen to your experiences so you repressed them to fit in and be accepted.

Matthew: I presume that's not what happened with you?

Jez: No, if you have the Yearning to return to the original state of Being then another opportunity opens up. Though you still have all the drama of the Personality, when that light of Choice-less Awareness shows up, it's accepted, nurtured and applied. When it's accepted it doesn't disappear so easily.

I was clearing my attic out yesterday and found a box full of my old journals. They were packed full of thirty years of observations of this life: insights, Openings, Understandings, Suffering, all documented. That guy who wrote it all was very driven, he wanted to see every aspect of the Personality: its past, the family it grew in, its Emotions and beliefs. It's clear now that writing about what I saw of my Personality became a kind of practice. The goal was to Understand it all, to master it. I felt that if I could do that, then I'd be free of its Suffering. Through the years I became gradually more aware of at least parts of my Personality; it helped me Understand my life a bit better.

Matthew: But you weren't Awake?

Jez: (Laughs.) No. Having occasional Openings and experiencing Choice-less Awareness with regards to some of your patterns is not the same as being awake. We talked about an Opening being like a spot of light appearing in a dark night; if Personality regains full control then that light disappears. Because I had the Yearning, that light wasn't rejected in me. Instead of disappearing, it grew. So there were more areas of Choice-less Awareness in my life, but still, they were just scattered spots of light in the vast field that was my Personality.

You could say I was still Dreaming, but I was having occasional flashes of lucid Dreaming. That's more than most people have, but still, that's all it was. So a life was lived in which I knew there was 'more', in which I occasionally experienced the 'more', but I was mostly still subject to the Suffering of the Personality. That Dream of Personality didn't start to be fundamentally challenged until I was in my forties.

Matthew: It's amazing to think that, despite all those years of being open to this and observing Personality, it didn't start to be fundamentally challenged until then.

Jez: That's a measure of the power and strength of the belief that we are Personality. It was drummed into us in childhood and ever since, everywhere we go, everyone we see reflects back that belief that was given to us. Unless we're very lucky and have contact with someone who has Woken Up, this is all we are likely to experience in the Group Personality. So that light of Choice-less Awareness may feel strong when it appears but it's tiny and fairly weak in comparison to the belief in Personality, even when you do all you can to nurture it.

Matthew: So, given that all the odds are against this happening, how does breaking through the Dream of Personality happen?

Jez: That's a huge question – we'll explore it in our next few talks. But we can start by saying that there has to be readiness in you for that Dream to fall away. When there's Readiness, (let's give the word a capital 'R' in this context), nothing can stop it happening. When an apple is ripe, eventually it will fall from the tree.

Matthew: What does that Readiness mean, practically speaking?

Jez: When there's Readiness, the functioning of Personality starts to break down, so in some way your life has to come to a point where this is ready to happen.

Matthew: We've all heard about breakdowns, but what do you mean by the Personality breaking down in this context?

Jez: At the centre of Personality is the Wound; it's like the nucleus, the seed upon which it grew. The Wound is an imprint of our dislocation, our separation from the Love source, so it holds intense trauma and pain.

Everyone's Wound is slightly different, because the circumstances of their formation and the Character to which they happen are different. We all respond in different ways to that loss of our state of Love; there can be feelings of extreme fear, confusion, terror, anger, grief or a mixture of any of these. These primal feelings, once repressed, go onto become Emotions which cluster at the core of our Personality. The Emotions we have in our everyday life all come from the root of these primal Emotions.

Occasionally you may experience a powerful life event such as separating from a lover or the death of a friend; the experience is so traumatic that it hits these primal Emotions and activates them. They rise up from the subconscious to the surface and then the root feeling that's behind the Emotion might be exposed. Think of it like an earthquake: There are all these forces moving under the earth's crust; when the pressure gets too great the crust is split apart and the forces break through to the surface.

An example of this from my childhood was when my parents were arguing fiercely and I felt extremely shaken and upset; that was because the strength of the event brought out those primal Emotions of insecurity and fear.

When the Wound is exposed we get a taste of how we felt when it originally happened. In the Original Relationship to Life, Love was not something we received from out there; we were already 'in' Love. We felt absolutely secure in this state. To quote Lao Tzu, we were 'nurtured by the great Mother'. When we lost that state – when we first felt the absence of Love – we felt adrfit, vulnerable and insecure. When the Wound is triggered, this is what we re-experience.

Throughout my twenties and thirties I was aware of a core of pain inside me that was far beyond what you might call 'normal unhappiness'. It didn't affect me too much on a day-to-day basis because it wasn't exposed. Most of the time I was just getting on with living this life, and it was a pretty good life.

Matthew: You were a successful author.

Jez: Yes. I loved my job; I was paid to use the creativity that was part of my Character. If you'd seen me back then you wouldn't have thought I was troubled; you'd have seen an out-going, creative guy enjoying a successful career. That's because, most of the time, Personality is doing its job of maintaining our identity and functioning in the world while these Emotions lie dormant, repressed at its centre. These breaches of the Personality's edifice are rare, because strong, threatening life experiences like this don't come along too often.

Matthew: So how did the breakdown of Personality happen for you?

Jez: Everything changed in my forty-fourth year: These breaches of the Personality's defence system started happening without any significant or threatening life event to provoke them. For example; one day I was giving a talk to teachers and librarians to promote my books. I'd done these countless times before so I was quite used to it, but before I began the talk I started to feel strange. It was as if something in me had fused: my hands became cold and my heart started racing; I felt abnormally stressed. It was as if something in me didn't want to be where I was, giving that talk, because I didn't have the ability to fulfil that role. It was as if all my energy was being diverted into dealing with the traumatic event that was happening, this energetic release of the Wound.

Matthew: What did you do?

Jez: I tried to apply willpower. My mind said: 'Come on – just get on with it, you can do it, you've done this hundreds of times before.' But the body doesn't care about what your mind wants; the body just expresses whatever's going on in the only way it can, in the form of symptoms. However, despite all this going on, somehow I managed to pull myself together enough to give the talk, but I was severely shaken. I had a few episodes like this over the following months; each time I was greatly disturbed. I knew something was seriously wrong.

These episodes were like hammer blows to the Personality. Its structural integrity was undermined and weakened; the ability to repress didn't work any more. And then came the final blow: the breakdown of Personality.

Matthew: Would you say it was your Readiness that allowed it to happen?

Jez: Yes, but I have to be absolutely clear here: It wasn't 'my' Readiness in the sense that it had come about through my intent or volition. I didn't make Readiness happen any more than I made the Openings, the Yearning, or Choice-less Awareness happen. Having that Readiness is not up to you. A caterpillar doesn't one day choose to become a butterfly; that transition has nothing to do with the caterpillar – it's just life doing its thing. It's all grace, but as someone once said, sometimes it's a 'fierce grace'.

Matthew: What do you mean?

Jez: I mean that the breaking down of the Dream of Personality is not a pleasant or easy experience. We'll go into this in the next talk.

7

BREAKING DOWN

The Personality is dismantled

'You have put so much energy
Into building a prison for yourself.
Now spend as much on demolishing it.
In fact, demolition is easy,
For the false dissolves when it is discovered.'
– Nisargadatta Maharaj

Jez: You've lived identified with Personality your whole life. This is what you've known yourself to be; it's provided a way of feeling safe in the world. When the connection to Personality starts to break down, all that begins to fall apart.

Matthew: That's the first time in a while I've heard you talk about Personality offering something positive.

Jez: Personality is a vehicle to operate in the world. It protects you, gives you strength, identity and functionality. The trouble is, if you believe it's who you are it also brings Suffering, because identification with Personality means you're not resting in the Original Relationship to Life. That's the deal, that's how this works.

If life plants in you the Yearning to Wake Up, then Seeing through Personality is the only way it's going to happen permanently. Therapy and Personal Development courses endeavour to reformat the Personality so that it's more effective and happier. What we're talking about here is finding out who you are beyond Personality. To do that, Personality and its Dream (the life it creates) have to be dismantled, broken down. Going through that can be incredibly disorientating, even terrifying.

Matthew: Breakdowns are so feared in our society, you don't hear them talked about much.

Jez: You're right; in the Group Personality 'normal unhappiness' is accepted as an unwanted but expected part of life. As much as we try to escape it, no one can permanently avoid it. The Personality is used to dealing with this by employing strategies of Distraction, hope etcetera.

A breakdown is different. While it can happen to anyone, it's relatively rare. It's not part of normal unhappiness; the Suffering involved is far greater, and those strategies of Distraction and hope for dealing with normal unhappiness have no effectiveness whatsoever.

Matthew: There's a stigma attached to having a breakdown, isn't there?

Jez: Yes, cancer is more readily talked about these days than breakdowns. Apart from death, breakdowns are the greatest fear in the Group Personality. There's a reason for this: when we use the word breakdown, it's the functionality of Personality that's being referred to. This means it loses its control, and as I've said throughout these talks, one of Personality's main objectives is to be in control. It can't do a thing about the fact that it's breaking down. None of its strategies can distract from it; the Personality becomes powerless.

Matthew: But despite all of that, most people eventually recover.

Jez: Yes, most people take drugs to numb themselves from the psychological pain and wait for the Personality to gradually win back control. The whole traumatic experience is buried in the subconscious (as much as it can be). Victims of breakdowns limp back to their lives and try to pick up where they left off. From extreme unhappiness and Suffering they return to the normal unhappiness of the life of a Personality which, by comparison, is infinitely preferable. Although they've survived the breakdown and come out of it more or less intact, nothing much has been learned or gained from the experience in terms of this Enquiry.

Matthew: Are you suggesting that, if you have Readiness, you can learn from a breakdown, that it can even be beneficial in some way to Waking Up?

Jez: Yes. Readiness has two aspects to it: The first, as I've already mentioned, is that the psychological system of the Personality is ready to break down. The second is the Readiness of the person to whom it happens. Imagine if that person has had some Openings, some glimpses beyond Personality. All their life they've been trying to understand this thing that they've taken themselves to be. When a breakdown strikes and Personality stops functioning normally, it's laid bare. Think of it like a clock: You don't concern yourself with how it works when it's doing its job and displaying the time. If the mechanism breaks down and the clock stops, you can take out its workings, observe the gears, cogs and spindles and get an insight into how it does its job.

So a breakdown can offer an opportunity for Choice-less Awareness to observe and understand the Personality, an opportunity that wasn't there before. Then it's possible that the whole system can be Seen very clearly, and in Seeing it – in making its operation conscious – it starts to become harder for you to be pulled back into the Dream it's creating.

For example, let's say you go to see a brilliantly written stage production and the lead character is played by a superb actor. The craftsmanship is so fine you're pulled into the story: You start to care about the character; every twist and turn of the plot engages you. The whole experience is so powerful that, for as long as it lasts, you actually suspend belief that it's a play. That's the magic of theatre: It can make the artifice of the imagined world it portrays seem real.

Now imagine that the talented actor in the lead role is a close friend of yours; you know intimate details about his life, his marriage, his children. That knowledge works against your ability to be immersed in the drama of the play, because every time you see your friend, you know he's not the character he's portraying. You can't suspend belief, you can't forget that the guy on stage is your friend.

In the same way, when the Personality is Seen, your identification with it is undermined. The more you know your Personality, the harder it becomes for you to be pulled into its 'act'. You can't go unconscious any more, you can't forget that it's a play, a story you're watching: the Dream story of Personality.

So a breakdown offers an opportunity to See the Personality. When that opportunity is used, you could call it a 'Spiritual Breakdown,' because it can lead to a dis-identification with Personality. Firstly, because you become more aware of its whole show and secondly, because the awareness (that you are not it) is strengthened.

Matthew: Can you explain this a bit more?

Jez: On a very basic level, if you've taken yourself to be this Personality all your life, and then find – in a breakdown – that it isn't working 'normally', that challenges your connection to it. You're watching this operating system failing to do its job effectively, and then the question arises: 'Who is watching it?' That immediately shows you that you're not that Personality. How can you be, if you're watching it? So then the question arises: If you're not the Personality, then who are 'you'?

Matthew: The Choice-less Awareness watching it, maybe?

Jez: Yes, that would be one way of expressing it. You're not the Personality; you are the Consciousness (in the form of Choice-less Awareness) watching it. But what you've made there is an intellectual conclusion – it's not coming from Understanding. Having not been in that position yourself – other than during the short period of your Opening – that's all it can be right now. But if you were in that situation of watching Personality breaking down, it wouldn't be just an intellectual conclusion; it would be an energetic Understanding. That means it would have tremendous power to actually change your life, the way you live, who you think you are.

Matthew: Will you tell me about the breakdown that happened to you?

Jez: Yes, but bear in mind that my story isn't a template for everyone; this is just how it happened for me. And it's not really important.

Matthew: Really? How can you say such a life-changing event is not important?

Jez: It's not important to me. If you're not identified with Personality, you lose all fascination with its story. Once you're 'out' of it, what does it matter how you got out?

Matthew: It might not matter to you, but people like me, who are interested in the subject of Awakening, enjoy hearing stories about others' experience of it because they might show us a way out.

Jez: It can be helpful in that it demonstrates the principles of how it happens, but what I'm saying is: Don't get hung up on the details. Also, let me clarify a couple of things before I tell you what happened to me. The breakdown I experienced was not psychotic in nature; there were no delusions or voices from God. Rather than enter an unreal, hallucinatory world, I saw fully the reality of the life I was living and the Personality that was creating it. A Spiritual Breakdown doesn't create psychotic delusions; it reveals the 'everyday delusions' of Personality.

This can happen in different ways; the breaches of Personality that I've talked about can continue, causing a gradual erosion of the functioning of Personality, like a rock being slowly worn away by the sea. In this case a person can keep up the appearance of a normal life; they can still function in the world as if nothing unusual is happening.

But a Spiritual Breakdown can also involve a more immediate

destruction in which the whole show seems to falls apart at once; this would be analogous to an earthquake shattering the rock. In this case there's a much more dramatic collapse of that Dream the Personality is creating and the person is unable to continue much semblance of a normal life. This is the kind of breakdown that happened to me. (Laughs.) I wouldn't recommend it!

Matthew: How did it begin?

Jez: Four months after that first disorientating episode at the talk, I was driving to the southwest of England with my wife for a holiday. It had been a period of mounting stress because these episodes were starting to interfere with me carrying out my job. I saw the holiday as a chance to get some relaxation, which hopefully would put right whatever was wrong with me. After about thirty miles I pulled into a service station for some petrol; on the way back to the car my knees buckled beneath me and... the best way I can put it is my whole Personality just fell apart.

This time there was no coming back from it. I couldn't pull myself together; the centre from which I'd previously operated was still there, but in a very basic, primitive form. As you can imagine, this was accompanied by tremendous anxiety for me, and this was making others around me uncomfortable. Families were becoming upset; people were staring at this grown man, collapsed on the ground, sobbing.

Paramedics were called. They had no training to deal with this; they didn't know what to do with me except take me to the hospital to be checked out. The doctor there was the same: I think because I didn't have any serious physical problems he thought I was wasting his time with some kind of panic attack.

Matthew: What happened next? How did you get home?

Jez: The doctor had given me a tranquilliser, which just about allowed me, with my wife's help, to get home on the train. From there on my life was put in limbo. Without that centre – that part of me through which I interacted in the world – operating as normal, it was almost impossible for me to function.

Matthew: But you could still operate to some extent...

Jez: Yes, in the safety of my own home I could still function, but to a much lesser degree. I had no appetite and was losing a lot of weight; my heart was palpitating and making sleep difficult. I felt this terrible fear for no apparent reason. Also, I became very sensitive to stimuli – I couldn't even watch TV because it overloaded my senses. Silence was the only thing I could deal with; the world of man, of thought and busyness was beyond my capacity. I used to see people through my window going to work and think: 'I used to be able to do that.' It was as if I'd forgotten how to be me. At least, the me I'd been living for forty-odd years.

Matthew: Did you get any medical help?

Jez: I tried to be rational about the situation I found myself in. I thought: 'There's a whole profession dedicated to mental problems like this, I should find out if they can help me.' So I saw a psychiatrist, and found myself in the bizarre position of discussing with a stranger all the intimate, detailed observations I'd made about my psychology which I'd documented in my journals. I'd drawn a map of the whole life of my Personality going right back to the Wound: the primal beliefs, the Emotional patterns and physical symptoms. I think that surprised her; most people don't have that kind of objective knowledge of their psychology. Still, none of it had prevented this catastrophic breakdown happening.

I asked the psychiatrist: 'Am I going mad?' She told me I wasn't. 'What happens now?' I asked, 'Can you help me?' She said that she couldn't make the breakdown go away; the only thing I could do was wait for it to pass. So that's what I did. My life changed dramatically, from being pretty active in the world with my job, to becoming a virtual recluse waiting for 'normal life' to resume.

Matthew: Didn't you want to see people, to get support from friends and family?

Jez: No, for two reasons. Firstly, because it was so painful to be social: With no strong centre I found it really hard to relate to people, and I had absolutely no ability to pretend that I could. Secondly, because breakdowns are every Personality's worst fear, when people saw me in that state it brought up that fear in them. They didn't know what to say, or how to react, which wasn't in any way healing for me.

Matthew: So you retreated from the world?

Jez: Yes, I entered a womb-like situation; my house became my chrysalis.

Matthew: But I know from what you've told me, this wasn't a peaceful, restful retreat?

Jez: Quite the opposite. From the caterpillar's point of view, you can imagine that this stage of entering the chrysalis is catastrophic. His life, as he knew it, ends. He finds himself imprisoned in this chrysalis with no fresh air, no light and no friends or family around. He doesn't know what's going to happen next; he's at the mercy of life.

Matthew: But you knew about Waking Up and the whole Spiritual idea of life beyond Suffering?

Jez: Yes, and in the past I'd had these magical, blissful glimpses of Being, but as I said, they were temporary breaks in the Personality. There was no fear in those Openings because nothing was given up or transcended. They were just free gifts, and afterwards I returned to my everyday life with my Personality more or less intact.

This was different: There was no way back to that operating system which had protected and served me. I was left in this state of terror. I didn't know what relation this had to Waking Up; no one had talked about this in the Spiritual books I read.

Matthew: Were you prescribed medication to lessen the symptoms?

Jez: I was offered some kind of tranquillisers to help with the extreme fear I was going through, but I didn't want them. All my life I've felt that the best response to painful psychological feelings is to feel them; if you repress them you only have to deal with them later. So I made a decision: As long as I could bear the pain, I wouldn't numb myself with medication. I thought: 'Whatever this experience is, I won't protect myself from it. I'll go through it fully, even if it kills me.'

Psychological pain is the hardest thing to watch. We're programmed to pull away from pain, and that actually has the effect of adding more tension and making things worse. The pain kept me focussed sharply in each moment, just as when you cut your finger, it draws your attention to it. My wife has said that, however bad the

intensity of the pain became, she could see in my eyes that I never went unconscious. However painful the drama was I never cut off, I was always there, watching it unfold. In retrospect I can see this willingness to observe fully what was happening was Choice-less Awareness and full-feeling engagement with life arising in me. It was part of the Yearning to return home.

Matthew: Didn't doing that give you some form of hope because you knew it would lead you out of it?

Jez: No. You have to remember that even though Choice-less Awareness arose in me, I didn't know it would lead me out of the Suffering. Like I said, I had no map for this. I didn't know what was going to happen; I was just relieved to get through each day.

Matthew: But it did end.

Jez: Yes, but not in the way I wanted it to, and when I wanted it to!

Matthew: What do you mean?

Jez: When you're in extreme pain you just want it to end, immediately. This is simply a human response; Choice-less Awareness watches whatever is happening, but it doesn't take that inclination away. I was desperate for it all to end, for my 'normal' life to return so I could carry on with the career I had enjoyed and the stability of knowing who I was. That's what happens with most breakdowns, but when it comes to Spiritual Breakdowns you don't have the luxury of that. If Waking Up is going to happen, the breakdown has to undermine your identification with Personality for good. But that didn't happen until much later. First, there came an unexpected twist to the story.

One evening, the psychological Suffering associated with the breakdown I'd been stricken with for eight months intensified. The pain got so bad, it was as if it had been turned up to full intensity. I went to bed drained. I was so sick of being tortured and cut down by this breakdown, I think in my desperation and exhaustion I somehow let go into it. I entered it more fully. This triggered some sort of primal release, and then, in the middle of all that terrible, writhing Emotion... It stopped, and a light broke through the dark night.

WAKING UP

8

AN AWAKENING

A powerful experience of the Infinite

'I am awake for the first time
and all before has been a mean sleep'
– Walt Whitman

Matthew: You were saying that one night, the Suffering of your breakdown intensified and then the light broke through.

Jez: Yes. There's a good quote from Albert Camus that reflects what happened to me:

> *'In the depth of winter I finally learned*
> *that there was in me an invincible summer.'*

When I came downstairs the next morning my wife asked: 'What happened last night? The whole house feels like it's full of light.' I told her: 'I don't know, I went to bed in torment and somehow found myself in the arms of infinity'. That was the expression that came into my head; I used it when I wrote a poem about what had happened.

In the Arms of Infinity

Awakening strikes
Like a flash of lightning illuminating a dark night.
The story of 'you',
With its history of beliefs and Emotions,
And its future of desire and hope –
Dissolves in the arms of infinity.
Outside of the mind and its perception of time,
Free from the stranglehold of Contraction,
It's found that there's no separation from Love.
Each touch, each smell and sound,
Each breath, thought and feeling
Is known as Love happening within, through and around
What has been lived as 'you'.

In the timeless experience of Love
The chasing after desires
And the Distraction from Suffering
Suddenly become redundant.
Now there's nothing to fight for,
Nothing to escape,
Nowhere to go.

Meaning is now found in the simple Joy
Of being planted in the centre of the Mystery of life.
To experience this Mystery,
Through the form of this apparent 'you',
Is all that Oneness wants to do.

Matthew: This reminds me of our earliest talks about how we come into the world. Is what you're describing the same as the Natural State?

Jez: It's an experience of the Natural State of Being which we all live as babies, but there's a difference: In the Natural State there is Choice-less Awareness but there's no self-awareness.

Matthew: Because there's no self yet?

Jez: Yes. In a newborn baby there's no sense of a centre yet, and no consciousness that can observe itself. In an Awakening there's awareness through an adult's consciousness, which can fall upon it and then try to express it in words, as I attempted in this poem. I say attempted, because it's not easy to talk or write about; in fact it's almost impossible.

The Story of 'You' was all about Personality: its function, appearance, motivation etcetera. This all happens in the Relative Level where things can be observed, mapped and described. Language is a product of the mind and as such it belongs to the Relative Level; so discussing Personality is comparatively easy. As I've mentioned before, using words effectively to describe what's beyond the Relative, i.e. the Absolute Level, is not so easy; it's like trying to catch the sky in a butterfly net. And yet, here I am, flailing around with that net!

Matthew: But taking that on board, can you tell me more about what happens in the 'Relative' experience of a person to whom the Awakening has happened?

Jez: I have to stop you there to clarify something: The Awakening doesn't happen to a person. It happens because the viewpoint of the person, or Personality, is suspended. In that suspension, what already is, i.e. the Absolute Level of Oneness, is revealed.

Matthew: It's hard to know how to talk about it without using terms like 'a person having an Awakening'.

Jez: I know. From the perspective of the Relative Level, it appears that 'a person has an Awakening'. Despite my best intentions, as we continue into this discussion, the way I express things may seem to reinforce that viewpoint. But now I've made that point, we can continue. Just keep in mind the fact that, whatever it may sound like, the Awakening doesn't happen to a Personality. It reveals itself because the Personality is temporarily outshone.

Matthew: I get it. We have to talk about this from the Relative Level because that's all we've got.

Jez: Yes, we're playing this impossible game, but it's a good game and it's possible that, through playing it, something useful could be communicated to you.

Matthew: OK so let me try again: How does the Awakening manifest to the person who 'appears' to be having it? How did it feel for you?

Jez: The Awakening appears as a sudden, dramatic expansion of consciousness. Shockwaves pass though the contracted sense of self, opening perception and awakening energy in the cells and tissues of the body. For me there was mostly a great Stillness, a peace which contrasted with the hell I'd been living during the breakdown, but it may also be experienced as swoons of bliss, openings of chakras, intense heat or profound clarity of mind. These are the details, the form it comes in, but mainly there's a feeling of having woken up from a sleep.

Matthew: So is the Awakening event different from…?

Jez: I need to stop you again and clarify something which will help to shed light on what an Awakening is. From the Relative perspective the Awakening seems like an event that happens in time. I went to bed, and it happened at about 1.30 a.m.. However, from the Absolute Level, the Awakening appears because the Personality, which includes the mind and its perception of time, is unhooked from. So we're in this area of two apparently opposing things being true at the same time. From the Relative Level there is the appearance of someone having an experience in time, but that experience is of the Absolute, which is beyond time.

To shed some light on this, think about a baby in the Natural State: They have no concept of time (they have no mind yet which can hold a concept); they are not 'tuned' to the Relative Level where time is perceived. They're 'tuned' to the Absolute Level where there's no such thing. An adult does have a mind and awareness of something called 'time' but during an Awakening they are, like a baby, 'tuned' to the Absolute which is beyond the arising of time.

My point is that the Awakening only appears as an event in time from the Relative perspective. What is revealed in the Awakening is beyond time; however the Personality which is returned to can only relate to the finite world. So when an Awakening is discussed, this timelessness is translated into an event in time. It helps to remember this when we use the word 'event'. So you were saying?

Matthew: I was just wondering, what is the difference between and Opening and an Awakening event? They sound quite similar.

Jez: An Opening is a glimpse beyond Personality, just a short revelation; it may last seconds, or at the most maybe an hour. Because Openings are so fleeting, it's possible – once they've passed – that the experience of them can be repressed, consigned to the subconscious. We found out that this is what happened to some Openings you had when you were younger.

An Awakening is a more powerful, longer-lasting experience of life beyond Personality. Because of its power, it can't be repressed. You are subsumed in an experience of Oneness so strong that, when it's passed, it's impossible to ignore. An Opening is like someone flicking a light on and off again on a dark night; an Awakening would be like that light staying on for much longer so its effect, and the illumination it brings, is much stronger.

You can measure the difference between and Opening and an Awakening by the fallout the person experiences after the 'event'. From what you've told me, what happened to you on the village green was definitely an experience of the Absolute, but it seems like the only real effect it had on you was the occasional arising of Choice-less Awareness. So although it was a powerful experience, it was not analogous to actually Waking Up from the Dream. You could say it was more akin to those moments during sleep where you hear a noise and almost wake up. The Dream is momentarily broken, and then immediately returned to once the disturbance has passed. Subsequent moments of Choice-less Awareness would be analogous to similar, but smaller disturbances of sleep.

So what I'm saying is the Dream is not fully broken, it is quickly returned to. This is what happened after my childhood Openings by the river: I just cycled home and carried on with the life of a teenage boy; I had my tea, played with my brother and watched some TV. Although, like you I'm sure, there was a sense of wonder and happiness for a while.

Matthew: So how are things different after an Awakening?

Jez: You don't just walk away from an Awakening so easily, so unaffected. The Dream has actually stopped, at least for a while, so that makes it harder to fall back to sleep again.

Matthew: You say 'harder', but it still happens then?

Jez: Yes. I remember being in a kind of afterglow for a day or two, and then... It was somehow lost. Not forgotten, just not experienced any more. In most cases I've heard of, the experience passes. It may last for days, weeks or even months but that clear perception of the Absolute usually slips away.

Even though an Awakening is a powerful, extraordinary 'event', afterwards there's a gravitational pull back to what is known, to the safety and comfort of the perspective of Personality. This causes a closing down of the perception and experience of Awakening. You have to remember, despite my Openings and search, I'd lived pretty much identified as this Personality for over four decades. The Personality is a well-protected, strong system. It's not going to just lie down and give up that easily. After the Awakening experience of Oneness, there's the fallout, as the infinite collides with the idea of separation.

Matthew: What was the fallout for you?

Jez: First of all, there was a sense of wonder, of blessedness that this had happened.

Matthew: I've read that some people experience a lot of fear...

Jez: Yes, I've heard that; it all depends on what had come in the life before. For me, I'd already faced so much fear in the breakdown, this Awakening was a blessed relief, a temporary break from all that. Also, having opened myself to the teachings of Oneness, I had some context to make sense of what had happened. This is why I've said that studying the subject of life beyond Personality, while not causing an Awakening, can certainly help in the aftermath of one. Without that grounding in the concepts, the sudden turning upside down of what we've known as 'reality' can, in the return to Personality, shatter our sense of security in the world and stir up great waves of fear.

Matthew: From what I've read, in some people there can also be a lot of energy released and a sense of certainty and strength.

Jez: Yes, there can be a kind of fervour and excitement; the person can appear 'high' on the event. The Awakening is experienced as being extraordinary because the intensity of its light is extraordinary by comparison to how we usually live in the Contraction of Personality. This can cause a kind of zealousness, excitement in the person and a desire to tell everyone about it.

Matthew: Did this happen to you?

Jez: To a degree, but I soon found out that no one was interested. (Laughs). The last thing Personalities want to hear about is an experience beyond Personality. Besides, there was too much else going on. Awakenings are free gifts that point the way to liberation even more powerfully than Openings. But then – after the 'event' – the real work begins: the transformative effect they have on your life. It's not something you do, but it happens. Openings and Awakenings are messages from the Absolute Level, but the ability to live what they reveal concerns the Relative Level of the body, the mind – the operating system of the person.

9

SURRENDER

When the Personality loses its control

'Yield and overcome,
Bend and be straight,
Empty and be full.'
– Lao Tzu

Matthew: So, from what you've told me, the Awakening didn't end the Suffering of the breakdown?

Jez: No. An Awakening is stronger than an Opening – it might last days, weeks or even months – but it doesn't break through the Dream permanently. In my own case, as the perspective of the Awakening wore off, the Suffering of the breakdown started coming back.

Matthew: Can you clarify the difference between a breakdown and an Awakening?

Jez: It's a good question. The word 'breakdown' refers to the breaking down of the functioning of Personality as an operating system. In an Awakening the functioning doesn't break down but it's a powerful experience of Seeing *through* Personality and beyond it. That doesn't mean it's disappeared; you could say that you're temporarily unhooked from it.

When that happened for me in the Awakening I was left with bewilderment and confusion that arose from the mismatch between what I'd glimpsed and the Suffering I'd returned to. It was similar to the situation I'd found myself in after the Openings that started in my teens: I knew there was a place beyond Suffering, but I didn't know how to stay there.

Matthew: We're back to my question of how do you break out of the Dream of the Personality, aren't we?

Jez: Yes, because it's the fundamental question that underpins this whole Enquiry. 'How do we get rid of Suffering?' It's the question that kick-starts most Spiritual Seeking... and finding the answer is what ends it.

Matthew: Are you going to give me the answer?

Jez: I've been giving you the answer from our very first talk. But do you have the Readiness to hear it, beyond an intellectual level? However genuinely this question is asked, even by sincere Spiritual Seekers, most people don't want to hear the answer.

Matthew: Why is that?

Jez: Because the Suffering we're talking about being free of is an outcome of identifying with Personality, so to be free of it requires you to venture beyond the control of Personality. And that's something this entity called Personality doesn't want you to do. The Personality wants to survive; it doesn't want to be seen through and dismantled. It doesn't want you to ask why you're feeling depressed, why you're addicted, why your mind never wants to rest. Rather than look at the root cause of those problems, Suffering is dealt with by looking the other way: by taking tranquillisers and medicine to make the symptoms disappear, by numbing oneself with drink, getting out of one's head on drugs or chasing happiness, success and all the other forms of Distraction. There's a whole machinery in place to Distract you from your Suffering, to stop you questioning the Personality. What I'm talking about here is going in the other direction, walking towards the Suffering and feeling it.

Escape from Suffering is normalised in the Group Personality, but as I've said, that doesn't mean it's natural. We come into this world in the original state of Being, with full-feeling engagement with whatever we experience. That's what we've lost, but that's what is required if the Dream of Personality is to break down.

Matthew: Some teachers say: 'You just Wake Up,' and all this talk of some sort of process is unnecessary. They say there's no future, there's only the present moment, so how can there be this gradual process of breaking down?

Jez: One of the myths of enlightenment is that you instantaneously Wake Up out of the Dream and all the Suffering vanishes forever. It's a pleasing idea, but our relationship to Suffering is much more complex than that.

Matthew: Can you expand on that a bit more?

Jez: Let's have a recap: Openings and Awakenings are instantaneous shifts of perception to the timeless, Absolute Level. In the return to the Relative Level you're confronted once again with time and cause and effect, and with that comes your identification with Personality and its history. That's what stands between you and the permanent connection to what's glimpsed in the Openings.

Matthew: Because we live in this Relative Level?

Jez: Yes. Like everything else, human beings are a manifestation of the Absolute Level, but we're built to exist in the Relative Level. I'm talking to you, sharing with you; that requires the appearance of a 'you' and a 'me'. I'm feeling the warmth of this tea in my cup; that requires fingers, blood vessels, blood, a bodymind system that feels temperature. We are infinite beings but we appear on this earth with a body and the power to think, judge and to love each other. All of that arises from the appearance of separateness in the Relative Level. That idea of separateness started as a self, and after the Wound that self developed into the Personality; then all the Suffering began. So, as human beings built to function in the Relative Level, we live through the Dream our Personality creates – and that includes its Suffering.

Matthew: Unless you have an Opening or an Awakening?

Jez: Yes, then there'll be a temporary break from the Dream, a glimpse into the Absolute perspective, but when the Opening or Awakening ends... that perception will be lost.

Matthew: How do you know it will end?

Jez: Because identification with Personality is so strong, so ingrained, that unless it's broken, the Personality will pull you back into its Dream. When someone says, 'You just Wake Up,' it's technically true, because there's a moment when the identification with Personality and its Dream is there, and the next moment, it isn't. But the word 'just' is misleading and inaccurate, because what is not addressed in the phrase 'You just Wake Up' is how Readiness brings you to that moment in which that identification falls away. The apple won't fall from the tree until it's completely ripe, until it's absolutely ready to let go.

Belief in the Dream and attachment to it is broken down in time, in the Relative Level of a human being with psychology and a past. The Absolute perception is always there as a potential; the breaking down of identification with Personality in the Relative Level is simply removing what obscures it. If that doesn't happen, you may be blessed with more Openings or Awakening events but you will always return to the Dream and its Suffering, because the machinery creating it is still in place.

Matthew: The way you talk about this breaking down of the attachment to the Dream makes it sound like a Spiritual practice: It has the same goal as a practice – freedom – and it happens in time.

Jez: There are very important differences between the two: A practice is something you *do* to attain a result. A Spiritual Breakdown and breakthrough – that devastating confrontation with Personality – isn't something you *do*; it's something that just happens. A practice has the goal of freedom from Suffering in an imagined future, but the Spiritual Breakdown can create the environment in which that freedom is actually delivered. A practice is like a controlled experiment to try to achieve that result. A breakdown is the loss of control, in which that freedom can be revealed.

Matthew: So to be in that Readiness involves a loss of control…?

Jez: Yes, and possibly increased Suffering. As the control of Personality lessens, so all the repressed Emotions can come up. Most Spiritual Seekers don't want to hear this; understandably, they're attracted to the belief that you just Wake Up instantly, because then they won't have to confront their past. They're in this for some idea of bliss, and here I am talking about the Suffering getting worse!

Matthew: It does seem crazy to go willingly into Suffering. I mean, who'd want to do that? Only a masochist, surely…

Jez: It does seem crazy. The Personality screams: 'Whatever you do, don't go there…' But people who do go there aren't masochists, or mentally deranged; they're just acting on an impulse that doesn't come from Personality.

Matthew: You mean the Yearning?

Jez: Yes. Yearning is the vital ingredient that can turn a breakdown into a breakthrough. That innate pull to return home to your state of Being is so strong it can override all these instincts of self-protection. There are many people sincerely Seeking Spiritual fulfilment, a freedom from Suffering, but not everyone has the Yearning that wants it like a drowning man wants air. So hearing me talk about how identification with Personality has to be broken down is a test to any Spiritual Seeker. If you don't have the Yearning, then you'll make your excuses and turn back. You'll find reasons to dispute what I'm saying and hang on to a belief in either a gradual path through a practice like meditation, or an instantaneous Waking Up – because that seems a lot easier than facing your Personality and watching it break down.

It's easy to get stuck on the Spiritual path. What this means is the openness to this Enquiry has run dry, the Personality has taken back control and your unfolding is arrested. You've amassed a lot of spiritual beliefs, you might have gained some Understanding along the way, but you don't progress any further. A lot of people get stuck in that spiritual wasteland, like buds that haven't quite bloomed into flowers.

Anyone with real Yearning and Readiness won't be put off by what I'm saying. They'll just be glad of more information and encouragement from a fellow traveller to light their way as they face whatever they have to face on their path. Because in the end, only someone who's been through some kind of Spiritual Breakdown and passed out the other side can offer any useful guidance to someone going through this. This knowledge is beyond theories and psychiatric textbooks; the Understanding of this can only arise from personal experience.

Matthew: Did you have any guidance or help like this yourself?

Jez: The only thing I found that helped me was a passage in a book about Carl Jung in which he talks about going through his own breakdown; he called it a 'creative illness'. The idea that the illness I was in the grip of could be creative was a turning point. I started to have a different relationship to this thing that had brought my life to its knees: I began to have a deep respect for it. I saw it as a teacher because it could teach me things no other experience in the Relative Level could, because no other experience was so radical, so powerful. Just as the Openings and Awakening taught me about the Absolute Level, so the breakdown revealed the workings of Personality in the Relative Level.

There's an idea that when you die, your life passes before your eyes. In a Spiritual Breakdown the history of the Personality can come up; repressed Emotions ingrained in the bodymind are exposed, not all at once but progressively. And of course, eventually we start to experience the one thing we've avoided, our worst fear...

Matthew: You mean the Wound?

Jez: Yes. I've mentioned how the Wound, which lies at the centre of Personality, can be exposed in really traumatic situations. Personality is built around defending us from this trauma so, if it happens, we don't face it for long and it's soon repressed. By not facing the Wound, we avoid its pain but never get to experience the Love and freedom that lies beyond it.

If the Personality's control has been lost, and it can no longer repress the exposure of the Wound, then you're confronted with it. We all have our own particular version of horror, which ultimately comes down to our experience of the separation from Love, the particular circumstances in which the Wound happened.

Like everyone else, I'd packed the trauma from my Wound away and learned how to get on with my life in spite of it. But it laid in waiting; throughout my life I knew it was there. When it occasionally showed its face, I looked at it as much as I could, even understood it psychologically, but that's just a mental confrontation. That's not the same as feeling the trauma, going into it, re-experiencing it.

Matthew: And you did this willingly?

Jez: I learned I couldn't do anything to make it go away, and when Doing ends, when resistance falls away, there is surrender. (Pause.) It wasn't a strategy; I didn't surrender, but surrender happened and when it did, something changed in my experience of the breakdown. I'm not saying I was suddenly free of it all – you have to understand that it went on for years – but I noticed there was an energetic change in how my life was lived. Although I still had to face whatever I had to face, I was at least in a kind of harmony with what was happening. I wasn't resisting it, so I wasn't creating more pain from that resistance.

A Spiritual Breakdown is like entering a fire: It looks like it's going to destroy you, but in fact it only destroys the false in you. If you are Ready and surrender happens, your identification with Personality starts to be burnt away.

10

THE SHIFT – Part One

When identification with Personality
drops away permanently

'We shall not cease from exploration.
And the end of all our exploring
Will be to arrive where we started
And know the place for the first time.'
– T.S. Eliot

Matthew: The question that keeps arising is 'How does one Wake Up out of the Dream of Personality permanently?' You've talked about Readiness, Yearning and surrender but I still don't feel you've actually answered the question...

Jez: What you're referring to is what I call the 'Shift'. This is the moment when identification with Personality is broken forever. Let's try a different approach to this question: How do you think that happens?

Matthew: I presume it's the culmination of the breaking down of the Personality. You've said that throughout your life Choice-less Awareness fell on the Personality, but just parts of it, like flecks of light in the field of grey. When a Personality is exposed in a breakdown and there's surrender to it, I imagine those flecks of Awareness gradually get bigger and take over the Personality until there's nothing left of it.

Jez: It's logical to think that, once Choice-less Awareness has seen through all the patterns and forms of Personality, then Suffering stops; then there's no Personality left, no Dream. This is how life usually works in the Relative Level when it comes to progress: A logical, steady progression continues until the goal is achieved. But the Shift doesn't happen like that.

Matthew: Why is that?

Jez: This is a very important point. The truth – that you're not the Personality – exists now, not just in a future that arrives when you've Seen through all of its layers and structures. Whether you're ready to experience and live that now is a different matter.

Matthew: This sounds contradictory to me because you said we need to confront those layers of the Personality.

Jez: Confrontation with them happens, and it can contribute to you being ready for the Shift, but that's not what actually frees you from the Dream of Personality. This is not about an accumulation of knowledge, insight or even awareness. It's about finding an entry point into the Understanding that you're already free; that you're not your Personality.

Matthew: If Awareness of Personality doesn't ultimately bring about a freedom from Personality, people might ask: Why practice it?

Jez: It's a fair question. To put it another way, the logic you're applying is: If no practice works, not even awareness, then you might as well do nothing. This conundrum can lead to a trap, because the mind is used to the logic of action followed by result: 'If I do this, I'll get that.' So now it starts to practice a kind of searching in reverse. It says: 'If I don't practice and I give up, I'll reach the goal.' But it won't necessarily deliver freedom.

Matthew: Why not?

Jez: Because it's still a practice, a Doing. There's still a Personality applying the logic of 'When I get this I'll be happy.'

Matthew: This is impossible!

Jez: To the logical mind, yes, it is.

Matthew: So you're left in a double bind: Doing nothing doesn't get you there and doing something doesn't either?

Jez: Correct, no practice can deliver this to you.

Matthew: But Choice-less Awareness is beneficial?

Jez: Yes, but remember, Choice-less Awareness is not a practice.

Matthew: Remind me why...

Jez: Because it's not something you *do* to achieve a result, it's something that arises spontaneously; there's no Personality intention behind it. The word 'Choice-less' has a double application here, because Choice-less Awareness is Choice-less with regards to what it falls on, but also Choice-less in that you don't choose to have it. It doesn't arise though willpower.

Matthew: So Choice-less Awareness is beneficial because...?

Jez: Because it can fall on the Personality, so all of its workings can be Seen. As we've discussed, when Personality is Seen, your identification with it is undermined. So what I'm saying is: Choice-less Awareness can create an environment in which deliverance from the Dream of Personality can happen, however – and this is important – that deliverance is not the result of a linear progression. It's not dependent on Seeing every layer and facet of the Personality. It can happen after Seeing one facet, or three, or a hundred; you can't know. It just depends on how ready the 'apple' is to fall from the tree.

Matthew: So what would your advice be to that younger you, who wrote those journals and tried for all those years to understand his Personality in order to get free of it?

Jez: I'd say: 'Keep on doing what you're doing.' What else can you do but follow that passion, that path? From that side of the Dream, all you can do is keep watching. Like I said, I had no choice about it anyway.

Matthew: OK, so to summarise, there's nothing you can do, or not do, to Wake up from that Dream. Choice-less Awareness can be beneficial but that's not something you do either. So, taking all that on board, I still want to try and pin this down: How does the Shift actually happen?

Jez: Of all the questions that arise in this Enquiry, this is the most difficult to answer. As I've said, explaining how the Personality functions is much easier because it all happens in the Relative Level where logic is applicable. Science works in the Relative Level: It's the investigation of things that abide by rules; it can be broken down into logical pathways, equations and conclusions. For example, in chemistry, matter can be observed under the microscope, analysed accurately and understood through the application of reason. We know that water is made from hydrogen and oxygen: This can be proven as a physical fact. Psychology is more nebulous than Chemistry because, rather than dealing with matter, it's dealing with mind. Thoughts, feelings and Emotions can't be physically put under the microscope but they can still be examined. With careful observation you can analyse and understand patterns of behaviour because there's logic to them. There's cause and effect: 'This happened and I felt that' etcetera.

In these talks we've mostly been discussing the Personality.

Although the material is perhaps unusual and alien to you, it can still be understood intellectually because of the logic that underlies it.

Matthew: Apart from when we've introduced the subject of the Absolute Level, like when we were talking about Awakening.

Jez: Yes, exactly. When we talk about Oneness, Being, Consciousness or Love things get more difficult. Logic starts being left behind, words become inadequate. Then we find that more poetic language becomes a better tool to point in the direction of what's being discussed. However, for the most part we've been dealing with the functioning of Personality, but now we've come as far as we can in discussing the approach to the Shift from the Relative Level of a Personality. We've talked about Yearning, Readiness, surrender and the breakdown; all this helps you See through your identification with it, but then the world of logic runs out. That's indicative of the Absolute coming in.

Matthew: What do you mean? Why is it coming in?

Jez: Waking up happens when the Relative Level of a person...

Matthew: Hold on, what do you mean by 'the Relative Level of a person'?

Jez: I mean the whole functioning of the mind which translates the Oneness into Duality – the sense of separation which we learn to operate as, the sense of 'Me-ness'. Waking up happens when the Relative Level of a person, that idea of separation, meets the Absolute Level of Oneness. Where these two realties meet, things become nebulous. The closer you get to the Absolute Level...

Matthew: I need to stop you again? Isn't everything the Absolute Level?

Jez: Of course.

Matthew: Well, if everything is the Absolute Level, how can you get closer to it?

Jez: You're right. Looking from the Absolute Level, as you've just done to make that comment, the idea of getting closer to Oneness is absurd. But I'm attempting to describe what happens in a Shift – which refers to a Shift from the Relative Level, i.e. from the perspective of Personality. From that viewpoint, there appears to be separateness, and then there appears to be something which is not separate, which is the Absolute. So we're engaging with concepts because of the Personality's belief that it is separate. Without that belief there'd be no need for these concepts, these discussions or for this book. I could just say 'You are Love', you'd nod in agreement and that would be it. But then again, there'd be no need to even say it...

Matthew: I see what you mean.

Jez: So, allowing for the limitations of language, I was saying that the closer our discussion gets to the Absolute Level, the more we leave the domain of logic and the mind loses its illusion of control. After you Wake Up, at first you don't necessarily know what's happened. You know you've 'arrived somewhere', but you don't know how you got there.

Matthew: OK, so I'll rephrase my original question: Looking back on your experience from this perspective, how did the Shift happen? You must have some recollection of that time?

Jez: In the next talk I'll tell you what I remember, but once again, bear in mind that this isn't a template for everyone.

11

THE SHIFT – Part Two

Synthesis of the Absolute & Relative Levels

'You have been hiding so long,
Endlessly drifting in the sea of my love.
Even so, you have always been connected to me:
Concealed, revealed, in the known, in the unmanifest.
I am life itself.'

– Rumi

Jez: After the Awakening I found myself back in the ruins of that broken-down life. As you can imagine, what I wanted to happen was for the breakdown to end and the Awakening to return. But like I always say, this Enquiry is about how life is, not how you'd like it to be. The fact was, as with my teenage Openings, I could do absolutely nothing to bring back the Awakening.

Matthew: So what happened?

Jez: There was just this... surrender. That's the word that comes to mind.

Matthew: Surrender to the fact that there was nothing you could do to bring the Awakening back?

Jez: It was more brutal, more radical than that. There was surrender to the idea that I might never get it back. As it wasn't happening, I thought maybe that life I glimpsed in the Awakening was never going to be a permanent experience for me.

Matthew: Despite the Yearning you've had all your life?

Jez: Yes, someone once said: 'Pain is wanting life to be different.' It's a glib, rather blunt aphorism but it does contain some truth. You can't fight what life gives you. For me, that ongoing perspective of what I'd glimpsed in the Awakening was not returning. I couldn't get it back. I couldn't even talk to anyone about it (apart from my wife) because no one wanted to hear or know about it...

So there was a giving up of the hope that I'd be delivered into that perspective permanently, and a surrender to living a life outside of it. This was the final let-go, the surrender of the idea of that Awakening returning. You could say my expectations were downgraded.

Matthew: To what? You still had some expectations then?

Jez: Yes, the Spiritual expectations had gone; the only ones left were practical. All I wanted now was to get back into my previous life, the one I lived before the breakdown, where I could function and operate in the world, do my job and be like other, 'normal' people.

When the extreme cathartic stage of the breakdown seemed to have lessened, I tentatively tried to get back into my life as an author, working on new books and doing occasional promotional events. It was like putting on an old suit; I'd been doing that job for 30 years. I knew how to do it, I was good at it, and at least it gave an outlet for my creativity.

Matthew: So you picked up your old life as if nothing had happened?

Jez: I tried to. That was the plan, but something felt wrong. I found I was not as at ease in the role as I'd once been. It felt like a part I was playing; I wasn't really 'in it' the way I had been before.

As the years passed I felt more and more uncomfortable carrying out that role; I started to feel like a fraud. This manifested as symptoms of ill health. The body doesn't lie; you can always rely on it to tell you when something you're doing isn't in alignment with who you are.

Matthew: But you didn't want to stop?

Jez: No. You have to realise that this semblance of a life was all I had left, and now that was being taken away! I fought for it for years; I tried to reclaim it. But just as with the Awakening, I had to surrender any idea of getting it back. It felt like jumping off a cliff, like a kind of death, and actually, it was.

Matthew: What do you mean?

Jez: I can see now that the life I'd been trying to force my way back into was the last stand of my Personality. When I let go of that, or rather, when that dropped away, it seemed to be the final straw. It was a death, not the death of the Personality but the death of identification with it. That was the Shift. It is a return to living a life in which there is a synthesis of the Absolute and Relative Levels.

Matthew: What does that mean?

Jez: Imagine a baby. To her parents she appears as a separate being, but this is a perception that doesn't arise in the baby. Her experience is that she's just part of everything that's arising around her in the physical world. So there's no division between the Absolute and Relative Levels; you could say that her consciousness experiences both at the same time, and this creates a kind of harmony which anyone around can feel. That's what I mean by a synthesis between the Absolute and Relative Levels.

As we discussed in *The Story of 'You'*, the longer we live in the world, the more we 'tune' to the Relative Level; gradually our developing minds learn to name it all and then everything starts to become separate. Eventually we arrive at that decisive moment when we *apparently* become separate too.

Matthew: You mean when we identified as the self.

Jez: Yes, identification with the self acts like a portal: Before it, there is synthesis between the Relative and Absolute realities; after it, that is lost and the Relative Level is mostly what's perceived. Just as we see ourselves as separate, within the confines of this body, so that's how we see the world. We see according to the mind and the sense of 'I'; we see mostly the duality. This means that, although we're unaware of it, we experience a division, a dissonance, a lack of harmony between the Absolute and Relative Levels. Why? Because we're operating as if there is only the Relative Level. The outcome of this is the Suffering of Personality. Because we've forgotten that we are One, we are Love, we suffer the illusion of thinking we are separate from Love.

Matthew: Unless we have an Opening – then we suddenly have an experience beyond the Relative.

Jez: Yes, then a more Spiritual life begins, in which there's recognition that there's something more – beyond this rational, physical world of things and names. We start to remember the Absolute that lies behind the Relative.

In an Awakening we have an even stronger experience of that Absolute Level, but because we've not fully lost identification with the Personality, that perception is lost. So there's still a dissonance between the Absolute and the Relative. This manifests as a return to the Suffering of the Personality; and having now experienced a taste of liberation, this can take on a greater intensity.

Matthew: So after the Shift, there's no disharmony experienced between the two levels?

Jez: None at all. When that identification falls away permanently in the Shift, the perspective of the Absolute Level becomes ongoing. So there's no longer any division between the Absolute and Relative: there's a synthesis of the two Levels. The Relative Level is understood to be the Absolute Level; the two become One again. Like the newborn baby, you inhabit the Relative Level in a physical body but somewhere, you're always tuned to the Absolute.

Matthew: What does that actually mean?

Jez: It means that, like the newborn baby, you're connected to the source, without the interference and distorted perspective that comes from being identified with Personality. However, as I've said before, an adult experiences Oneness in a different way from how a baby experiences it, because we can fully perceive the separateness of the Relative world as well. (This perception includes the apparent appearance of an 'I' with a name attached to it). We have a mind which can label and separate the world, but after the Shift, it's never forgotten that it's all just an appearance in Oneness.

When I talk about a synthesis between the Absolute and Relative Levels, remember it's just a way for me to try to express what this Shift is. It's just a concept I'm using. I wouldn't want you to think I go around thinking: 'Ah, it's wonderful to feel the synthesis of the Absolute and Relative Levels.' The concept is simply an attempt to translate the experience and feeling of the Shift into thought and information. I want to talk about concepts and their use with regards to this Enquiry at some point, but let's not get too distracted here.

Matthew: OK. I have a question about the Shift: How does it relate to what happened in the Awakening? What's the difference?

Jez: There are two main differences: First, the Awakening is temporary; the Shift is permanent. The identification with the Dream is totally cut; you can no longer fall back to sleep and be pulled into the Dream. So it's only after the Shift that you can truly say that Waking Up has happened. The Shift is the transition into the ongoing perspective that was glimpsed in the Awakening.

Matthew: But how do you know it's permanent? How do you know you won't wake up one morning...?

Jez: ...And not be Awake! (Both laugh.) It's a good question, not an easy one to answer but I'll try. The question included two uses of the word 'awake': awaking from sleep and Awaking from the Dream of Personality. The first use refers to the world of duality; it applies to the Relative Level of a human being in which two opposite states appear: the waking and the sleeping states. In the waking state we are conscious, we're perceiving the world through our senses. In the sleeping state we're unconscious.

The second use of the word 'Awake' applies to Consciousness, which, as you'll remember, originates beyond the human domain. To experience that impersonal Consciousness pertains to the Absolute Level that lies beyond the 'personal', Relative Level. Consciousness has no opposites; unlike small 'c' consciousness, it can't be turned off. There's no such thing as un-Consciousness.

Matthew: No, but your access to it can be turned off. You had access to it in the Awakening, and that wasn't permanent...

Jez: It's true. So now we're getting to the nub of this. Consciousness (with a capital 'C') is ever present, but access to it, the experiencing of it, isn't. Waking Up becomes permanent when access to Consciousness remains.

Matthew: So how does that access to Consciousness remain?

Jez: It remains when identification with Personality falls away completely. That's the key: In an Awakening it hasn't fallen away completely; if it had, then the state of Awakening wouldn't end. In fact it wouldn't be an Awakening; it would be the Shift.

Matthew: Which begs the question: How do you know that identification has fallen away completely?

Jez: Because my experience is that it has ended. In the end that's all I can say. There was a point when it hadn't ended, and Choice-less Awareness observed that fact. (It's pretty obvious because you're still engaged and ensnared in the Suffering of Personality.) Now Choice-less Awareness observes the fact that identification has fallen away. Other than that, there's no external proof of the Shift. There's no definitive test, like a pregnancy test, that can scientifically take a reading! Right now, you don't know if it has happened in my case, and my saying that it has doesn't mean much to you – it's just an opinion I'm holding. If the Shift happened for you, you'd know it; and then you'd be able to recognise that it had happened in this case. You would feel like I feel, that you could no more forget this perspective than you could forget that you have two arms.

Matthew: OK. So, unlike an Awakening, you're saying that the Shift is permanent. What's the second difference between an Awakening and the Shift?

Jez: It's about the nature of the experience: An Awakening arrives with a great fanfare as the Dream is suddenly Woken out of; this turns our perception of ourselves and the world upside down and inside out. In the body there can be bliss, heat, shaking and openings of energy. After the 'event', this dramatic expansive experience of the Absolute is lost, leaving only an imprint of it in the body-mind memory.

The Shift is different from the Awakening in that there's no drama like this. Like a change in the seasons, there's no single point at which you can say the transition has happened. For me it was such a low-key transition that at first there wasn't even the recognition that anything *had* happened. If you imagine a young child before identification with the self, there's no need or inclination to identify who or what they are. There's simply what arises without the translation of that into a thought or concept.

Gradually, through Choice-less Awareness, the Understanding arose that a Shift has occurred. Identification with Personality had fallen away, not just temporarily, but permanently. I experienced it as a quiet recognition of Being, which is extraordinary only in its ordinariness.

Matthew: It seems pretty extraordinary to me, so what do you mean by that?

Jez: Compared to life identified as Personality, which is most people's experience, it's certainly out of the ordinary. But from the point of view of the Absolute, we've always been this, so in that sense, it is ordinary. It is simply a return to our beginning, a return to who we already are.

12

ENLIGHTENMENT MYTHS

Exposing the idea of human perfection

'Do you think you can take the universe and improve it?
I do not believe it can be done.'
– Lao Tzu

Matthew: I need to clarify some terminology before we go on. Are you saying that someone who's had an Awakening is not Awakened?

Jez: Yes. An Awakening passes, so it's incorrect to say that someone who has had one is Awakened.

Matthew: But if the Shift has happened, then they are Awakened, because the dis-identification with Personality is permanent?

Jez: Correct.

Matthew: So, by that definition, you're Awakened? (Pause.) You look kind of uncomfortable...

Jez: The Dream of my Personality has been permanently awoken from, so the answer is yes... But I wouldn't normally use that term, or the other word – Enlightenment – in reference to myself.

Matthew: Why not?

Jez: Because those words are burdened by misinformation and this makes using them problematic. Let's use our Timbuktu analogy;* imagine I live in Timbuktu and I'm trying to describe accurately to you what it's like to live there. You've never been there, but you've heard many stories from people who say they have. When I talk about my experience of Timbuktu you hear it through the prism of what you've previously heard. That's how the mind works: It tries to understand the world around it by piecing together information it gathers from various sources. But when it comes to matters of the Absolute, this is not so helpful: That idea you've constructed of what it means to be Awake is not the same as the experience of being Awake. There are two reasons for this: First, the sources from which you've gathered this information can't all be relied on.

Matthew: You mean because not everyone who says they're Awakened actually is?

Jez: Correct: Some of those people who say they know Timbuktu haven't actually been there. They may be experts on all that's been written about it, part of their Personality's Dream may be the belief

---

* *The Story of 'You'* – Page 296

that they have been there, but none of this is the same thing as the experience of actually being in Timbuktu. So what they say about it can't be trusted. If it's not first-hand experience, it's just rumours going round.

Matthew: What about people who have been there, people who've had an Awakening experience?

Jez: Having visited Timbuktu, they may have some worthwhile things to say about it, but, as a guide, they won't be as reliable as someone who lives there. So if you listen to their account, there will be some truth in it, but also inaccuracies can come in. We'll go into this subject more when we discuss teachers and gurus...

Matthew: OK, and what's the second reason that I can't necessarily rely on reports I've heard about what Awakening is?

Jez: Quite apart from the reliability of their sources, when you hear those reports they're filtered through your Personality, so your idea of what this is, is partly derived from your interpretation of it. Most people see in this what they want to see; this is especially the case with the word 'enlightenment'. The literal meaning of the word 'en–lighten' is to dispel darkness or confusion; it's a beautiful and accurate application of the word. Symbolically the 'darkness' of the Dream (the Suffering) is dispelled by the light of Choice-less Awareness. But the word 'enlightenment' has taken on a different meaning; it's been overlaid with all sorts of beliefs and projections that aren't in alignment with the truth of what this is really about.

Matthew: Can you be more specific?

Jez: How would you describe an average person's image of someone who's enlightened?

Matthew: Some guy at the top of a mountain...

Jez: It's never a woman is it?

Matthew: No, it's quite a male-centric image. It's a guy who's reached a level of understanding that makes him almost superhuman. It's as if he has special powers and isn't subject to the same laws as 'normal' people like us.

Jez: That just about covers it. For those interested in finding out what is true, for those with a Yearning towards freedom, this belief causes no end of obfuscation and misunderstanding. For a start, it suggests that this sort of freedom can't happen to you, it's exclusive to some divinely appointed superhuman breed. The word 'enlightenment' has come to refer to an idea of human perfection. Waking Up has nothing to do with being superhuman; rather, it's about being fully human.

What does it mean to be human? Let's look at it this way: What's the difference between a human and a robot?

Matthew: A robot doesn't have feelings for a start.

Jez: Right, one of the essential characteristics of being human is our capacity to feel. Will you look up the dictionary's definition of the word 'superhuman'?

Matthew: It says: 'Having a higher nature or greater powers than humans have.'

Jez: Our nature is to feel: Having a 'higher nature' suggests that part of being superhuman is to be *beyond* feeling. And this is one image that many people have of what enlightenment is about: A person who's detached, beyond feeling.

Matthew: Hang on a moment; I felt a sense of detachment during my Opening on the village green.

Jez: Yes, detachment does arise; it's a detachment from Personality, from Emotion, moods and all the Suffering that identification with Personality creates. But – and this is a very big but – it's not a detachment from feeling the Joy, the sadness, the whole gamut of human experience. That's what I mean when I say it's about being fully human.

So this is a misinterpretation of the original meaning of the word 'enlightenment' and it creates a lot of confusion. The problem is compounded by the fact that many Personalities are quite content to believe this misinterpretation, this myth of perfection in which freedom is abstracted into a set of holy ideals that are inhuman, other worldly, from another plane. The Absolute isn't somewhere else; it is right here in this plane, in the form of the Relative Level. That includes all sorts of feelings and experiences of being human, but after Waking Up, it no longer includes the outcomes of identifying with Personality, because that is what falls away.

The idea of reaching a perfected state is hardwired into the Spiritual search and it's simply not accurate. It's a glittering toy for the mind to play with, to hope for, to fixate on. Enlightenment, in the definition that it's been reduced to, becomes just another set of hopes and beliefs for the Personality to distract itself with – an elaborate abstraction in the game of: When I get this I'll be happy.

Matthew: So if we use the term in the original sense, i.e. to en-lighten, that would be accurate?

Jez: Yes, but it would be impractical for me to use because I've no control over how the word is interpreted. I'd be using it to describe someone who's returned to the Natural State but, as I've explained, most people would hear it as a description of someone with superhuman qualities.

But the problem runs deeper than that: The original meaning of the word is fine when it's used as a verb, because when this understanding blossoms in you it does en-lighten, it does take away the 'darkness' (i.e. the Suffering) caused by identification with Personality. However when it's used as an adjective, when we say: 'This person is enlightened,' or 'I am enlightened,' a fundamental inaccuracy enters the picture.

Matthew: Why is that?

Jez: Because no one gets enlightened; that's not what happens. For someone to claim something called enlightenment there has to be a Personality there who is claiming it. In this understanding there's a Seeing through of the 'I' that could claim to be enlightened. So from this point of view, anyone who claims to be enlightened is simply displaying the fact that they have *not* seen beyond their Personality.

Matthew: But aren't you claiming to have Woken Up?

Jez: No, I'm not claiming that. That's the point. That's why I try to avoid such talk: Because that misinterpretation can be, and usually is, applied to it. No one has Woken up. A Waking up has happened, but it's not happened to 'me'; it's happened because identification with that 'me' has fallen away.

Think of it this way: If, as a baby, Lucy (our invented character from *The Story of 'You'*) had the power of cognition and speech, would she go around saying: 'I have achieved the Natural State'? That would be ludicrous: She has not achieved the Natural State, Lucy *is* the Natural State. Did Lucy do anything to be it? No, that's why it's called the Natural State. It exists before any Personality can claim it.

Remembering and returning to Being as an adult is essentially the same; the only difference is that we have self-consciousness, and know what it's like to be identified, to be lost, and we've come out of that lostness. Coming out of it does not turn us into some superhuman breed of man or womankind.

What we're talking about here is recognising what we already are. When this is known, all the myths and projections about enlightenment, and the people who play that enlightened role and believe they're somehow special, start to look a bit ridiculous. This realisation is not superhuman or other worldly; it's utterly human. Are newborn babies in the Natural State superhuman? No, they're simply human, and that's enough. It's only the Personality that wants more, that creates an idea of extraordinariness, of specialness.

Matthew: I do know what you mean. The word 'enlightenment' is used to describe some sort of perfected human state, isn't it?

Jez: Yes, but what does that mean? If something's perfect it implies that it's as good as it can be, doesn't it? Evolution has finished; there's nowhere else it needs go.

*Matthew: Right, but – if I've understood you correctly – the Shift means that the version of life that appeared before it **has** finished completely.*

Jez: Yes, the belief in the Personality has ended; it's been seen through once and for all. The Awakening is a passing glimpse beyond the Personality; the Shift is a permanent landing in that viewpoint. So the Shift itself could be said to be perfect in the sense that it's complete. But what comes up in the life of the person after that Shift isn't complete,

it's an open book. Life hasn't finis
you want to experience the Grand
there. But that isn't the case: Going t

I've been to the Grand Canyon
take the experience in because the ca
real. So then you walk on one of the t
the rocks and look at the vegetation. Cl
rocks changes their colour. Where does
to a point where you can say: 'I have ful
Canyon?' I don't think so. In this sense, the
a beginning.

My whole emphasis in these talks is   ...an you off the
projection of this realisation as some perfected, superhuman state.
I understand why this idea of perfection comes about, because after
the Shift life *is* lived differently, there's no doubt about that. Someone
who lives beyond Personality has a flow and ease in how their lives
are run. Someone who has dropped all strategies of pleasing, of
trying to gain love from others has an absence of neurosis, a peace
about them. Someone who knows and resides in the Stillness and
presence does appear different from the stressed-out normality of
the Tribe of Man. But to those who live in this Understanding, these
attributes are just outcomes of returning to Being. In fact, these
attributes, which we'll talk about next, are actually very practical.

This 'Spiritual thing' has been made so complicated by
man's mind, and you can trace it all back to this distorted idea
of enlightenment. In essence, this Spiritual thing is simple. You
can forget all that stuff about past lives, karma, altered states of
consciousness etcetera. I'll reduce it down into one statement: It's
all about Seeing life from beyond Personality. That's what this whole
book has been trying to point to.

Matthew: That's all it is?

Jez: Yes. The Personality, rooted in the mind, creates an illusion of
what you are. To become free you have to see through that illusion,
you awaken from that Dream. Then you live a life that's beyond
Personality. That's it.

Once you see this you'll know that all these projections and
beliefs about enlightenment are simply inaccurate and irrelevant.

...nd Personality you begin to understand for ...the real teachers, the people who really know, are ...t. Because when it comes to this Understanding there's ...e truth that, potentially, any human being can find.

Matthew: But there are so many different versions and descriptions out there in the world of what it is to find this...

Jez: Let's be clear, a lot of the material out there about Spiritual attainment and enlightenment is simply a reflection of the hopes, desires and escapism of the Personalities who write it. So we're not talking about that; we're talking about the writings by people, all through the centuries of man's existence on this planet, who have actually discovered life beyond Personality and lived it.

Matthew: But even the writings of the great teachers are quite different...

Jez: The variety in their interpretations is simply the result of the truth being filtered through different moments of history, different cultural reference points and different Characters. Part of the beauty of life is its diversity: The writings of Buddha have a different taste from those of Lao Tzu or Rumi; there's a different emphasis and feel to each of them. But while the approaches and expressions may vary, what is found, the root of it all, is the same. There's a quote from Gautama Buddha on this:

> 'Just as the great ocean has one taste
> The taste of salt,
> So also this teaching and discipline has one taste,
> The taste of liberation.'

How can what is found be different? We're all human beings. We're all made the same and we all suffer the same delusion... Until this is found, until we Wake Up from the Personality's Dream.

Matthew: So what you're doing here is sharing your interpretation of it...

Jez: Yes – what else can I do? I'm offering my observations of this from the experience of it through this Character, and part of that is dispelling the myths that abound about this subject.

To me the whole approach and emphasis to this is backward.

You ask me if I'm Awake; I want to ask you: 'Are you still asleep?' That's the angle I see this from. That's the most amazing thing: To keep yourself from the truth of this is an extraordinary delusion to uphold. I know, I did it for over forty years; the only difference between you and me is that I don't do it any more.

Matthew: You seem to be implying that to Wake Up from that delusion is not such a big deal.

Jez: It looks like it, if you're still in that delusion, but from outside of it, no, it's not a big deal. To live like this is as natural as breathing. That's why the word 'Awakened' sounds a bit grand to me, but it's a lot less loaded than the word 'enlightened,' and it points to a fundamental truth, which is that to see through Personality is to Awaken out of its Dream.

So now I'm going to tell you what it means practically to live in the original state of Being, as an adult. I'll describe my experience of it, and highlight where the misunderstandings come in.

13

WHAT REMAINS

The idea of a 'you' is played out in the
Relative Level

'Before I had studied Zen for thirty years,
I saw mountains as mountains, and rivers as rivers.
When I arrived at a more intimate knowledge, I came to the
point where I saw that mountains are not mountains,
and rivers are not rivers. But now that I have got its very
substance I am at rest. For it's just that I see mountains once
again as mountains, and rivers once again as rivers.'
– Qingyuan Weixin

Matthew: Some teachers say that after Awakening there's 'no one there'; the 'story' of that person has finished. From what you've said it seems that you wouldn't agree. Am I right?

Jez: The phrase 'There's no one there' is potentially misleading because it contains *some* truth, but the reality is a little more subtle than it suggests. The Personality is kept alive by your belief in it. When that breaks down, identification with Personality falls away. It's like when you cut the vine: The fruit dies. In the Shift, what is seen through is the Personality; it's finally recognised as a phantom built on beliefs, thought, Emotion, desires, hope etcetera.

Matthew: So there's no identification with Personality, but I don't understand what they mean when they say: 'There's no story'. What about the history of the person? That all still happened.

Jez: This is where we have to be really careful with terminology. There's a history that you remember: You passed this exam; you went to this university etcetera. So there's a trail of facts from your past which now appear as memories just as they did before; these don't suddenly disappear from the mind.

Matthew: So what is meant by the 'story'?

Jez: The experience of our lives is more than a series of events happening in the physical world. Our lives are made of who we think we are, and how that one experience and responds to those events. That sense of who we are, that finite idea of an 'I', is the Personality. And that Personality had Emotions, hopes, desires, survival strategies, Suffering etcetera, which it wove around and through those physical events. All of that is what's meant by the 'story': the hurt of a betrayal, the 'pleasing others' in order to be accepted, the feeling of achievement in passing an exam, the disappointments when our plans fall apart. The Story – let's give it a capital 'S' – is the Emotional history of the Personality.

For the purpose of providing practical examples of what I discuss in these talks, I've occasionally referred to my Story. Most people are attached to their Story, because it's all they've got; it's intimately tied up with their identity, with who they think they are. But what happens to a Story when there's no belief in it to uphold it any more? When the Personality is no longer identified with, it's no longer 'your life';

it becomes just a series of events that happened to that person you previously thought you were. If the dreamer is seen through, what happens to the Dream? It's seen through too. That doesn't mean you can't remember it, it's just that, after the Shift, that Story is no longer your identity; the identification with it has been broken. It seems as if it has happened to someone else, because the one who created it and clung onto it, the Personality, is no longer believed in.

Matthew: You say the Personality's no longer believed in, but you're still a person, you still function. How is that possible if the Personality is the vehicle through which we operate and function in the world?

Jez: A good question. The teacher J. Krishnamurti used the phrase 'life without a centre' when talking about this realisation. The centre he's referring to is what I'd call the Personality. After the Shift there's no 'Personality centre' living that Story of you, but there *is* a centre that operates; without it you couldn't function at all. That centre is the self.

Matthew: We talked about this when we discussed childhood in the previous book; can you remind me what you mean by the 'self'?*

Jez: The self is the original vehicle through which Oneness, in the form of a baby, interacts with the World of Separation. The baby learns that it can grab food, get attention by crying etcetera. All this activity happens through the self, a primal sense of being separate. The self has no beliefs or Emotions to guide and inform its activity, so in this sense it is neutral; it responds to life without an agenda, its Awareness is Choice-less.

After the Wound, the self gradually picks up patterns of belief, Emotion and thought and becomes the Personality. Now, Choice-less Awareness becomes Personality Awareness – that is, Awareness is no longer neutral; it's guided by the motivations of Personality. It sees what it wants to see – what makes it feel safer – and disregards anything which it finds threatening.

In the Shift, one simply stops taking oneself to be that Personality. That identification with it, which began in childhood, falls away. When that happens, the operating centre returns to its original, primal form: the self.

So there's a return to how things began. The identification

---

* *The Story of 'You'* – Chapter 10

has shifted back from Personality, to Being. It's a reversal of what happened after the Wound, when the identification moved from Being to Personality. What you're left with is Being, functioning in the world, through the self rather than the Personality.

What's the difference? The self is free of all the Emotions, beliefs and survival strategies which burden the Personality, so it can do its job really efficiently, without the creation of Suffering.

When teachers of Non-Duality use the phrase: 'There's no one there' to talk about life after Awakening, it can be misleading because it suggests that you somehow become invisible after the Shift. The truth is, there's no Personality running the show, but there is a self functioning and this of course manifests as the appearance of a person and a life that is lived. So from the outside, I look the same as before the Shift. In the Relative Level there's a sense of a self, but there's no identification with it; it's just a function that's arising. That's the nature of a human being: to appear to be separate. On the Relative Level there's the appearance to others that I am this self and from this point of view, there is a 'sense of self' too.

Matthew: There is?

Jez: Of course. There's a human being 'happening' here, just as there is over there in the form of 'you'. There's a sense of a person, of a 'me' talking to you and answering these questions, but there's awareness that this sense of 'me' is just a function which, on the Absolute Level, has no real currency. So there's the playing out of the *appearance* of a self, a sense of me-ness in the Relative Level, and there's the awareness that it's just an appearance; something that's arising. There's no one there to own it, to identify with it.

Matthew: As we said before, you could say that you are the Choice-less Awareness watching it all?

Jez: You could say that. Some people call it Consciousness, or Love; these are just concepts and labels. But who is this 'you' that identifies with Awareness or Love or Consciousness? There's just Awareness, Love or Consciousness. The idea of a 'you' is played out in the Relative Level, but that's just a game, an appearance. That's what in India they call 'Leela', the play of life. The best way I can describe it is in this poem I wrote after the Shift happened:

The Wave

Dressed in turquoise, froth and spray
I swell in fascination with myself.
I have somewhere to go –
I know that I will be happy when I arrive,
So I keep moving, I keep turning
Endlessly confirming
I am a wave.

I am shouldered by others just like me,
All rolling in the same direction,
Each believing that someone up ahead knows the way.
And being so many of us
How can this be wrong?

But then,
The ocean becomes calm and still.
The momentum which gave me purpose,
The movement which defined me,
Stops.
I subside, I dissolve,
I fall back into the ocean.
i am no longer a wave –
i am the ocean
The ocean is me.

*

In time,
This form rises up again.
The ocean looks the same, but everything has changed.
i do not strive to be different from how i am,
i cannot make myself any greater or lesser –
i can only be the form which the ocean gives me.

i cannot choose where i'm going –
i can only flow where the currents pull me.
i have no destination,
Everywhere is here.

i am the back and forth,
The up and down,
The stillness and the rage.
i am the wave and the ocean.

BEING

14

UNCONDITIONAL LOVE

Love that is untouched by Suffering

'"You" don't become loving –
That "you" disappears
So that Love can be.'
– Rikka

Jez: To counteract all the myths of enlightenment that you've been indoctrinated with, I'm going to attempt to give a practical account of what it really means to Wake Up from the Dream of Personality. I'll approach this from a few different angles over the next few discussions. We'll start with the difficult subject of Love, which means I need to talk about control. The Personality is on a continual mission to dominate life, to control it and deliver experiences that will make it feel safe.

Matthew: What do you mean by 'safe' in this context?

Jez: Ultimately it means to find Love, but on a day-to-day level it means to feel safe from the Suffering that comes from the disconnection from Love. There are two poles to this: First, to feel safe, we need to distract ourselves from that Suffering. That's why the Personality loves to be busy, thinking, planning, achieving etcetera.

The second pole is the searching for that Joy and Love that we've lost contact with. It's linked with happiness: When we feel safe, we feel happy. Everyone has their own version of happiness: 'When I get this house, this job, this income, this partner – I'll be happy.' As we've discussed,* these strategies are future orientated and they're all ultimately doomed to fail. As long as you're identified as Personality, that deep, abiding sense of happiness, fulfilment and safety you're Seeking in those projections is always going to remain on the horizon.

Matthew: Why is that? Why can't the Personality feel safe?

Jez: Because Personality is born out of separation. The Wound is the loss of your Original Relationship to Life, the loss of that experience of living as Love, and what grows from that sense of separation is Personality. So ultimately the Personality can't feel safe or connected because Personality is the illusion of disconnection from Love. Why can't the Personality feel Love? Because it is the embodiment of the idea of disconnection from Love.

Matthew: You say the 'idea of disconnection from Love' because, on the Absolute Level, we are Love, right?

Jez: Yes. Outside of the Dream of the Personality, there's no disconnection.

---

* *The Story of 'You'* – Chapter 33

Matthew: All this talk of disconnection from Love makes me think of evil.

Jez: You're bringing religious imagery and beliefs into this; without all that emotional spin, it's just a fact. You could see this disconnection from Love like a cable that's been unplugged; it happened after the Wound when we learnt that human Love is conditional and that to feel safe we have to Contract from feeling.

Matthew: You're saying that, unless you have Awakened, there's a Contraction from Love.

Jez: There's a Contraction from feeling, which precipitates a Contraction from Love.

Matthew: Are you suggesting that, if I feel Love, let's say for my partner – it's not really Love?

Jez: As we've discussed,* Love is one of those words that's used very freely; it means different things to different people. If you're talking about the Personality's idea of love, which is based in the idea of needing the other person to fulfil us, then that's not the sort of Love I'm talking about. That's what the Personality has turned Love into: It's become conditional.

However, if you're feeling Love which arises spontaneously in the heart, not the head, then in that moment you're not coming from Personality. There's no need in it, there are no conditions placed upon it. You can tell the difference, because in that moment there's no Suffering. However, unless you have Woken Up from the Dream of Personality, then those moments will always be fleeting glimpses.

Matthew: If we're outside of the Personality in a moment like that when feeling unconditional Love, then where are we located?

Jez: For that moment at least, you're plugged back into Being; that's why Love has always been a sacred path to finding this. It's the Personality and its Contraction which is obscuring our experience of Love. There's a good quote from Rumi on this:

> *Your task is not to seek for love, but merely to seek and find*
> *All the barriers within yourself that you have built against it.*

---

* *The Story of 'You'* – Chapter 30

Love has become a 'thing' that we need, that we try to get, possess and control, but all that has nothing to do with unconditional Love which is experienced as part of Being.

Love can't be manipulated; the wave can't control the ocean. If it tries to, it will always fail. Why? Because the wave is just a part of the ocean, so to find safety by trying to be more than the ocean, by trying to dominate it, is impossible. It's looking for safety in the wrong place. The wave – the idea of separation – can only feel secure when it releases that idea, and experiences what it is: the ocean (Love). Then all of the Doing, striving and controlling falls away and what's left are the attributes of Being: Choice-less Awareness, Stillness, Joy and full-feeling engagement with life. As we covered in the first book,* this is what we all experienced as newborn babies, but after the Shift, it's lived with the sensibilities and mind of an adult.

Matthew: But what does 'living those attributes' actually mean in practice?

Jez: We'll talk about how each of these attributes manifest in an adult life in the following talks. Here, let's take one step back and focus on the Love – or in our metaphor, the ocean – in which all this arises.

After the Shift there's a conscious recognition of the Original Relationship to Life. There is surrender to the fact that you are the child and life is the Mother and, on the Absolute Level, She's always showering you with unconditional Love. We're given everything we need to live this life: energy to run our bodies, air to breath, Joy to feel, food to eat... the list is endless. So in the Relative world this is how Love can feel, like a relationship between a child and a Loving mother.

Matthew: The way you're talking about a relationship between a child and the Mother all sounds a bit dualistic...

Jez: In Oneness there is only Love, but in the Relative Level there's the appearance of being this separate person, and with that comes the appearance of relationship – including a relationship between you and life. So like I said, in the Relative world this is how Love can feel. This is why some Indian traditions use the term 'Sacred Mother'. It's a way of symbolizing the Original Relationship to Life in which there's absolute trust that we're cared for and nurtured by life.

---

* *The Story of 'You'* – Chapters 4 & 5

Matthew: What about if something horrible happens to you on the Relative Level, like being verbally attacked by someone?

Jez: You've introduced a really important point. When talking about the Absolute Level in *The Story of 'You'* I used the somewhat poetic phrase: 'All is made of Love'. But when duality gets to play itself out In the Relative Level, Love finds its opposite: the 'absence of love'. In human relations there is always the possibility of encountering actions that arise from the Shadow* side of Personality – from fear and hatred. That is when violence enters the picture. Everyone begins their lives in the Natural Sate of Stillness and Love; violence (that is not led by the survival instinct) is a sign of how far someone has become divorced from that original state of Being. It arises from the person's own Suffering and loss of that experience of Love.

So, if after the Shift, you experience violence in people, there will be awareness of that. It will be seen for what it is: an outcome of the disconnection from Love.

Matthew: But awareness of that wouldn't stop you feeling violence if it was directed at you?

Jez: Of course not. Just because you've Woken Up it doesn't mean that being verbally attacked by someone is going to be a pleasant experience. It would be the same as if it happened before the Shift – it would feel like hatred coming at you, because that's what it is.

Matthew: So where does Love come into all this? What is the difference after the Shift?

Jez: If the person being verbally abused is Awake, then the abuse will not be taken personally; the Emotional reaction which is behind the attack will not be met with an Emotional reaction from the one being verbally abused. There will be a response, but it won't come from the 'absence of Love', it will come from presence, from Love.

Don't get me wrong, I'm not trying to paint some image of perfection. Being verbally attacked wouldn't feel nice and the person would not enjoy the experience – who would? Being the target of violence of any sort doesn't feel good; I'm just making the point that experiencing that violence wouldn't lead to a reaction.

---

* *The Story of 'You'* – Chapter 27

Matthew: We've talked about the difference between a response and a reaction before: Can you clarify this again?

Jez: Yes. It's an important topic because it highlights the subject of Emotion and how it's the product of Personality. Let me give you an example: A Personality with low self-esteem might use the experience of a verbal attack to further ingrain feelings of low self-worth and sadness. A Personality with anger issues might use such abuse to further entrench their hatred and anger towards others. So the abusive situation is taken personally; it's picked up by the Personality, it's reacted to – this means that it triggers the Suffering and Emotion that's already there.

By contrast, a response is informed by the knowledge that what's being acted out on you by the aggressor is usually not personal to you. Something you've said, done or represented has simply been a trigger for their Emotions to come in your direction.

A response has reason, perspective and distance. It's not informed by the Personality and its history of Suffering, by its belief in being unworthy or its need to feel superior. A response comes from beyond Personality. It comes from Being; a place where Love is unconditional, where it has not yet found an opposite. This means that a response has no violence or hatred in it. However, what that response might be... Who could say? It would arise spontaneously in the moment.

Matthew: What about an extreme case of physical assault... What would happen then?

Jez: There will be a physical response of self-defence; but even this will not be reactive, meaning it will not come from Emotions. Even if there is violence, it will simply be the self-protection, survival instinct being activated. We'll go into this subject more when we discuss Non-Doing.

Matthew: What about if the threat didn't come from people, but from life itself? What if you were struck with a horrible illness; how does Love come into that scenario?

Jez: Human beings are born with a will to enjoy and live the life we've been given – that's part of how we're made; so on the Relative Level it's absolutely natural to not want to die early of a painful illness. However, in the original relationship to Life, there's also the recognition that, just as 'the Mother' (as we've been referring to life) gives us our existence, She will also take it away. How or when that happens is up to 'Her', not us.

This is why surrender is such a big part of this. The Shift teaches you that, on the Absolute Level, any idea of control is an illusion because there's no 'you' who could have control. Part of being a wave is the recognition that, at any time, you could quietly subside back into the ocean.

Matthew: There's a lot to think about there.

Jez: Don't think about it; just let it sink in without thinking. This is all theory to you now; until you find out for yourself, that's all it will be. I'm just pointing, from many different angles, towards what this Shift is. Examining how Love manifests *in* the Relative Level is a good angle to explore that.

Matthew: We've talked about unconditional Love. What about self-Love? How does that fit into all this?

Jez: We have to use that phrase with caution because it can sound like we're talking about being egotistical, and what I'm referring to has nothing to do with that. What's the definition of 'egotism' in the dictionary?

Matthew: 'The fact of being excessively conceited or absorbed in oneself.'

Jez: Egotism is just the opposite pole of self-criticism and lack of self-Love; it's another response to the Wound which the Personality can adopt. You don't see children in the Natural State being egotistical or lacking self–Love; these are simply different responses to losing that experience of oneself as Love.

In the case of egotism, the Personality feels inferior and that manifests as needing to prove itself to be OK – to be powerful, successful, dominant. There's nothing intrinsically wrong with any of those qualities; what we're discussing is a situation in which there's a *need* to be dominant or powerful or to prove oneself. All that tells you is the person doesn't feel worthy, or acceptable without proving themselves, so it comes from a position of lack.

With low self-esteem there is also a feeling of inferiority, but there's no will to fight against it or disprove. It's a common outcome of the Wound which manifests as low confidence, self-criticism, depression etcetera. After the Shift happened to a friend of mine, she told me: 'I always felt unloved, but I was so loved by life.' In the Natural State there's just Love; the idea of withholding Love for oneself, or needing to prove oneself better than anyone else, is just not possible. There's no reason for such aberrations. So what I mean by the phrase self-Love is simply life being lived without those patterns of self-criticism – a life in which Love is felt, in and as oneself, just as much as it can be felt for other people.

Matthew: I think for some people it would sound kind of egotistical to say that.

Jez: To whom would it sound egotistical? Only the Personality with its warped ideas of how we should act, following a code the tribe has adopted which says: 'Don't be big-headed.' To conflate a natural arising of self-Love with egotism is to totally misinterpret this. Egotism is just another Personality sickness; the Love I'm talking about is beyond Personality.

It's completely natural to Love this self and this Character which arises as part of it; it's only when Personality comes in that disapproval starts being applied to what we are. The idea that how we are made can be wrong is a belief which has its roots in the Wound when, for whatever reason, we experienced disapproval. From the perspective beyond Personality, this all becomes absurd. Who are we to say that we're somehow intrinsically wrong, not loveable, not acceptable as we've been made? I'm not talking about all the aberrations that can arise after Personality has been identified with, all the violence and hatred which come from the dislocation from Love. I'm referring to who we are before all that begins; I'm talking about our original nature. We are as perfect as the rocks, the trees or the animals, simply by virtue of the fact that we've been made this way.

Matthew: The emphasis in the world, especially in religious contexts, is more often put on loving others than oneself, isn't it?

Jez: Yes, but the idea that we can Love others whilst not having self-Love is totally back to front. There's a natural order to this: In the Original

124

Relationship to Life we receive Love from life and it fills us up. Sharing is a natural outcome of being so filled with Love that it overflows to those around you. You become so full of it that you can't *not* share it.

After the Shift I first noticed this unconditional Love arising when I was with my Dad. Throughout his life we had a decent enough relationship but it wasn't particularly close. Near the end of his life, he wasn't in good health and certain difficult sides to his Personality could intensify, so it wasn't always that pleasant to be with him. After the Shift something changed in my relationship to my Dad. Because I didn't need approval or anything else from him, I was able to accept the difficult sides of his Personality. In practical terms, this meant I didn't criticise him or try to change him.

Matthew: But what if he was really mean to you?

Jez: If he was being unloving to me, I would either ignore it or leave the room. Self-Love means you can never allow yourself to be a victim of 'emotional violence', even mild forms of it. I accepted his right to be as he was and I accepted my right to move away if his Personality was not loving to me. However, I found that this acceptance changed the whole dynamic of our relationship: The Love I felt for him as my father didn't waver. It didn't come and go depending on his behaviour; it became unconditional, and I know he could feel it. If people pick up that you're judging them disapprovingly, they'll instinctively not warm to you. No one likes to be disapproved of. However, if they can feel that you accept them as they are, something in them can relax, and often they let you in more. Despite the difficult circumstances, it made the last year I spent with my father the closest I ever had with him.

Matthew: What you're saying seems to suggest a very positive outlook on the world, as if Love can prevail.

Jez: And then there'll be world peace, right?

Matthew: That would be nice!

Jez: But if we see things as they are, not from the hope of how we want them to be, then that idea of world peace remains just a nice idea – at least, as things stand at the moment.

Matthew: Why do you say that?

Jez: Because, as we know, most people don't live from this Understanding – they live from the Personality. While many people try to love their fellow man, living from Personality opens the door to the possibility of every atrocity we see in the world. Once someone Contracts and closes their hearts, they can become capable of all sorts of acts of violence.

So I don't have any false ideas of terrorists having this Understanding and putting away their guns and bombs, because I'm cognisant of how Personality works. I know that most people won't give up their beliefs and religious ideals, because they make them feel safe. What I'm trying to point to in these books isn't a Utopian dream. It is the perception of Love, but that perception includes the recognition of the manifestation of Love's opposite in the Relative Level, where Personalities get to play out their narratives of Suffering. So unless there's a dramatic change in mankind and suddenly everybody discovers a Yearning to return to their original state of Being, that idea of world peace will remain just an idea.

At the moment this Understanding is underground, it's not widely known; but none of that really concerns you. The only thing that matters is *your* Yearning, *your* discovery of the Love that you are. To return to the original state of Being, any expressions of un-Love in you, such as hatred, jealousy, gossiping – has to be seen, Understood and ultimately transcended.

Matthew: To me, all this talk of Love makes what you're saying sound religious.

Jez: You have to become aware of your own lack of connection to Love, not because of any religious idealism to be a 'good' or religious person; it's for a very practical reason. We're born in Love, to lose our connection to that is to lose our freedom, our Joy on this earth. Any violence or hatred you have for others is just hurting you in the end because it's blocking your Love, strangling your Original Relationship to Life. So this Enquiry is not religious in nature, it's Spiritual – it relates to the discovery of Love, not in some externalised idea of a deity, but in life itself.

15

STILLNESS

The inactive, passive expression of Being

'Silence is the language of God;
All else is poor translation.'
– Rumi

Jez: After the Shift, the attributes of Being* start to manifest in one's life again. We've talked about the opening of the heart and the arising of unconditional Love; a natural outcome of feeling the safety and relaxation of that is the experience of Stillness. Like discussing Love, talking about Stillness directly is difficult. Many years ago I wrote a poem that might help shed some light on it:

Stillness

All is finished before it's begun.
No poem needs to be written,
No song sung.
No wisdom shared,
No ignorance dispelled.
No love to find,
No Suffering to escape.
No states to be realised,
No past to be atoned for,
No future to be hoped for.
In Stillness
Everything is,
Just as it is.

Matthew: It all sounds very peaceful, but I think some people will say: '"No poem needs to be written, no song sung"? Who'd want to live a life without art?'

Jez: You're describing a view from the Relative Level. Art arises in the Relative Level and it's very important to us because it helps us reflect on, express and understand the Relative Level. Stillness, however, is an experience in humans of the Absolute Level. It's one step back from that world of manifestation, before any impulse of creativity arises.

Matthew: Hang on, you wrote a poem about Stillness! Doesn't that contradict what you're saying?

---

* *The Story of 'You'* – Chapters 4 & 5

Jez: (Laughs.) Ah… the paradoxical nature of this Great Mystery! Stillness is just one expression of Being – the inactive, passive expression of it. When I wrote that poem, I was moved by creativity into a more active expression of it. If you remember, when we discussed the original state of Being in babies, I said that Stillness can remain at the centre whilst activity appears on the periphery in the self. If you look closely at a baby being fed or playing with a toy, you can see them looking out at the world from that place of Stillness.

Stillness is part of Being. We see Stillness in babies because they haven't yet identified as a Personality; this means that all the Suffering that grows out of that identification isn't there to obscure it. The baby is in Stillness because of its innocence; after the Shift our approach to Stillness is through experience. We have known that Suffering of being identified as Personality, but now that identification has fallen away.

Before the Shift, Stillness can of course be experienced, but it is always fleeting. You'll have tasted it momentarily in your Opening on the village green.

Matthew: I'm sure you're right, but if I try to tune into that experience now my mind goes fuzzy. I can't do it.

Jez: That's because Stillness exists before the manifestation and the filter of the mind. So to experience Stillness is to experience life from a very different angle, one that's not dominated by the interpretations that mind puts on what is seen.

Matthew: I know what you mean: It didn't feel like it was me who was looking at life. I felt 'more than me'.

Jez: Exactly – it wasn't the perspective of you, the 'you' that's created by the mind; it was simply Choice-less Awareness. Stillness arises when that 'you', which is the Personality, falls into the background. Then the practice of meditation, in the sense of trying to reach Stillness, becomes redundant. There's no need for a rock to try to be more like a rock; it already is a rock.

Matthew: But most people don't know they are 'a rock', right?

Jez: Right, and so Stillness, which is part of everyone's original state of Being, is sought – because the experience of it has been lost. Because we've lost it, there's a Yearning for it. As we've discussed, Stillness is the aspect of Being that's been adopted by society as the traditional image of enlightenment. This is probably because of all the statues of Buddha sitting in meditation looking so blissful.

Matthew: That's another attribute of the classic idea of enlightenment, isn't it? Perpetual bliss...

Jez: Yes, the experience of bliss can be one aspect of Stillness. It can be felt in the form of increased energy in the body, swoons, deep relaxation and thoughtlessness. I used to regularly experience what I'd call the 'hole in the head'. That's exactly how it felt, like there was a hole in the centre of my brain from which thinking would usually arise. When this hole opened up there was a delicious feeling of thoughtless bliss. At those times, to be around thought and busy minds became painful, almost violent, because the silence was so deep and open. My wife has experienced the same thing; I remember she once said: 'Don't talk to me, I'm deliciously unthinkable.'

Bliss, however, is not perpetual. It's a state – in other words, it passes. If it were perpetual, it would be totally impractical; you wouldn't be able to think or act effectively in your daily life. From the world's point of view it appears like you become a kind of idiot, because, to a great degree, you're unhooked from thinking. So as much as the world might fetishise the idea of perpetual bliss in their adopted image of 'Enlightened Beings', it's not something that they really want. Buddha has become a popular icon in the world because most people like the idea of Stillness and bliss, but actually it's a threat to most Personalities. Why? Because in the world you're valued by your productivity, your ability to achieve and succeed. In the state of bliss you achieve absolutely nothing – that's what's so beautiful about it: You become gloriously useless.

For Stillness to manifest we have to go beyond the Personality and its internal dialogue in the mind, but our whole culture is built around going in the opposite direction; we're encouraged to constantly think, achieve and be busy. However, deep inside all of us something craves Stillness because we have a memory of it from the Natural State.

Matthew: It's like we want it, but we don't want it at the same time.

Jez: We want the benefits of Stillness in terms of relaxation and health, without the Personality having to give up control.

Matthew: Stillness is something people are trying to achieve when they meditate.

Jez: Yes, and 'trying' is usually the operative word. In many cases meditation is something done by the Personality to imitate the state of Stillness. It *tries* to be Still; it makes an effort to be peaceful! That's the absurdity of this. It's like me saying to you: 'I want you to try very hard and put every effort into being relaxed. Are you relaxed yet? (Laughs.) Come on, you're not trying hard enough! Relax more!'
  Even if you do manage to lull the body into a state of Stillness during meditation it's usually not for very long because the operating system of the mind and the Personality doesn't like being told to shut up and let go. The Personality wants to be in control and letting go into Stillness is losing control. So when we try to meditate, the mind often starts going faster; the first thing that's witnessed is the internal dialogue, the onslaught of nagging thoughts and judgements.

Matthew: Although many people try to find some Stillness in their lives, in my experience it's rare to meet really peaceful people.

Jez: Yes, I think it's true to say that most people aren't resting in that Stillness side of their nature! That's why it's looked up to and almost fetishised in the idea of the enlightened guy who sits there on the mountaintop in 'perfect' meditation, devoid of all thoughts. This image has engendered the belief that the mind is the enemy, that it's something you have to kill in order to find peace. I suspect it comes from a misinterpretation of Buddhism. We've talked about how the mind, when overrun by Personality, becomes hyperactive and sometimes negative. Thoughts become critical of oneself and others; there's a constant internal dialogue from which you can't escape. This is why, in some spiritual circles, the mind is considered to be the root of Suffering.

Matthew: So, you're saying the mind is getting the blame but it's actually the Personality that's the culprit?

Jez: Yes, although I wouldn't use the word 'culprit'. It's interesting that words like 'culprit' and 'blame' are coming up when we're talking about Personality; they suggest that it's somehow 'wrong' or 'bad'. As I've said before, identifying with Personality isn't 'wrong', it's just something that happens. There's a huge difference in those two approaches. If you make Personality 'wrong', you're falling into the same trap as saying that the mind is the enemy; you're back to fighting with yourself and that's simply another manifestation of Suffering.

You need to observe the Personality without Emotion, without an agenda. You need to observe it with Choice-less Awareness, as something that just happens. Then you'll recognise that identifying with it has major consequences which cause Suffering in human life. To blame the mind for that Suffering is like being a chronic overeater who blames his condition on the hand that places the food into his mouth. The hand is not at fault, it's just functioning, holding and letting go of food. It's doing what it's designed to do. The problem comes in because it's doing that under the command of the Personality and its addiction to food.

The mind is just a function that expresses the Personality that it's working under: If the Personality is full of anger then the mind will be full of resentful, hateful thoughts. If it's fearful then the thoughts will be full of worry, if there's self-loathing, then critical thoughts will predominate. It can feel like the mind is the tyrant, but actually the Personality is the source, the root from which all those thoughts are arising.

Matthew: So you're saying that the only way to find the lasting experience of Stillness you're talking about is to Wake Up?

Jez: Yes. That's not to say that there can't be *moments* of – for example – strong feelings, but the connection to Stillness at our centre is never lost. It is the still point which watches whatever is arising. The location of that is outside the domain of Personality.

Matthew: What happens to the mind when that connection to Stillness remains?

Jez: When identification with Personality falls away, the activity and content of the mind changes.

Matthew: How?

Jez: Firstly, you're no longer hooked into those Emotions from the Personality, so there's nothing to feed those thoughts of hatred, fear, worry or anger and they start to dissolve. If there's no hatred, then hateful thoughts aren't generated; their creation has been stopped at source. Similarly, without any patterns of lack of self-Love, self-critical thoughts can't be created. So, in this way, you can see that the content of the mind changes: It's unburdened by all these negative thought loops.

Matthew: You're calling them negative? Surely that's making them 'wrong'?

Jez: I mean they're negative in the sense that they cause Suffering, so it's a judgement on their nature; but there's no Emotion in that judgement. I don't see them as 'wrong', I see those kinds of thoughts as outcomes of identifying as Personality. Thoughts can be creative, powerful, full of insight and wisdom, or they can be full of hatred, fear, criticism and resentment. I judge thoughts to be negative if they're having a negative effect on the person having them. These kinds of thoughts are the manifestation and the theatre of Suffering and they fritter away your precious life force. Can you imagine how much energy it takes to run those thoughts constantly? Without all that useless activity the mind can become more efficient; there's more energy for it to do what it's required to do (such as problem solving) and to have thoughts that aren't arising from the Suffering of Personality.

Matthew: So, just to be clear, the idea that thoughts stop altogether is another one of those myths of enlightenment?

Jez: Yes. In Stillness, thought recedes and what we call meditation becomes a natural flowering. So there can be moments of 'no thought', but thoughts don't stop altogether. We're made with a brain and the capacity for thought; thinking is part of living what we are as human beings. It's just that after the Wound, thought becomes overrun with the Suffering of Personality. That's where 'negative' thoughts and thinking patterns come from. After the Shift, without that burden of dealing with the Emotional baggage from the Personality, the mind can start functioning more efficiently – it can reach its potential. You might observe it being more perceptive, eloquent or sharp. Then thought can become a powerful and beautiful tool for your creativity.

Matthew: You talk about the mind and its thoughts as if they're nothing to do with you.

Jez: They aren't.

Matthew: It feels like they are.

Jez: Yes. Before the Shift you identify as Personality and as the mind but, after the Shift, that identification falls away. You realise the mind that's thinking these thoughts is not *my* mind, just as this is not *my* body. There's no idea of possession going on any more. If there's no ownership then any thoughts arising are life's thoughts. For example, that's what's happening in these talks; to put it poetically you could say that this mind, this intellect, is being used by Being to talk about itself.

Matthew: That begs a question: Were the thoughts you had before the Shift 'life's thoughts' too?

Jez: Yes, of course, but they were thoughts that arose in a system which hadn't yet realised they were life's thoughts. So often those thoughts had a different nature.

Matthew: You mean they could be expressing Suffering, Emotion etcetera?

Jez: Exactly. After the Shift, rather than expressing the Personality, the mind is free to fully express the Character, so you can find that creativity increases.

The point is, the mind can be quiet in Stillness or active in many different ways, but it's unable to torment me with useless, jabbering negative thoughts because it's no longer the servant of the Personality. It falls back into its natural place: It's active when it's needed, and passive when it isn't.

The idea of perfection in spiritual circles – of having no mind, no thoughts – is a reference to the arising of Stillness, in which thoughts can dissolve into the Absolute. But Stillness is only one expression of Being. The rest of the time, of course there's mind activity. As I said, that's how human beings have been built, and this is all about being what you are. To try to be what you aren't, to try to be perpetually mindless in meditation, can actually be a kind of violence because it's an imposition on the way this life is. Ironically it can just create more dis-ease, more self-criticism with thoughts such as: 'I'm really useless at meditating', 'I hate my restless mind' etcetera.

Matthew: You said that self-criticism goes after the Shift, but does all criticism go?

Jez: If you mean the desire to gossip or put others down, then yes. In fact, all obsessive fascination with others' Personalities, and what they're doing, disappears.

Matthew: It's a good job for the social media companies that not everyone Wakes Up – it could spell the end of them!

Jez: Not necessarily, because what I said was: 'the fascination with others' disappears. So you might still observe what's going on in the world but your relationship to it is different. There's no obsession with it, no addiction in it. You can't get hooked on these things because there's no compulsion to Distract yourself or put people up or down.

Matthew: But I know you still have opinions about things.

Jez: Absolutely. For example, I'm of the opinion that was a good interjection, because it helps me refine what I'm trying to say.

Matthew: There's an idea going around that judgement is bad – like when people use the phrase: 'Don't judge me.'

Jez: That statement – 'Don't judge me' – involves making a judgement that the other person is judging you. So, in a sense, the statement is implicitly hypocritical.

Matthew: So you don't agree with the idea of not judging other people?

Jez: (Laughs.) I'm going to make a judgement now: There's nothing wrong with judgement! It's vital that we have the facility to judge. Discernment is a very important function of human life; the idea of turning that off is absurd. We make judgements all the time in life because we need to. It started with our early ancestors as a survival mechanism; for example: 'This water is rancid, so I won't drink it.'

Matthew: I know what they mean when they say: 'Don't judge me!' though. I have a friend who's very judgemental and it's really horrible when he puts that on me.

Jez: Yes, because it's coming from the Shadow side of his Personality, from Emotion and a need to put you down. Putting others down or making them 'wrong' makes the Personality feel more secure because it makes them feel 'right.' This is where the word 'judgement' gets a bad name. So when people say: 'Don't judge me,' they're talking about Personality's habit of *negatively* judging others. That means it's not a balanced judgement, it's biased. Quite understandably, what they mean when they say: 'Don't judge me,' is: 'Don't judge me from the negative aspects of your Personality.'

That kind of biased judging becomes impossible after unhooking from Personality. What's left is discernment, the ability to See what is going on in people. In fact, with Stillness at the centre and the mind unburdened by Emotion, this discernment gets sharper. But it is always guided by Love; there's no intent to blame, hurt or 'make wrong'. This applies to other people as much as oneself. It's really that Stillness and focus manifesting in two different directions, inwards and outwards.

16

PURPOSE

Does it exist after the Shift?

'Love knows no answer for it does not question.'
– Silent Lotus

Jez: Do you feel you have a sense of purpose in your life?

Matthew: Yes, although sometimes I'm more connected to it than at others. For example, when I worked for a political party, I felt I was helping make the country a better place. Also, after a lot of false starts I feel I've found the right job, I feel I'm doing what I'm meant to be doing. So it brings me a sense of purpose and from that, I guess, happiness.

Jez: So for you there's a link between purpose and happiness?

Matthew: Yes. I think a lot of people would link having no purpose with being aimless and depressed. Wouldn't you agree?

Jez: Yes, I think that's the prevailing view, but these things are seen very differently after the Shift.

Matthew: So do you think there's no purpose in human life?

Jez: It depends what we mean by purpose, because there are different categories of purpose. If you look at this biologically, the primary purpose in human life is to survive and procreate; it's a part of the Original Relationship to Life. The wildebeests you see on the wildlife programmes run away from the lions that are stalking them, they don't stroll away casually; they run as fast as they can. They also migrate thousands of miles just to find fresh grass and water. All this is driven by the instinctive will to survive.

Biologically human beings are programmed the same way: The will to survive drives us to take care of our survival needs. If you're hungry you'll focus all your energy on finding food; if you need money to provide shelter for your family you'll look for a job that will earn money to do that. So carrying out these actions related to survival can give us a sense of purpose. If we get the job, and bring in the money, we feel fulfilled. So that's a purpose linked to survival. It's important to mention because, as I've said, it's part of the Original Relationship to Life and it's a part that, unless we become suicidal, we don't lose.

Socially we can have a purpose too. For example, the bus driver who drove you here was fulfilling a social purpose. People need to travel to work to earn money to live on; the driver facilitates that. In the same way, police officers are there to enforce the law and maintain order in society; doctors take care of medical conditions and maintain public health. So socially it's possible to find a sense of purpose through the service we provide in our jobs.

It's clear that purpose appears in many forms in human life: in survival, procreation and in the roles we adopt in society. However, when we ask: 'Does your life have a sense of purpose?' we often use the word more metaphysically. For example, if you're religious you might say that your life has a spiritual purpose: to serve God.

Matthew: And if you're not religious? What about you? Would you say that, apart from survival and procreation, Waking Up is the ultimate fulfilment and purpose of a life?

Jez: First of all, you have to remember that we all have the survival instinct but we're not all born with the 'Waking Up' instinct. Just as not every woman has the desire to be a mother, not everyone has that Yearning to Wake Up. However, if that Yearning *is* there then – like a broody mother is desperate to be pregnant and give birth – so that Yearning can only be fulfilled by rediscovering the original state of Being. So, until that happens, the quest for the resolution of that Yearning gives a sense of purpose and fulfilment to your life.

Matthew: And once it's been resolved, what then? Is there no purpose in life after the Shift?

Jez: That's a big question, and to answer it we need to define exactly what we mean when we use the words 'purpose' and 'fulfilment' because, although they're closely related, from this perspective they're very different things.

Let's look at fulfilment first: As I said in our talk about Stillness, on the Absolute Level there's nothing to do, nothing to prove, nothing to achieve. In other words, there's nothing to fulfil. As I've said, Personalities have used this aspect of Being to create the classic image of the enlightened person:

Matthew: Up in a mountain cave, cut off from society, meditating all day long...

Jez: Right. I can't help thinking that if you want to exist tuned to that Absolute Level all the time – with no manifestation of the Relative

Level in terms of everyday human life – then you might as well take away the Relative Level and enter the Absolute fully...

Matthew: You mean... die?

Jez: Yes, experience the Absolute absolutely! (Laughs) But if we come down from that mythological mountain and enter the real world – which includes the Relative Level – things are different. Fulfilment of this life is found not just in the Stillness which is within us, but also in sharing Love through interaction with others in the world.

Matthew: You mean in relationship?

Jez: Yes, in being a lover, a friend, a brother, sister, teacher...

Matthew: As you mentioned, for many people fulfilment is also often found in being a parent.

Jez: Yes, evolution drives our species to reproduce, and being a good parent and nurturing the next generation brings a huge fulfilment for most people. The body of a mother yearns to reproduce and that's expressed hormonally as broodiness, so giving birth gives a kind of biological fulfilment by carrying out what the body is programmed to do. But, of course, it doesn't stop there: The relationship between the parents and the child is all part of Love being expressed and shared in the Relative Level.

There's also another form of sharing Love which brings fulfilment: sharing Love in the form of your talents. Everyone has different skills and gifts: A painter has an impulse to paint, a comedian yearns to make us laugh, a businessman wants to run a successful company and so on. It's a beautiful manifestation of the variety of life in the world of duality.

Matthew: It's part of Joy, isn't it, to want to share your talents with others?

Jez: Absolutely. Sharing is a very important part of human life: It's part of our connectedness, it's one expression of Love. It's always been like that; you can imagine a Stone Age artist drawing images of the hunt on the cave wall, the cook roasting the slain beast over the fire and the storyteller sharing stories of the hunt.

If you think about it, there are two sides to the act of sharing:

The sharing itself (from the giver) and the receiving of what's being shared (by the receiver). So, to use our Stone Age scenario as an example: The members of the tribe appreciate that the hunters have risked their lives to bring food to eat. Everyone sees the drawing on the wall and recognises the skilful depiction of a beast. When the cooked food is passed to the hungry, tired hunters and when the stories about the hunt are told, it feels good because everyone is receiving the gift of the sharers' creativity. Their talents and artistry help the tribe bond and build a sense of community. The hunters, the artist, the cook and the storyteller are appreciated; this means that their gifts have been received, and that in turn makes them feel good because it's a form of Love and respect.

This is the way of human life in the Relative Level; in giving, the giver also receives. From the appreciation of the receiver there's a sense of fulfilment and Joy. It's a beautiful cycle of giving and receiving, but...

Matthew: I thought there was going to be a 'but' somewhere...

Jez: It's beautiful, but only if the Personality doesn't get involved.

Matthew: What do you mean?

Jez: The separation from Love – or more accurately, the falling away of the knowledge of ourselves as Love which happens in the Wound – leaves a hole inside us. The Personality does whatever it can to find the Love we're missing and uses whatever love it finds to fill this hole. This includes the love that's received from the appreciation of our gifts and talents.

Matthew: That sounds like a good thing, like the Wound is being healed...

Jez: On the surface it may seem like that, but the Personality isn't being healed because it's coming from a position of need.

Matthew: What's wrong with need?

Jez: That need I'm talking about is actually a symptom of the estrangement from Love that began in the event of the Wound. Without an intrinsic, inbuilt sense of worth and Love, we need the appreciation of others to feel good. If that Love was already in us, there'd be no need of it from outside.

Matthew: So you're saying it's natural to receive and enjoy Love from others but if there's a need for that Love, it becomes a different thing?

Jez: Yes. Let's take the example of a painter: If she is driven by a need to be loved and appreciated, then her talent for painting acquires a specific purpose: the purpose of gaining love to fulfil that need. She thinks: 'If I create a good painting, in the future, when people see it they might like me – they might love me.' The freedom of the original creativity becomes compromised; it's now serving the needs of Personality. The whole dynamic changes because her creativity is then driven by fear...

Matthew: Because there's always the possibility of other people not liking the painting?

Jez: Yes, if the picture is liked, the Personality's pain is soothed; the artist feels happy, at least for a while. If it isn't liked – if it's rejected – then that pain of the Wound, her original hurt, will be stirred up and activated. So, by contrast you can see how art that's untied to the needs of the Personality is unbounded. Without that need, creativity is free of fearful thought, free of hope and time. It's simply an expression of Joy happening in the present.

Matthew: It's what they call 'Art for Art's sake.'

Jez: Yes. A good example of this principle is found in Van Gogh's life. He only sold one painting in his whole lifetime, the rest of his nine hundred or so paintings were not made famous or sold until after his death. Did this stop him painting? Did it make him try to paint in a fashionable style that might have more chance of being sold? No, a true artist doesn't paint to fulfil their ego, to receive appreciation or because of grand ideas about purpose. A true artist paints because so much creativity is welling up inside them that they can't *not* create.

I love Van Gogh because, apart from the stunning beauty of his paintings, he represents this principle so beautifully. He wasn't Awake, he suffered terribly with the psychology of his Personality, but he's left this beautiful lesson for us in his life. He points beyond purpose.

Matthew: So you're not using the word 'purpose' in the practical context of, say, earning money to feed your family?

Jez: No, I'm referring to how Personality's sense of purpose is linked to fulfilling its needs of making it feel worthy, loveable, special. The Personality likes to think it has some grand purpose; it's the driving force behind the belief that 'When I get this I'll be happy.' So the sort of purpose I'm talking about is linked to a future goal in which you'll be more rich, successful, happy. It's a sense of purpose that the Personality imposes upon our lives to give them meaning, to make us feel safe. We think that what we do in the world matters, that it's important.

Matthew: Don't you think that's true?

Jez: Only on the Relative Level. You could say that to live our Character fully and exercise our talent is important in that it's a fulfilment of life in the form of 'you', but from the Absolute point of view, there's no purpose and what you do isn't important.

Matthew: That's a hell of a statement!

Jez: Animals don't have a mind, and they have no purpose. A bird doesn't make up goals to give itself a purpose and make itself feel important. It doesn't think: 'When I fly to Africa, then the other birds will respect me.' (Laughs.) It just gets on with being a bird. If that involves flying to Africa, if that's what life has programmed it to do, then that's what happens. If it involves the Stillness of sitting on eggs in a nest all day, then that's what happens.

When you Wake Up you realise it's not what you do that matters. It's your Being that matters, not your Doing. Our culture flirts with the concept of 'being in the moment', but there's no Understanding of what that really means, which is to realise that what you do is ultimately not really important. It's the Being part that matters. If the Being part is there, then the doing part will take care of itself.

Matthew: I'm feeling a lot of resistance to this.

Jez: No Personality wants to take this on board; it's the very opposite of what Personalities are about. The core beliefs that Personality buys into are: 'You're special', 'There's a reason for you to be here', 'You're important', 'Your life has purpose'. It's as if the life of a person isn't enough; we have to have a fabricated idea of purpose slapped on top of it.

Matthew: So you think your life has no purpose?

Jez: None at all – other than the living out of itself.

Matthew: I find this quite confronting; I've always thought of having purpose as an essential part of life.

Jez: As we grow up we're trained to need a purpose to validate our lives. Why do we need that? Young children don't need a purpose. If they build a sandcastle on a beach, there's no great purpose in that action; there's no ultimate goal to be reached other than the creation itself. It's just Joy being expressed in the form of play.

Matthew: OK, but surely in adult life there are some legitimate uses for purpose beyond survival. What about in Seeking this? Didn't you say at the beginning that Waking Up was a kind of purpose?

Jez: Yes, but that only applies before you Wake Up. The character in the Dream can ascribe purpose to its affairs, but that idea of purpose only means something within the construct of the Dream. So the quest for Waking Up was only important when I was still identified with the Dream.

Matthew: But what about these books we're creating? Don't you think it's important that you share this?

Jez: On the Relative Level you could argue this book has importance and purpose because it's the expression and fulfilment of this Character called Jez. So that's just like saying: 'This flower opened and shared its fragrance, so that's important, that was its fulfilment. It's what it was designed to do.' So on that level, yes, it's important I share this. But beyond that – no, I don't feel there's any great purpose and importance to it.

Matthew: But people might really benefit from this book; doesn't that give it a purpose and make it important?

Jez: I think that would be a beautiful outcome, and yes, I would be pleased if that happened. As we spoke about earlier – the other half of giving is receiving, and in that cycle of sharing is connection and Love. But I don't have any grandiose ideas about this; I'm not trying to save the world. Life created this book of talks through this Character. This book, and whatever happens out of it, is nothing to do with 'me'. That's down to life.

So, in summary, what I'm saying is: There's no purpose but there *is* Love, in the form of this incredible play of life and your interaction within it. Attaching purpose to that is just the mind trying to keep the Mystery, the unknown, at bay. After the Shift, meaning is found simply in the Joy of being planted in the centre of the Mystery of life and experiencing it.

17
CHOICE

Choosing happens, but there's no chooser

'A lover knows only humility, he has no choice.'
— Rumi

Matthew: The way you say there's no purpose and what happens has nothing to do with you sounds rather fatalistic…

Jez: Does it? Let's see how the dictionary defines 'fatalism'.

Matthew: It says here: 'The belief that all events are predetermined and therefore inevitable.'

Jez: As I understand it, fatalism sees us as separate individuals who are dumped into this life in which a force called fate predetermines everything that's going to happen to us, as if there's a script and we're all just actors playing it out.

Matthew: Which begs the question: 'Who's writing the script?'

Jez: If you were religious you'd say it was God. He's the guy upstairs, the author of this whole show, coming up with the dialogue and the plots. It's a view of life as a kind of imprisonment, because we have no free will; the future is all mapped out and given the label 'destiny'.

The perspective after the Shift disagrees with this; here it's seen that apparently, we do have the ability to affect and change events in our lives. Events are not predestined; anything could happen. A choice could arise to do a handstand now but there's no script existing with the direction: 'At ten forty-five Jez performs a handstand in response to Matthew's question about fatalism.'

Matthew: So if you apply this to evolution, there was no script saying that evolution would go the way it did – it's just a natural process, responses to random environmental changes.

Jez: Yes. For example, woolly mammoths only evolved their thick coats as a response to the Ice Age. Without the Ice Age they may have just been slightly hairy mammoths.

Matthew: Of course, a fatalist would argue the environmental conditions that led to the Ice Age were themselves predestined.

Jez: Right, the script says: 'At this point in the earth's history there will be an Ice Age.'

Matthew: You're saying that there's no such script; which implies that we have free will...

Jez: That's the big question, isn't it? Does mankind have freewill?

Matthew: Yes. What's the view on it from beyond the Shift?

Jez: You'll notice that earlier I said there's an 'apparent' ability to affect our reality; for example, for me to perform a spontaneous handstand. I used the word 'apparent' because, from this viewpoint, it's known that it's not our own choice.

Matthew: What does that mean?

Jez: It means that there is no 'I' here that could choose to do a handstand; that 'I' is what is seen through in the Shift. So this viewpoint agrees with fatalism in that ultimately we don't have control or choice, but it disagrees with the idea of destiny. What I'm saying is, anything can happen, I could perform a spontaneous handstand, but the point is: It wouldn't be me doing it. There is only the appearance that it's me.

Matthew: I can grasp this conceptually, but I feel a great resistance to it.

Jez: There's a good reason for that: The self was built upon its apparent ability to make choices. In choosing one food over another in babyhood the self takes its first steps in asserting individuality and a sense of control over the world in which it lives. This power of choice is the driving force which, through the years, helps to build the identity we come to know as our Personality. In adulthood we become permanently aligned with some of the choices which have been made – such as what religion we believe in, or which political party we vote for. It's all very much part of our identity, our autonomy – our sense of power.

All these choices arise in the Relative Level, where there's an appearance of an 'I' which seems to have something called choice. When our eyes open to the Absolute Level, the identification with Personality falls away and the illusion that we have choice dies with it. The best way to sum this up is to say that choosing happens, but there's no chooser.

Imagine you have a dream one night in which you possess a superpower; say you have the ability to fly. In the dream it appears real; no one can tell you that you can't fly because your experience is that you can. In the dream you can even prove to others that you can fly. However, when you wake up in the morning, you experience a different reality: The dream has gone. You no longer have that superpower.

Matthew: So, let me get this straight. You're saying that free will is like a superpower that the Personality has, within its own Dream?

Jez: Yes, exactly, and once you Wake Up from the Dream of Personality the illusion of free will is gone.

Matthew: This is mind-boggling!

Jez: Let's approach it from a different angle: Who's left to make a choice if the Personality is seen through?

Matthew: I don't know. It kind of does my head in just to think about it!

Jez: That's because you're seeing from the perspective of Personality. How can the Personality see beyond its own existence? It's like your eyes trying to see themselves.

Matthew: It's the only perspective I've got.

Jez: Is it? What about the perspective that arose on the village green? It's not a perspective that 'you had', because in that Opening there was no 'you' there to 'have' it. That's what the Opening was: A glimpse beyond the perspective of Personality.

Matthew: Something happened as you said that... I was back on the village green in that experience, and 'Matthew' wasn't there, but something was.

Jez: Last time we spoke about your Opening you described it as the experience of being 'More than me'... That's an interesting way of putting it. It's really another way of saying you were 'more than Personality'. So you *have* experienced this, or strictly I should say, 'This perspective has been experienced.'

Matthew: I guess that's true, but it feels like my mind can't quite grasp it. It's like trying to grab hold of slippery soap with wet hands...

Jez: It can't get hold of it, because that experience on the village green was beyond the mind – although you could argue that it was, at least in part, interpreted and perceived through the mind. The experience itself was of knowing beyond the known. What I mean is, it didn't arise from an accumulation of knowledge; it wasn't created by drawing on your memory from the past. It was an experience of knowing beyond all that, in the now.

Matthew: Like when one has an original thought?

Jez: Exactly. So can you tune into that experience on the village green again?

Matthew: Yes, but hasn't that now become part of that knowledge from the past stored in my memory banks?

Jez: To an extent yes, it's been labelled 'Spiritual Experience' and filed away amongst millions of other memories from your past. But this memory is different: It has the potential for holding a certain resonance because its content, its perspective, is also available to you right now, because it's beyond time.

Matthew: I experience it as a change in perspective.

Jez: OK, so from that perspective, try and answer the question: 'Who is left to make a choice if the Personality is seen through?'

Matthew: Nobody... Or maybe you could say: 'Life.'

Jez: Exactly.

Matthew: So when you say: 'There's choice but no chooser,' you're saying there's no Personality making the choice.

Jez: Right. A Personality doesn't own the choices that appear to be made by it; it all belongs to life, or we could use the word 'Consciousness'.

Matthew: I can just about recognise that from my Opening. Is this only seen in Awakenings and Openings?

Jez: No, you can see it at any time. Any artist who honestly observes the act of creation knows that the choice of which colour to use in a painting, which word in a poem, or note in a melody cannot ultimately be claimed by them. The artist knows what to do, where to put things, but they don't know *how* they know. In the moment of inspiration the 'artist' temporarily disappears.

This can be observed in any situation. Do I know what I'm going to say next in our conversation? No, the words arise and are attributed to 'me', but I'm not responsible for them.

*Matthew: I can sort of see what you're saying on an intellectual level, but I can't help feeling that you **are** responsible.*

Jez: Let me try putting it another way. If you were to watch a film of yourself riding a bicycle you'd see that your body was making a series of tiny adjustments of position in order to maintain balance. Is it you making those tiny adjustments? Are you consciously thinking: 'Move your body three centimetres to the left as we turn this corner?' Or 'lean to the right for a split second?' No, those adjustments are being made, but it's not 'you' consciously making them.

This reminds me of a story about a centipede. He's walking along minding his own business, when a beetle says to him: 'I always wonder: You've got a hundred legs; how do you know which one to move at the right time?' The centipede replies: 'I've never thought about it before,' and promptly trips up!

You can apply this questioning – 'Who is really in charge, who's making decisions?' – to any activity. For anyone who's willing to honestly observe their experience this can be a huge pointer beyond Personality because it works in reverse: If you can observe the fact that you're not the one making choices, then you surely have to start questioning the Personality that *claims* to be making them.

Matthew: I don't think that sort of questioning happens very often, for the simple reason that it feels like we're making the choices.

Jez: Yes, from the Relative perspective it *feels* and looks like we make the choices. It looks like I've chosen to pick up this pen, but did I choose it? Did I choose to have that thought or did it just arise in my brain which then moved my hand to pick it up? If you trace it back, in the end you find that you can't claim that thought, or the choice to follow it.

Matthew: So it's the illusion of choice.

Jez: That phrase is an excellent summation of what we're talking about. Where did it come from?

Matthew: It just appeared in my head.

Jez: So you can't actually claim it, even though the words came out of your mouth.

(Pause.)

Matthew: No, I guess I can't.

Jez: Whether someone perceives this or not is all down to their Readiness. If 'you' are identified with Personality then 'you' will obviously claim the creation of that phrase which came out of your mouth. 'You' will claim the choices being made by 'you' and any suggestion otherwise will appear ridiculous.

Matthew: Do you perceive this all the time?

Jez: Yes. After the Shift this isn't just glimpsed in moments of inspiration where the sense of 'I' is forgotten in the flow of creativity; it becomes permanent. Of course, I'm not consciously thinking about it all the time; it's taken for granted.

Matthew: It's the inverse of the Personality taking for granted that it **is** *making the decisions.*

Jez: Exactly; we're through the looking glass and Seeing the world backwards. (Laughs.) Nothing can be possessed any more – a beautiful painting is created but no artist is left to claim responsibility for its creation.

Matthew: Not even Picasso?

Jez: Not *even* Picasso – this applies to geniuses as much as the rest of us! Mozart didn't compose those symphonies and Shakespeare didn't write those plays either! (Laughs.)

Matthew: So the same goes for this book?

Jez: Absolutely. Remember my poem about the Wave?

> *i cannot choose where i'm going –*
> *i can only flow where the currents pull me*

For the wave to think that it's in any way responsible for its form, or where it's going, is absurd. However the wave is manifesting – the spray it gives off, the shape it assumes, the direction it rolls – it all belongs to the ocean.

Matthew: So you're not responsible for all these words, all this Understanding you're sharing with me?

Jez Of course not, that would be ridiculous! Do you remember how this book came about? One day we had a talk, and you said we should record it for an article on your magazine website. I came up with a list of subjects for future talks and gradually the idea of turning them into a book emerged. At every stage hundreds of decisions were made, and in one sense none of this had anything to do with me.

Every time we approach a new subject, I don't really know what I'm going to say. In fact I often have the feeling that it will be impossible to capture this Understanding in words. For me it feels like walking over a cliff into thin air and trusting the ground will appear underneath my feet. Somehow, so far, the next step has always appeared.

Matthew: And if it didn't?

Jez: Then there'd be no book.

(Pause.)

*Matthew: In a way that makes it all the more special that it **has** appeared.*

Jez: That's exactly how I feel. I'm full of wonder about it.

Matthew: It sounds strange to hear you say you're 'full of wonder' about your own book.

Jez: You're not meant to say that are you? In the world of Personality that sounds arrogant, and in the world of Personality, it probably would be big-headed to say that...

Matthew: It would be called pride.

Jez: Right. Pride can be a way that Personalities make themselves feel stronger. By owning things, they pump themselves up with 'their' achievements. That's what we mean when we say someone's egotistical isn't it? Everything's self-centred: It's all about making them look good. But you have to remember that after the Shift, after Alice goes through the looking glass, different rules apply. Let me ask you a question: 'How can you be called proud or arrogant, when you're not claiming anything?'

Matthew: If you're not claiming anything that you're creating, then from the world's viewpoint you wouldn't be called proud; you'd be called mad!

Jez: Yes agreed, it sounds utterly mad from the perspective of Personality.

Matthew: Not just mad, but dangerous. Because if you're saying you have no choice then you have no responsibility for your actions. And that means you could do anything – you could kill someone and then just say: 'It's not my responsibility; I didn't choose to do it. Life did it.'

Jez: It's not a defence that would stand up in court is it? (Both laugh.)

Matthew: No, but it's a fair point.

Jez: Is it? It presupposes that I'm going around with the desire to commit murder and that this Understanding – that we have no choice – suddenly gives me license to fulfil that desire.

Matthew: OK, but what if someone did have those tendencies and then Woke Up to this Understanding?

Jez: You're really drilling down into this question, and that's the right approach to have. We've talked about the Shadow and the violence that can be hidden within it.* All of that is part of the Personality,

---

* *The Story of 'You'* – Chapter 27

and unhooking from Personality involves unhooking from those tendencies.

Matthew: You mean they wouldn't arise any more?

Jez: They could possibly still be there, but, from my experience I'd say that they'd be profoundly affected by the Shift into the perspective of Oneness.

Matthew: How?

Jez: This brings us back to our discussion about violence. Most religions tell us to love one another, to be good and do good. It turns out there's a real basis for this. With the heart open in Being, any idea of violence – unless it's in self-defence or for survival purposes – is impossible. Why? Because there's no possibility of hatred when Love is running the show. Just as the possibility of being violent to yourself wouldn't arise, nor would the possibility of violence against another.

In the arena of religion this non-violence becomes a dogma, a goal to aspire to – a moral code to follow. But *trying* to be Loving, when there's a huge Shadow with hatred lurking in it, is only going to work as long as repression and control are applied. (And even then, I would say a love that is forced is not Love.) So aspiring to be 'good' or 'loving' just becomes more Doing. After the Shift, Love is not something that's done; there's no Doing in it. It's just a natural part, in fact the central part, of Being.

Matthew: That all sounds very positive but I suspect that the idea of living without choice would sound frightening to most people, like driving a car and letting go of the wheel.

Jez: You talk about it as if most people live *with* choice – unless they Wake Up. The fact is, though most people don't know it, everyone lives without choice. What they live with is the *illusion* of choice; the appearance that they're at the wheel. After the Shift, that illusion goes – that's what changes. From the outside things look the same: It appears I'm making choices constantly, it appears these choices create my likes and dislikes. For example, I happen to like Blues music. This is a preference arising in my Character. Where does that preference come from? If I trace it back, am I really responsible for it? Did I choose to like Blues music? No, that's simply how life is manifesting in the form of me. You like Eighties pop music, which mostly I can't stand. (Laughs.) That's how life is manifesting in you. The only difference is, in me, life is manifesting good taste! (Both laugh.)

Matthew: Without getting into a diversion about musical taste, you're saying that preferences arise, but they aren't really ours?

Jez: Yes. And of course, just because life gives you preferences, it doesn't mean it will always deliver them to you. Sometimes things don't go the way we want them to. For example, after the breakdown I knew I had to stop playing that role of the author. I didn't want to stop; my preference was to continue.

Matthew: But you did give it up.

Jez: Yes, or to be more accurate: It was given up. So you see it's a question of perspective: From this point of view, whatever happens is known to be the play of life. Life gives you preferences which may not coincide with what life brings you. It also gives responses to what life brings: You may feel sad, happy or angry with what life delivers to you. If you're no longer identified with Personality, it's known that these preferences and responses are also not 'yours'; they're all just the play of life. When this is seen, surrender happens, because the one who thinks it's in control just falls away. 'You' don't do it of course, but surrender happens. It's simply a return to the Original Relationship to Life we lived as babies in the Natural State.

Think of a river flowing down a mountain: It doesn't have to concern itself with which path to take, where to turn, where to fall, when to speed up or slow down. Gravity does all that. Gravity knows where to take the river; the river doesn't have to do anything except flow. From the outside it may seem like the river is choosing the route down the mountain, but we all know that isn't the case.

This Understanding of no choice isn't an intellectually held position. It isn't something you learn; it's not a belief. It's simply what is Seen after the Shift.

18

THE KNOWING

What governs a life when Personality
is no longer in control?

'There is a voice that doesn't use words. Listen.'
— Rumi

Matthew: Can we talk a bit more about what it means practically for someone to live without choice?

Jez: Well actually, we all live without choice.

Matthew: OK, to live conscious of the fact that we have no choice. I've been thinking about it and wondered if it equates to the experience of having inspiration? You know, that feeling when you instinctively know what to do.

Jez: Yes, that's it. When we discussed unconditional Love, I said that we receive it in many forms. This inspiration, this instinctive knowing, is one of those forms. It can lead to us knowing 'things' – i.e. having Understandings about how things work – or it can relate to knowing what to do. I use the umbrella term 'the Knowing' to refer to both aspects of it. After the Shift, the Knowing becomes much more available.

Matthew: Tell me more about it: How does it feel to live like that?

Jez: I think most people know how it feels to have it fleetingly. When you feel inspired, you're not confused are you?

Matthew: Not at all; it makes life easier, a lot less stressful because I know what to do. Most of the of the time it's like there are two sides of me; two voices debating with each other – you know: 'Do this' and 'Don't do that...'

Jez: So then you're confused; you're kind of divided?

Matthew: Exactly.

Jez: Have you ever wondered why intuition isn't available to you more of the time?

Matthew: Not really, I suppose I take it for granted that's just the way it is. It makes it special when I do feel it.

Jez: I'm suggesting that your Personality is the reason it's not there most of the time.

Matthew: I guessed you would, but why are you saying that?

Jez: As we've discussed, Stillness is one of the attributes of Being. I'm proposing that when you have those moments of intuition, there's a quality of Stillness in you. Why? Because it takes Stillness to be able to 'hear' or have access to that intuition. There's a lovely quote from Ram Dass relating to this:

The quieter you become, the more you can hear.

Matthew: It sounds logical...

Jez: Let's try approaching this from the opposite direction: When you're in moments of stress, do you ever hear that intuition?

Matthew: Generally, no, but in the highest stress – like emergency situations – I've noticed I can suddenly become very efficient and know what to do.

Jez: I know what you mean. What happens there is the intensity of the situation actually throws you beyond confusion into Stillness.

Matthew: But generally, you're right: Lower level, ongoing stress seems to block that intuition – and that's just when I need it to give me a bit of guidance.

Jez: As you say, it's because mentally you're too busy. Emotion and stress are consuming your attention and obstructing the Stillness from which the Knowing arises.

Matthew: But you can have really screwed up Personalities who obviously have phenomenal intuition and inspiration. I'm thinking of someone like Van Gogh, who we mentioned earlier...

Jez: Definitely. He's a good example of how you can have intuition in specific, isolated areas of your life. Van Gogh obviously 'heard' and followed intuition when he was painting; he had clarity and single pointedness in the act of creation. However, in the rest of his troubled life, it's clear that he was distracted and 'divided' by what some people believe to have been bipolar disorder.

This is why, for someone like Van Gogh, painting is like a religion. It's the most healing, important part of his life because it's perhaps the only time he feels connected, focussed and undivided.

He knows what to do – what colour to pick, what brush technique to use – and that gives him a feeling of wholeness. It's just dealing with the rest of his life that is the problem.

What I'm saying is, Stillness is part of Being. That means it's always there as a possibility; but when we're engaged with Personality, it's in the background – it's an unfulfilled potential. In a state of relaxation, when all the frantic activity of Personality quiets down, Stillness comes to the foreground; then intuition can become available to you.

Matthew: Religious people would interpret it as God or the Holy Spirit talking to them, advising and taking care of them.

Jez: I understand that viewpoint because that's how it feels. We are being taken care of. Like I said, Indian traditions call life the Sacred Mother; it's another way of representing that feeling of being taken care of. It's just a symbol, but it's one that's natural to use because in human life, the original experience of being loved and taken care of is by our mothers. That doesn't mean you have to believe that there's some actual mother or father figure, a God or Goddess up there in something called heaven watching over us.

Matthew: You'd use more neutral terms like 'Life' or 'Consciousness.'

Jez: Yes.

Matthew: But it amounts to the same thing?

Jez: Absolutely, it's unconditional Love being felt, but I'm simply not attaching any beliefs to it. This Enquiry is about Seeing what is, beyond belief. Belief is a product of Personality and, as I said, it's the Personality that actually blocks you hearing this intuition and experiencing the Knowing.

Matthew: How does this Knowing relate to what people mean when they talk about the Higher Self?

Jez: It depends on how you use that phrase; what do you mean by it?

Matthew: To me it refers to the best part of us – the part that knows what's the 'right thing to do'.

Jez: When you attach the phrase 'the right thing to do' to the idea of a 'Higher Self' it suggests a moral standpoint – i.e. there's 'the right thing to do' which comes from the Higher Self and, by implication, there's 'the wrong thing to do' which comes from some baser part of you. Presumably you'd call that 'Lower Self'.

Matthew: It's like the angel and devil sitting on each shoulder telling us what to do.

Jez: Yes. To see this more clearly let's apply it to a specific scenario: Imagine you've been trying to lose weight and someone offers you a slice of a delicious chocolate cake. The 'Lower Self' (the devil on your shoulder) says: 'Go on, have a piece, forget your diet, enjoy yourself. You know you'll love it!' Meanwhile, the 'Higher Self' – the angel sitting on the other shoulder – says...

Matthew: 'Don't eat it – think of your waistline. You'll only regret it!'

Jez: Doesn't this all sound a bit familiar? All the 'trying to be good, virtuous, better', or the impulse to be 'bad': naughty, indulgent, lazy or whatever it is. Where do you think all that comes from?

Matthew: From our discussions it all sounds like everything you ascribe to Personality.

Jez: Exactly, it's all the theatre of Personality being played out: the needing to please, the repression of unacceptable parts of ourselves to the subconscious. It all comes from the Wound. It has nothing to do with the Natural State. It comes from division, from the relentless thoughts thrown up by the mind, from the neuroses of Personality.

Matthew: OK, let's forget the phrase 'the right thing to do' and replace it with 'the best thing to do'.

Jez: That's better, that's what I'm talking about. That has nothing to do with a 'Higher Self' or the 'Lower Self'. It's beyond all the angel/ devil, good/bad divisions that come from the mind of Personality; it comes from Consciousness.

Matthew: But surely Personality is part of Consciousness?

Jez: Yes, everything appearing in the Relative Level is part of Consciousness, so of course that includes Personality; but Consciousness is expressed in many different ways. In the Relative Level everything has different qualities. For example, rock is opaque, glass lets through light, but they're both made of matter, atoms, energy... Consciousness.

This doesn't just apply to physical objects, it also relates to psychological states in the human condition. Personality has a different quality from the Natural State; it's much denser. If you equate the Stillness of Consciousness to light, you could say that the Natural State lets more light through than Personality does. So, when Consciousness isn't compressed down into this thing called Personality, more Stillness is there, and this can manifest as the Knowing.

Before the Shift, I wasn't so in touch with the Knowing because my Personality was still in command, but I found that writing journals was a way of calling it forth, opening the portal to it. Even though I didn't have access to it most of the time, I knew it was there, and I trusted it. I had the Yearning for it, so I did everything I could to find it.

Matthew: But now it's there all the time?

Jez: I would say most of the time. That doesn't mean I always know what to do, but when I don't, I know to do nothing. It's like living in a kind of 'receiving mode'. It's an ongoing trust in life to tell you where to go, what to say, or not say at any moment. (That's what's happening right now!) Normally the Personality and its motivations are guiding so much of our lives. It says: 'Don't go there – if you do, this might happen' or 'Don't do that, it makes me feel insecure.' The Personality has an agenda: its own survival. It doesn't want you to do anything that makes it vulnerable. It doesn't want you to feel repressed Emotions; it wants to Distract you from your Suffering. When those strategies and motivations are no longer engaged, there is Stillness, and then Consciousness says: 'Do this now,' and so you do it. It's simple, there's no prevarication, no fight, just trust in that Knowing.

An example of the Knowing can be seen is our relationship to food. In the Natural State the body tells us what it wants to eat, when it wants to eat and how much it wants to eat. This is part of our Original Relationship to Life; the body instinctively knows what's good for us, it knows what we need. As we grow up we can lose contact with what our body tells us. We may learn to crave sweet or fatty foods (like the chocolate cake we mentioned earlier), because they give comfort and Distraction from our Suffering. So that connection to the Knowing, that ability to hear it, is compromised by the activity and needs of Personality.

After the Shift, this reverses – you start living according to the Knowing, not the addictions and patterns in your mind. Your body tells you to stop eating when it's had enough and, instead of overriding those directions, you follow them and stop eating.

What I'm saying is that, if you take Personality out of the equation, if you're not identified with it, you're not bombarded with that inner chatter all the time. You hear the Knowing, and you follow it, even if it tells you something you'd rather not hear.

Matthew: So after the Shift that can still happen?

Jez: Oh yes. Like I said, there are still preferences; the self has all sorts of likes and dislikes. That doesn't disappear after the Shift; that's part of the Character, part of our uniqueness.

Matthew: So what happens when the Knowing tells you to do something that you find uncomfortable?

Jez: Choice-less Awareness becomes aware of the message that the Knowing is giving you, and also of the fact that there's a preference arising; that you might rather something else happen. But... so what? You do it anyway.

I'll give you an example: The Knowing told me to undertake this project with you, to collect and synthesise what I've found on this journey and share it. This casts me in the role of a teacher, which is not something this Character is particularly inclined to take on. I'm basically quite a private person; I don't normally talk about this sort of thing publicly.

Whatever happens, it's not up to us. Don't forget: All this talk of likes and dislikes, following or not following is simply how it appears in the Relative Level; from the Absolute Level, the truth is that we have no choice. The Knowing appears, and it is followed. None of this has anything to do with 'you'.

19

NON-DOING

Action which arises from Being is effortless

'Creating, yet not possessing,
Working, yet not taking credit.
Work is done, then forgotten.'
– Lao Tzu

Matthew: From hearing you talk about Stillness and the lack of choice, it would be easy to think that, after the Shift, one sits around doing nothing all day, but I know that's not the case with you.

Jez: It could be; after the Shift I became good at doing nothing. As the phrase goes: 'Don't just do something, sit there.' This wasn't always the case: Before the Shift I was always busy with some aspect of my job. It was a time of high productivity, but there was an element of escape to it. Writing and illustrating picture books was something I loved to do, and it fulfilled me creatively, but that busyness also protected me from stopping, from confronting certain parts of my life that were not free. Shortly before the breakdown my wife said to me: 'You're always busy; if you don't start slowing down you're going to die young.' In a sense she was right: It was the breakdown that stopped me in the end and led to the death of identification with Personality. Life is very compassionate: If you have the Yearning it will reach you in anyway it can.

Matthew: I never see you doing nothing, because we mostly meet when we're working. My experience of you is that you're very focussed.

Jez: I find that, if I do something, I do it fully – when I stop doing it, I stop fully. What we're talking about is balance. Stillness is a quality that exists at the centre, so there can be activity on the periphery, but it's balanced by the Stillness from which it arises. When there's no activity, you could say the Stillness is experienced more directly: in silence, in gaps between thoughts, sometimes even in bliss.

So, to summarise: Being finds expression through the inaction of Stillness but also through its opposite pole – action. Free from the tension, patterns and needs of Personality, action that arises from Being is effortless. Without willpower, struggle or force, things happen. Doing becomes 'non-Doing'.

Matthew: Can you remind me what you mean by 'Doing'?

Jez: Doing refers to any action that arises from the strategies of the Personality to carry out its functions and maintain its dominance. Anything that's motivated by the need to prove oneself worthy, loveable, acceptable, or the need to Distract oneself – that's all Doing. So, in that period before the breakdown when I was constantly busy with my job, that was Doing.

Matthew: Even though you were being creative?

Jez: Yes, even creativity can be used to Distract oneself. My creativity came from Joy but there was a lack of Stillness in it. The activity was not balanced by the inactivity of Stillness; that's why I'd call it Doing. So despite the fact that it made me highly productive, it was, like any form of workaholism, a manifestation of Suffering.

When identification with Personality drops away, all of that Doing becomes redundant. The need to Distract oneself from Suffering, to prove oneself worthy or loveable is an outcome of the Wound. After the Shift, there's nothing to prove and no impulse to Distract oneself from anything.

Matthew: So you could define non-Doing as: 'Action that doesn't come from the Suffering of Personality.'

Jez: Exactly, non-Doing originates in Stillness. This means that, unlike Doing, it has no tension in it. It's not action that's motivated by fear, by not being enough. It comes from fullness and Stillness, which means it has a flow and grace to it. You know how, when you're working under stress, you become less efficient? Here it's the opposite; you can become super-efficient and effective in whatever you're engaged in.

Matthew: It sounds like what sportsmen and women call 'being in the zone'; and lots of people are using the term 'being in flow' at the moment.

Jez: When someone's playing sport with a skill that's so flowing and beautiful, they're not really thinking about what they're doing; all their training just comes together instinctively in the moment. After the Shift it's like having more ongoing access to that.

Matthew: How does this relate to the Knowing?

Jez: As we've discussed, the Knowing comes from Stillness too. The Knowing tells you what to do; non-Doing is the carrying out of the action it tells you to do, whether it's someone giving a speech or a footballer scoring a beautiful goal. All of it is beyond conscious thought, it's just instinct.

Matthew: It's reminding me of what you said about the creation of this book, how it just kind of happened.

Jez: Yes, the creation of this book is a good example of this. The Knowing is the source of these words; non-Doing is the speaking of them, the phrasing, the transposing into concepts etcetera. All of that just kind of happened.

Matthew: I know what you mean; there never seemed to be any stress or tension in it.

Jez: Action which arises from Stillness has a different quality to it. All the energy which the Personality spent in creating and controlling its Story is released and made available. So it means you become more efficient. Without the mind's habit of linking action to achievement and purpose, you can have fun interacting in the world without stress. The Knowing tells you what to do, and you simply enjoy the experience of doing it.

If you watch a young child there's no stress in their play because it has no purpose. The child doesn't play in order to feel Joy; the play is an *expression* of Joy. After the Shift you play in the manifestation of the world like a child, because the Personality is no longer imposing its motivations and Emotions on your actions. This poem by Chuang Tzu expresses this beautifully:

The Archer's Need to Win

When an archer is shooting for fun
He has all his skill.
If he shoots for a brass buckle
He is already nervous.
If he shoots for a prize of gold
He goes blind, or sees two targets –
He is out of his mind.
His skill has not changed,
But the prize divides him.

He cares; he thinks more of winning
Than of shooting –
And the need to win
Drains him of power.

Matthew: I think we all know that feeling. It reminds me of being at a party recently; I was talking about politics to someone I was trying to impress.

Jez: How were you trying to do that?

Matthew: I suppose by showing how knowledgeable I was, but it all rather backfired. I could feel my mind getting ahead of itself, I started babbling; my thoughts became unclear. I don't think I quite gave the impression that I wanted to! (Laughs.)

Jez: It's great you can laugh about it. One of the biggest obstacles to Waking Up is arrogance and self-importance. Awareness has to rise beyond the Personality in order to laugh at its ridiculousness, its need to be special and to be applauded.

Matthew: I presume you'd say that my wanting to impress the guy at the party was all Doing?

Jez: Yes, the tension of the Personality's need to impress him obstructed your naturalness. It's a crazy situation because it's not that you *aren't* knowledgeable about politics; the problem was that you needed to *demonstrate* your knowledge. If you didn't care how that person felt about you, your knowledge would have been freely available. However, it's worth noting that without that need to impress, you may *not* have displayed your intelligence either, because there'd be no need, no impulse to show off.

Matthew: But I might have?

Jez: Yes, but for entirely different reasons.

Matthew: Such as?

Jez: Because life has made you that way, with a good brain. Life wants to do its thing: It wants to express itself in the form of Matthew and the intelligence it has given you. In the Original Relationship to Life you don't ever have to worry or over-think because the Knowing always tells you what to say, where to be, how to act. There's no need for a front, for a projection of how you want to be seen. If you're projecting a front, that just means there are two versions of you: a 'real' you, and an idealised you.

In this Understanding you become One; you become integrated. You don't need to act a version of 'you' to get anything. What is arising as 'you' is accepted, there's no conflict, no division. You don't feel you need to change it, or if you do, it's done consciously.

Matthew: What do you mean?

Jez: Well for example, how I am with you is not how I am with everyone. You and I are engaged in a contract: You've given me the message that you're interested in and open to this subject – so, when we're together, I talk freely about this. If I did that with everyone it would be inappropriate. Most people don't want to know about this; they find it disturbing, confusing or even annoying. I have no interest in changing their views or having all that projected onto me, so I may avoid engaging in conversations that may lead to this subject. I have nothing to prove so there's no impulse in me to go there. Without all those motivations from Personality you act appropriately to any situation.

Just as Personality has an inbuilt function of self-protection, so does the Original Relationship to Life. The Knowing, as applied to action, is like having a sensor constantly monitoring what's best for you: What is Loving, when you need to move, what you need to say or not say. After the Wound this function of discernment and discrimination can be lost; this leads to great confusion. It's like we've lost our anchor and the world is throwing us around like a boat in a storm.

Matthew: OK, I get the idea of non-Doing, but there's something about it that's bothering me: It's a feeling that's been bubbling up since we talked about choice.

Jez: Go ahead.

Matthew: With all this non-Doing and no choice you seem to be suggesting there's nothing to be done. We talked about this in relation to art but what about when you come to the subject of morality? I can't help feeling, in this world where there's so much hatred and Suffering, that it's morally wrong to take such an apathetic stance.

Jez: Non-Doing is not a stance that's taken by anyone; it's action that arises spontaneously. No one is choosing it. As we keep coming back to, Being is something that arises when that 'me', with all its opinions, is left behind.

Matthew: So are you saying that after the Shift, the idea of responsibility in the world goes?

Jez: After the Shift *you* are gone, so there's no idea of *your* responsibility or *your* choice. However, this is not to say that feelings of responsibility can't arise – it's just that, if they do, they're not owned by anyone. If some form of injustice is encountered, it's possible that an impulse to act could arise in response to that injustice. But that impulse would have arisen from Stillness, not from the Personality or some moral imperative.

Matthew: What's the difference?

Jez: I'll give you an example. When I first lived in London I had a girlfriend called Jenny who rented a room about a mile away from where I lived. One night she called me, clearly in a state of shock. Her landlady's boyfriend was drunk and physically assaulting her. Jenny asked if I could come round and help. Not the sort of call you want to be receiving at ten o'clock at night!

Matthew: What did you do?

Jez: I finished the chapter of the book I was reading, had a cup of tea, then rushed straight round there! (Both laugh.) Seriously, I'm not some kind of macho man but I went straight round, because in my mind I had an image of the defenceless landlady being attacked.

Matthew: So there was a sense of injustice?

Jez: Yes, I had no desire to get involved in someone else's fight, but that sense of injustice moved me to act.

Matthew: What happened?

Jez: When I turned up, this drunken guy started directing his aggression at the only other male in the room – me. He started coming at me, so Jenny called the police. I remember my body mustering all its strength to hold him down until the police arrived.

Matthew: Anyone might have responded like that; what makes it non-Doing?

Jez: The difference is there was no Emotion or need to prove myself behind it; so even if I had to be physical as I restrained him, there was no violence behind my actions. If my Personality had had a need to prove my virility – to my girlfriend, to her landlady, to the man or to myself – then I might have taken out a lot of repressed anger on him. Without Emotion driving the encounter, it was simply a series of spontaneous responses: the movement to go round and help, and then to restrain the guy.

Matthew: Would you respond the same way now?

Jez: I don't know. While I was pinning the drunken guy's arms down he decided to head butt me in the face. So that was quite a powerful lesson from life of what can happen when you get involved in other people's business... Maybe now I'd let someone else deal with it, or maybe I'd do the same thing again, I don't know. The thing is, you have no idea how non-Doing will lead you to act. It's spontaneous action; it's not up to you.

Matthew: You're linking acts of social responsibility with the motivations and Emotions of Personality, but surely not all altruistic acts come from Personality. What about giving to charity for example?

Jez: Charitable, apparently altruistic acts can be done for all sorts of non-charitable reasons: to make money, to make oneself look good and promote an idea of piety, to assuage some sense of guilt, to feel superior etcetera. I'm not saying all acts of charity in the world come from such ulterior motives; many people act from brotherly or sisterly love when it comes to good causes. I'm just making the point that any intervention or action that arises from Stillness has no ulterior motives behind it, and I'd call that non-Doing.

Matthew: If I understand this correctly, what you're talking about is action that is kind of pure?

Jez: Yes, pure in the sense that it's untouched by Personality. That actually gives it a greater power to have effect, because the intent behind it is not compromised by Emotion.

Matthew: What does that mean in practice?

Jez: In the example I gave of my encounter with the drunken guy, if I'd been pulled into an Emotion of anger, I'd have been less aware and less effective in terms of dealing with his aggression. When you're Emotional you're not fully present; the Emotion, which comes from the past, has invaded your senses and obstructed your ability to be present and aware in the moment. You're not seeing the big picture; you're seeing the Personality's viewpoint, which is informed by Emotion. As soon as you act with Emotion, you're coming from a place of weakness.

However, this is not a Self-Help course to train you how to be more effective in whatever you do. Non-Doing is not a goal; it's simply one of the spontaneously arising outcomes of losing identification with Personality.

20

FEELING

A return to full-feeling engagement with life

'The sage is guided by what he feels, not by what he sees.'
– Lao Tzu

Matthew: You've said that after the Shift, the attributes of Being, such as Stillness, manifest in one's life. Can you tell me about the other attributes?

Jez: When we talked about Openings we discussed how Choice-less Awareness – which naturally arises as part of an Opening – can start appearing in your everyday life. This can bring changes, because Choice-less Awareness can expose patterns of behaviour that you were previously unaware of.

Matthew: In my case it showed up how my friend always dumped his negativity on me...

Jez: Right, before that insight you felt that negativity on you, but you hadn't made this pattern conscious and you didn't have the clarity to actually do anything about it and change the situation. After your Opening, you became conscious of what was being put on you, and this led you to decide to not see him as much.

Until the Shift, moments of Choice-less Awareness like this are intermittent; they arise in flashes of clear Seeing which momentarily break through the Personality's ongoing level of perception. After the Shift, that view from beyond Personality becomes permanent. But, let's be clear about this, it doesn't make you omniscient. You don't suddenly become an oracle that can answer all questions about life – that's just another one of those absurd enlightenment myths. This insight is mostly in one area: the area of the activity and appearance of Personality. It's a bit like having x-ray vision: You gain the ability to see through the motivations and actions of Personality, be it others' or your own. This is not usually the case. Normally, it's easy to see other people's Personalities but not your own. The Personality has a blind spot about Seeing its own actions and activity. Personality Awareness sees what it wants to see, and disregards whatever's threatening to it.

Matthew: Because it doesn't want to be exposed?

Jez: Right. One of the main functions of Personality is to protect itself from exposure, because once it's been seen through, it starts losing its power and its illusion of control. Choice-less Awareness removes that blind spot, and then the actions and functions of your own Personality become clear to see.

Matthew: This explains why I sometimes feel that I can't get away with anything when I'm with you, that you see right through my Personality.

Jez: Do you want to get away with something? (Laughs.) I'm teasing; the fact that we've gone this far demonstrates that you have a certain amount of willingness to become aware of it.

Matthew: I think what I'm saying is, in the rest of my life I'm sure my Personality is not so seen by other people. With you it feels like there's nowhere to hide.

Jez: There isn't! This isn't something I Do; the fact is I can't *not* See your Personality when it's playing all those games it plays. For example, over the years we've discussed how, occasionally, your Personality likes to show off how well connected or clever you are. Do you know why you do it?

Matthew: Sometimes I name drop because I think, 'This is my life – why should I hide it? Why should I pretend I don't have these connections...?'

Jez: Who you know or don't know is not the point here; we're looking at your *motivation* for announcing those connections.

Matthew: I think it's because I don't want to take for granted how lucky I am to meet so many interesting people. As you know, I used to work in a literary agency that represented some really big authors...

Jez: Here we go, namedropping again! (They laugh).

Matthew: No wait, I'm trying to make a point here! Maybe I name drop sometimes as a reaction to everyone else who worked at the agency. I noticed they seemed to take it all for granted. I decided I didn't want to do that...

Jez: Can you see what's happening? You're throwing out all sorts of half-related associations and justifications.

Matthew: (Pause.) I'm not, am I?

Jez: Yes. It was like speaking with a politician who does that thing of talking around a question to avoid giving a straight answer.

Matthew: You're right... I don't know why I do that.

Jez: Ah... There's a straight answer: You don't know why you do it.

*Matthew: Why do **you** think I do it?*

Jez: It's a Distraction technique. The Personality will throw anything out to change the subject, to avoid what's really going on. That's what Personality Awareness does: It looks at what it wants to see and looks away from what it wants to avoid.

Matthew: But why would I do that?

Jez: This subject is obviously making you feel unsafe. Showing off is one of the ways Personalities use to deal with patterns of feeling inferior. It hurts to feel inferior, because you feel out of control, and it makes the Personality feel less safe. To counteract that hurt, the Personality uses any method it can to redress the balance and make it feel safe. Pumping itself up by displaying its cleverness or announcing association with celebrities, however distant, is a way it tries to do that.

Matthew: I've just realised something: I remember that unsafe feeling when I was transferred to that private school when I was a boy.* Suddenly I was a small fish in a big pond; everyone seemed richer, posher and more intelligent than me. I felt insecure, I guess... and threatened.

Jez: It's very likely that's where this began. It ended up as one of your Personality's strategies that shows up from time to time, looking for my support. But when you start announcing: 'Look how well connected and clever I am,' I can't be pulled into that game of agreeing with you and stroking your ego. My response, which is usually amusement, just mirrors back to you the ridiculousness of that strategy. There's no malice in it, no intent to put you down or catch you out. There's no it bias in it; that's why this Awareness is called Choice-less. It's like a light: When it's shining, anything that comes into its field of influence is illuminated.

* *The Story of 'You' –* Page 90

Matthew: I don't feel there's any malice in it from you. I always end up learning something from your observations, even though I might have to swallow my pride. I can see the ridiculousness of that pattern, but you're right – underneath it there's a feeling of inadequacy.

Jez: This brings us to the next attribute of Being: full-feeling engagement with life. Before the Wound, children still have Choice-less Awareness; they haven't yet learned to edit their experience of life. This means that whatever happens – be it pleasurable or painful – is felt fully. Nothing is repressed or turned away from; our engagement with life is total.

When Personality starts to edit what it doesn't want to see or experience, that's when we begin to lose our full-feeling engagement with life. For example, when you tried to distract me just now, your Personality was trying to edit out of your experience what I was pointing out to you: the fact that you have a pattern of showing off. When you recognised and heard what I was saying you stopped editing your experience; you connected with the feeling that was behind that pattern, which was a feeling of inadequacy.

Matthew: It's true – and when that happened, I suddenly felt connected, more alive.

Jez: The more feeling there is, the more aliveness; that's the equation.

Matthew: I remember you used the example of a toddler you saw running on the beach.

Jez: Yes, feeling the sand between his toes, the sun on his skin, the sea-salt in the air... Through his senses, he was fully engaged with the experience of being on the beach, and this resulted in the other attribute of Being: Joy.

This example of the boy on the beach is just one end of the scale; Joy comes in many forms. At one extreme there's bliss, at the other it might be experienced as quiet contentment. This Joy is the primal feeling that arises from our engagement in the Original Relationship to Life. In simple terms what this means is: We've been built to breathe, eat, sleep, communicate, share, walk; to live this life through the machinery of the body and the senses. When this happens, an innate Joy arises in the bodymind system.

Matthew: So you're not just talking about experiencing that Joy during special events, like reconnecting with loved ones or seeing a beautiful sunset?

Jez: No, as long as we're open to our feelings and our senses are experiencing life through them, Joy can also arise in everyday life in all sorts of circumstances. Let's take the example of cooking a vegetable soup: First of all there's the satisfaction of engaging with the vegetable seller at the market and choosing the ingredients. Then there's the creativity and experience of actually making the soup: the pungent smell and hiss as the onions start to sizzle in the oil, the gentle stirring of the wooden spoon in the pot, the first test taste on the tongue and finally the sharing of the soup with friends...

Matthew: But surely, you could also feel all that before the Shift?

Jez: That's true, you could feel that Joy, but the point is: In Personality there are many factors which can come in and obstruct that Joy. For example, imagine your partner has invited some friends around for dinner. You had plans – you're in the middle of a great book, you fancied a glass of wine and a quiet evening in – but your friends haven't visited for ages so you feel obliged and you agree to them visiting. Now the whole activity becomes a pressure: You go shopping and the people walking in front of you in the busy market annoy you because you don't really want to be there. What you want to be doing is sitting at home, quietly reading your book, sipping wine. When you get home and start cooking, your creativity is compromised because you feel hassled and rushed. Your usual intuition eludes you and you start making mistakes: You cut your finger on the knife, you put too much salt in the soup and ruin the taste.

When your friends arrive you resent them for being there, you resent your partner for inviting them and you're annoyed with yourself for agreeing to them coming. Your guests pick up on this and there's a tense atmosphere, the soup tastes bad, and the stress of the whole business gives you indigestion. The whole event has become drained of Joy.

Matthew: So you're saying that, after the Shift, this scenario wouldn't happen?

Jez: The situation in which the friends were invited could have happened of course, but your response to it would have been different: There would have been awareness and acceptance of your need to be alone, and maybe you would have honoured this feeling, despite your partner's plans. Or, you may have been adaptable and willingly put aside your own plans because it suited your partner. Either way, there would be no Emotion in it, no resentment and no loss of the Joy of cooking the soup and the sharing of it with your friends.

Without the involvement of Personality with all its problems, pretence and Emotion, Joy becomes a more regular experience because it's a natural outcome of engaging in life. Most areas of life are an opportunity to feel Joy: the feeling of earth under our feet as we walk in the country, the palette of fiery colours we see when the leaves turn in autumn, the feeling of connection between friends....

Matthew: I don't want to sound cheesy but there's Joy when you and I spend time together...

Jez: I know what you mean: We share, we laugh, we engage. All that connection is part of Joy. What blocks this Joy, which we knew so well as young children, is the Suffering of Personality: the worry, pathological fear, resentment, self-criticism and depression etcetera. Once you're unhooked from Personality, none of that's created, so there's a lot more space for that Joy to be felt.

Matthew: This seems to fit with the archetype of the enlightened person always being full of Joy and happiness. But not all experiences are Joyful...

Jez: Right, although Joy becomes a lot more active, it's obviously not the only feeling that arises through engagement with life. As human beings it's natural to feel a whole range of feelings. Feeling sad can be just as much an engagement with life as feeling Joy. With Choice-less Awareness, there's no choice of experiencing some feelings but not others; there's no longer any repression. Whatever arises is felt and felt fully.

Matthew: I remember it really hit you when your father died earlier this year.

Jez: Oh yeah. After returning from the hospital on his last night, a wave of grief suddenly swept over me. As I've mentioned, I found a real closeness to my Dad later in life and I was devastated that this had been cut short. So naturally, I was grief-stricken. I was sad about the times in the past where we hadn't been so close, and also about the times we wouldn't have in the future.

Matthew: There's an idea that Waking Up somehow protects you from feeling psychological pain.

Jez: That's another enlightenment myth. Waking up doesn't protect you from these feelings. Why should it? As I've said before, this is not about being superhuman, it's about being fully human. That means you simply are what you are. A human being is built to feel; without repression and the Contraction, that's what happens. So after Waking Up there can still be pain, sadness, anger etcetera but it's not caused by the ongoing Suffering which Personality creates.

Matthew: Can you clarify what you mean?

Jez: I mean that the pain would not be caused by neurotic worry, paranoia, feelings of being unloveable, self-criticism, recurrent Emotion etcetera. That sort of Suffering is ongoing, and self-perpetuating. The identification with Personality is causing the Suffering and so, unless there's a Shift beyond Personality, it continues.

    The kind of suffering that can continue after the Shift is 'normal suffering'.* For example it can be caused by the advent of illness, death and heartbreak. It's more infrequent, and when it does occur, it doesn't usually persist so long.

Matthew: Why is that?

Jez: Because when there's Choice-less Awareness, there's no rejection of it; feelings aren't repressed. That's the natural response to a feeling: You don't push it away, you feel it. One night, around the time of my father's death, I howled like a dog, or rather my body did. Awareness just watched as the grief passed through my bodymind system. Grief went on of course; that takes time, but that aspect of it was released. When the feeling is felt fully, it finishes its natural

---

* *The Story of 'You'* – Page 236

cycle of life; the energy is freed up and then there's no residue.

Matthew: It reminds me of children in the playground. When they fall and hurt their knee they cry as if it's the end of the world and a moment later, they're happily playing again.

Jez: Exactly, this is Being in action: Whatever arises is felt fully, there's no repression, no one choosing to feel some feelings and not others. If there's pain or sadness, that's what's felt, and then one returns to the possibility of Joy.

ADAPTATION

21

ADAPTATION

The changes that happen after the Shift
in your experience in the world
and your relationship to it

'If one is sick of sickness, then one is not sick.'
– Lao Tzu

Jez: I've described life after the Shift through the various attributes that arise, such as Stillness, unconditional Love and non-Doing, as well as the realisations that, on the Absolute Level, one has no purpose and no choice. However, there's something missing in this description: The fact that, after the Shift, there's a period of adaptation and this has its own specific consequences. Will you look up the definition of that word?

Matthew: Adaptation is: 'The process of change by which an organism or species becomes better suited to its environment'.

Jez: The 'environment' we're referring to in this context is life beyond Personality. Adaptation (with a capital 'A') refers to the bodymind system adapting to living in a totally new way, without being under the governance of Personality.

One of the first parts of Adaptation is the realisation of the fact that the world does not understand or recognise what has happened to you. Let me explain... After the Shift, you experience the Original Relationship to Life. You're no longer Seeking fulfilment of something you've lost; you're no longer psychologically outside of life's embrace, you're inside it. However, as far as the world is concerned – in one respect at least – you become an 'outsider'.

Matthew: In what respect?

Jez: Every tribe has certain characteristics that the people who belong to it share; they're what bonds them together. Followers of religions share their belief systems, countries share national characteristics and history, and families usually share genes and generally share the experience of living and growing together. Tribes offer the security and protection of community, the comfort of knowing: 'We're all in this together.'

Of course, sometimes people abandon their tribe. For example, you might lose your faith and leave a religious group; you may move to a different country and lose your connection to your national tribe. When this happens, you forfeit the sense of solidarity and protection which belonging to the tribe afforded you.

The tribe I'm talking about, the meta-level of the 'tribe of mankind', shares the experience of living on planet earth. The tribe of mankind obviously has all sorts of sub-tribes, but it shares one other meta-trait, and that's identification with Personality.

Matthew: I've never thought of it like that.

Jez: That's because, although you've glimpsed the view from beyond Personality, it's not your ongoing perspective – so why *would* you think about it? Thoughts are a reflection of where you are located; if you believe you're the Personality then your thoughts arise from that perspective. In these talks I'm taking you beyond your normal perspective.

Matthew: You've got me thinking now... Maybe somewhere there's a world where human life forms exist, in which Waking Up is the norm and living identified as Personality is the exception!

Jez: Maybe, but it's certainly not the case in this world. This experience, here now, is that the tribe of mankind shares the trait of identification with Personality. So in this sense – and in this sense only – when you Wake Up out of that identification, you leave the tribe of mankind. The world that's created by humans is not run according to this perspective, it's not geared towards Being; it's all run by Doing. It's run from the group belief that you are your Personality, and everything created by this tribe reflects and serves this belief. Everything facilitates, encourages, protects and glorifies Personality; this in turn keeps you firmly rooted and invested in that belief.

When you Wake Up you find yourself in a curious position. On one hand you feel this incredible affinity with everyone because you know that on the Absolute Level, we're all One. We're all brothers and sisters with the same Mother. We're all children of Life. However, in the Relative Level, when it comes to belief in the Personality, you're constantly reminded of the fact that you're not 'in the 'club', you have well and truly left and become an outsider.

Adaptation has to occur to align yourself to where you are now, in a perspective beyond Personality, and that perspective is constantly shown up by the world around you, which is run on totally different rules.

Matthew: How are you constantly reminded that you're not 'in the club'?

Jez: Technology is a good example: From this point of view you see how advances in technology, especially in connectivity, are used in the service of Personality. If you go out into the street now in any cities you'll see a tribe of zombies walking along staring down at their screens. Being constantly connected to the Internet is a great way for the Personality to keep occupied, to stop Being and feeling in the present. Now you can get apps to help find what you're looking for in the supermarket, so instead of being present in the aisle, looking at signs and understanding your environment, the computer on your phone tells you where to go. This is a good symbol of what's happening: The relationship is no longer between you and your environment, it's primarily between you and a screen. The computer acts like a filter between you and your life; it's just another way to avoid being present to what's going on around you.

Matthew: But there are Mindfulness apps now to help you be present! (Laughs.)

Jez: To me that's like sitting in the sea and looking at a photograph of water on your phone, trying to imagine you can feel its wetness! (Both laugh.) You see what I mean about the screen being a filter between you and life?

A friend recently told me that she noticed that her twenty-three-year-old daughter was uncomfortable making eye contact when they talked. Her generation are so used to communicating through texts or one step removed as an image on a screen, they're forgetting how to connect intimately, face to face. This is a classic example of Personality avoiding feelings and relationship, because feelings are threatening to it. Activities of the Personality, such as addiction to technology, are mostly taken for granted in the tribe.

Matthew: But you use technology...

Jez: Yes. I view technological advancement as a wonderful manifestation of the creativity of the human mind, so I use it and enjoy it but it doesn't control me. There's no possibility of addiction to it, of using it to disassociate myself from my surroundings. Without the need for Distraction or disassociation, technology is used for functional purposes only – which of course can include entertainment.

Matthew: How else are you reminded that you're not 'in the club'?

Jez: It happens every time I see advertising. The world is run according to future desire – that's what all advertising is based on: the belief that 'When I get this I'll be happy'. You're not 'in' if you're not wearing the latest fashion, you're not 'with it' if you haven't got the latest upgrade to your phone. After Waking Up you can See that silent pressure going on in the Group Personality very clearly. Advertising is a game of manipulation; the admen read the psychology of the tribe and manipulate its fears and desires to make it buy their product. After the Shift, without those desires and fears, you see through the whole game; you can't be manipulated any more.

Matthew: You mention the disappearance of future desire, but what about the future and the past in general? Enlightenment stories would have us believe that these disappear into something called the 'eternal now'.

Jez: We usually think of time as being linear; this is a representation of the Relative Level's perception of time. In this model, the Absolute Level appears as a vertical line cutting down through that horizontal line. That phrase: 'the eternal now' refers to the perception of the Absolute Level. That perception doesn't preclude you thinking about something we call the past or the future in the Relative Level. We learned to do this when the self was developing; it's an ability we need to operate in the world. However, despite the popular idea of 'living in the present', most Personalities are constantly living in their mind's projections of the past or future, through worry, regret, hope etcetera. That's something else altogether.

After the Shift, that ability to project into the past and future is not laden with all the Distraction and neurosis of Personality and it falls back into its natural place. So it's a mental function that's used when it's needed and not used when it isn't. The past is not leaned on, it's not needed to prove anything, the future is no longer overlaid with the hope and Distraction of 'When I get this I'll be happy.' You're no longer the summation of your past, or the hope you project into the future; you're simply what's appearing now.

Most people spend a lot of their day in the past or future with perhaps occasional moments of Stillness or thoughtlessness, resting in the now. After the Shift, that set-up reverses. Sometimes, this can make you less efficient in the world, because you can be less tuned to skills needed to operate out there. Projecting into the future can actually become difficult; for example it can be an effort to pack for a trip, to think about what you might need in ten days' time.

Matthew: Really?

Jez: Yes. In this moment, 'ten days' time' doesn't exist, it's a thought, a concept, but it's a concept that you need if you're going on a trip and need to have something to wear when you arrive! Birthdays are interesting too. People load a lot of Emotion onto them: You're one year older, what are you going to do that's special? Are you going to have a party? What do you want as a gift? etcetera. In Relative terms, yes, it's technically the date of your birth, a marker in your life, but in Absolute terms it's just another moment. It's no more special than any other moment.

So you can see how the Adaptation is about learning to live from a totally different perspective, and the particular lessons you have are sometimes dictated by what your Personality was like. For example, I used to be quite naive when it came to people; I was too trusting, I always gave them the benefit of the doubt and this sometimes resulted in me being a victim of their Personalities. This was a blind spot which came from a need to see the best in people; it was an example of my Personality's selective awareness. Now I see Personalities as they are; I have no illusions about where people are coming from. If they're coming from a place of Love, I feel it and enjoy it. If they're coming from Contraction, from the loss of Love, it's obvious to me. I can See it and I can't be a victim of it.

Matthew: What do you mean?

Jez: Let's use you as an example: Everyone has their own way of releasing stress; you tend to get very speedy, you start having rapid thoughts and you fire them off like a machine gun. You're aware of it now as I say this, but you're not conscious of it when you're doing it.

Every Personality has its own particular form, its own characteristics: Some people are pleasers, some are perpetually miserable, some are show-offs, some have low self-esteem etcetera. Very few people are conscious of the form of their Personality – that's why those habits continue. The Personality wants us asleep; otherwise we might Wake Up from the Dream. One of your particular

Personality's characteristics is to become very busy in your mind as a way to discharge stress.

Matthew: I don't know why I do that.

Jez: It's basically a technique your Personality uses not to feel. I've noticed it increases in intensity when there's something going on in your life that's stressful for you. Some people become quiet and reserved in difficult times; you go in the opposite direction. As long as you're in your head, throwing out all these thoughts, you're not feeling. Remember, for the Personality, feelings are unsafe, feelings are dangerous; feelings are a way that Personality can lose its control. You probably picked up this habit this when you were young; for some reason you must have learned that your feelings were unacceptable. So you replaced them with activity that was acceptable, which in your family was thinking; using your intelligence.

Matthew: You're right: In my family, intelligence and thinking are highly valued.

Jez: You can see how becoming conscious of that and Understanding how it informs your Personality helps you lose identification with it, because the more you can see this habit, the harder it is to be pulled into playing it out. But let's not get stuck in that; this is not a therapy session!

The point I'm making here is that once you've Seen through your Personality, Seeing through other people's becomes second nature – and once that happens, you can no longer be a victim of them. You have a right to be exactly how you are, but I have a right to not be a victim of how you are. So that means, in your case, I'll speak up about your habit of stress relief through mental busyness so that you become conscious of it. And hopefully slow it down – or, even better, stop it! (Both laugh.)

Matthew: It's just happened: Since you explained this I feel different, slower. And I've become aware of a slight wave of sadness about a situation happening in my relationship to my family.

(Pause.)

Jez: By pointing out your pattern I tripped it up; then you started contacting the feeling which all that mental noise was distracting you from. As you dropped into feeling you became present, more Still; more quiet.

Matthew: With me you can point this sort of Personality stuff out, but what do you do when it comes up with someone you don't know so well?

Jez: I would vote with my feet – I'd move away. This is not something you Do; it's not a practice, it's just something I've sometimes observed happening when I'm around others. It's all part of Seeing: When you See clearly where things are coming from, you have the ability to decide what you want to let into your experience. I say 'you', but of course it's not really 'you' making a decision, it's life.

Matthew: Do you have any more examples of what changes after the Shift?

Jez: I've noticed that my diet has changed over the last few years: For example, I rarely eat ready meals or fast food nowadays.

Matthew: Why is that?

Jez: Because I realised it wasn't nourishing food. There's one quality that characterises nourishing food: the amount of energy that's in it. Fast food is designed to appeal to your taste buds. It's cheap and widely available, but it's had most of the energy processed out of it. Once you See and Understand the mentality of where this food is coming from – primarily the pursuit of money rather than the sharing of the earth's healthy produce – that attraction for it can fall away.

Food is obviously a big area of addiction; I'm not just talking about people who are seriously overweight. Most people have some level of addictive relationship to food; I certainly did. When you don't need that comfort any more, those sorts of habits can drop away.

What I've described here are a few examples of how life beyond Personality offers a very different perspective on this world. This brings us back to my original point of how Waking Up turns you into an outsider. When I was young, in one way you could say I thought the same kind of thoughts as everyone else. My thoughts resonated with the group mind because they arose from the same perspective, which is that we are this thing called 'Personality'. That is how we're brought up: We're trained to think like our parents and the tribe think, to adopt their worldview.

But there were times when I had a feeling that something was wrong, that life didn't fit this model that I'd been taught. It was just a feeling. I had no Understanding of why I felt that. Feelings are important, but if you're young and everyone around you sees life in one way, it's very easy to think that you're the one who's wrong, that it's your perception that's faulty. But eventually, as a teenager, I came across some books that talked from a perspective that I recognised. For example, I heard about the life of Buddha and I realised that I wasn't mad; other people saw things differently too.

After the Shift you know you aren't mad. You understand where the world of man is 'coming from' and you know that you don't 'come from' the same place. The way the world is run doesn't relate to you. So there can be this feeling of being an outsider, as if you come from another species. It's a bit like being undercover: on the surface my life looks like everyone else's. I eat, cook, earn money, pay bills etcetera, but there's a profound difference: I have no belief that I'm a Personality.

In the past, people who entered into this Enquiry left the tribe and lived in monasteries or ashrams. They removed themselves from the usual world of man and lived with people who were of the same orientation. When this realisation happens in the middle of the world you're confronted with the fact that you're not surrounded by people like you. You're living in a tribe that, in one fundamental aspect, doesn't resonate with you. From the viewpoint of the world, most of what I've discussed in these talks is madness; from the viewpoint after the Shift, it's the world of man that appears utterly mad.

Matthew: What do you mean?

Jez: The addiction to thought... needing to find approval from others... Distracting oneself to avoid feeling... being forever engaged in neurotic thought about the past or future. To come from violent thoughts (you see it everywhere you look, in the media, politics, entertainment) is, from this point of view, totally mad. But in the world it's an accepted, normal madness and when you accept madness, it becomes reinterpreted as sanity.

Matthew: So none of this 'madness', as you call it, arises in you after the Shift?

Jez: That's a really important question. The answer is: 'Yes, that madness can still arise.'

Matthew: I'm confused. If it's the product of Personality, and you have no identification with Personality, how can it arise?

Jez: It can arise as part of the Personality's Residue. (Let's give this use of the word a capital 'R'.) This is a huge subject and it needs a discussion of its own.

22

RESIDUE

The energetic memory of the Personality
in the bodymind system

*'There is nothing to do but much to undo. It's about aligning
yourself to the truth which is always present. We are so bent
out of shape, bodymind wise, that is our toxic conditioning.'*
– Aldous Huxley

Matthew: What do you mean by Personality Residue?

Jez: This organism called 'you' has been living as this Personality ever since childhood. In many ways, the longer that identification is lived, the stronger it gets as the memory of our Natural State drifts further into the past.

Through the years, the Personality becomes an incredibly strong entity, built on deeply entrenched beliefs, hopes, desires and Emotions. This sense of 'me-ness' is expressed, re-asserted and defined in the various roles we play in life. Our history adds up to our particular Story of Personality. This system of energy, with its name and its history, has a density and momentum. After the Shift, when identification with Personality falls away, that momentum wants to continue. That's the Personality Residue.

Matthew: Hang on, you're saying that the Personality's momentum continues after the Shift?

Jez: Yes. We think that being Awake is synonymous with having no Emotional history left. That's a nice, neat spiritual ideal, but real life paints a different picture. The record of the Personality's Story is encoded into the bodymind system, and in the Relative Level it can still manifest. It's as if the system has to catch up with where it is now; it has to align and adapt itself to living without the Contraction. This means that one part of the Adaptation concerns the Residue of Personality, arising in the new landscape of life that is revealed after the Shift.

Matthew: So this Personality Residue can be beliefs, hopes, desires and Emotions...

Jez: Yes, also thought patterns and addictions... Every Personality is different so some of these will be more dominant than others. Before the Shift you may have had an addiction to drugs, food or sex. Maybe there was depression, obsession, or a predominance of anger, sadness, or fear. Perhaps you had the belief that you weren't good enough, or that you were better than everyone else. All of these characteristics of your Personality become redundant after the Shift. Why? Because they grew out of the separation from Love that happened in the Wound...

Matthew: And that separation is no longer experienced?

Jez: That's right. However, those Emotions, beliefs and patterns are so deeply etched in the self that they can have a momentum. The whole orientation of this organism has changed but these characteristics, which are now redundant, want to continue. The Story of Personality is recorded in your body and your psychology: in the organs, tissues, cells and in the mind. Waking Up is instantaneous, but the bodymind system exists in the Relative Level where the law of cause and effect operates in time. So there can be a mismatch between the bodymind system and what has been realised. It's as if the physical and psychological levels of what you are haven't caught up with the Spiritual level. So in the Adaptation, there's a process of harmonisation between these two levels; the harmonisation happens through the release of what is stored in the physiology and psychology. So this appearing of Personality Residue is part of the harmonisation process.

Matthew: How long does this go on for?

Jez: There's no definite time. I've heard that Adaptation can last seven or even ten years; every case is different depending on what Residue is left.

Matthew: What about in your case? How long did it take?

Jez: I can't answer that because there are some areas in which the Residue is still being released.

Matthew: The traditional idea is that none of these things, like Emotions, touch someone who's Awake.

Jez: That's the model we've been given, isn't it? The idea is that you Wake Up and the whole system is wiped clean of all its Emotional history; it's yet another one of those enlightenment myths.

Matthew: I suppose we've been led to think that someone who's Awake lives in the Absolute, beyond such mundane things.

Jez: Yes, that's the root of the misconception – it's totally bogus. The Shift is a return to Being; that means the illusion of being separate from Love has fallen away. However, as long as you're alive, you're operating in the Relative Level, in which there arises a 'sense' of separation. That is part and parcel of the experience of being human. In the Relative Level, this is how duality is experienced. The idea that this 'appearance of separation' suddenly stops happening after Waking Up is absurd.

As children growing and developing in the world, that sense of separation operates through the self. After the Wound, the self picks up Emotions, beliefs, addictions etcetera and gradually crystallises into the Personality. In the Shift, identification with Personality falls away, and you return to the root on which the Personality was built...

Matthew: The self.

Jez: Yes, and as I've said, the self operates in the Relative Level where everything functions under the natural law of cause and effect. Living identified as Personality is the 'cause' – the self contains the 'effect' of that, i.e. the Residue. It's the whole archive of Suffering that's recorded in the organs, tissues and cells.

The most obvious example of this would be if, before the Shift, you'd been addicted to alcohol. In that scenario, the body will obviously show the physical damage caused by that addiction in the liver, while the mind might still contain the memory of the unhappiness, the estrangement from Love that created that addiction.

All the Personality's deeply hidden patterns can be exposed after the Shift, which means they can be healed; their life cycle can come to an end.

Matthew: So you're saying that exposure of the patterns, as happens in the breakdown of the Personality before the Shift, doesn't necessarily lead to healing?

Jez: Correct. In the breakdown, everything that's been repressed in one's psychology can be exposed, so it can be a really difficult, painful and disorienting time. Choice-less Awareness can fall on some of what's exposed, and this contributes to the identification with the Personality being seen through.

Matthew: But that's not what you mean by healing?

Jez: No. Just Seeing that Suffering is not the same as healing it. The Healing I'm talking about (we'll give it a capital 'H'), applies to when that history of Personality is cleared from the bodymind system. We'll talk more about Healing in the next discussion.

Matthew: So, to be clear, you are saying that this Healing of the past that you're referring to doesn't need to happen in order to Wake Up?

Jez: No. We've talked about this before but it's an important point so it's worth clarifying. Waking Up is about your relationship to the Absolute. If we think we are identified as Personality, then we're not in harmony with the truth of who we are. This produces the experience of Suffering in the Relative Level. When Personality is seen through, one returns to the same harmony with the Absolute that a newborn baby has. This, in turn, has an effect on your experience in the Relative Level of your everyday life, because the Suffering that arises from the belief that you're your Personality is no longer created. But the Residue of that belief from the past can still be present in the bodymind.

So Waking up is not caused by the Healing of that Residue. Waking up happens spontaneously when the Personality is dis-identified with. Healing is what happens *afterwards* as an outcome of that.

23

HEALING

The history of the Personality is spontaneously cleared from the bodymind system

'In order to be effective, truth must penetrate like an arrow – and that is likely to hurt.'

– Wei Wu Wei

Jez: Let's start with a dictionary definition of the word 'healing'.

Matthew: It says here: 'The natural process by which the body repairs itself'. Also: 'To restore to health'.

Jez: What do we mean by health or sickness in the context of this Enquiry? I'm proposing that the only way to really live a healthy life, both physically and mentally, is to live in the Original Relationship to Life. Conversely, to live a life identified as Personality is ultimately not healthy.

Matthew: Seeing as most of the planet lives this way, that's a heck of a statement!

Jez: I know, but after the Shift this just becomes an obvious fact. From observation of your own life, and those around you, it becomes clear that identification with Personality causes both mental and physical sickness in everyone. I'm not referring to 'normal suffering' – that is, illness with genetic or environmental causes; I'm referring to sickness that arises as part of the Suffering of Personality.

First, let's look at mental sickness: anxiety, stress, paranoia, neuroses, worry, constant thinking, guilt, self-abuse, depression, anger issues, phobias... the list goes on and on. Although the medical profession recognises these issues as forms of psychological illness, they're so common that they're almost accepted as a normal part of being human; their cause is often put down to the 'stresses of modern living'.

Matthew: But you're saying they're caused by identification with Personality?

Jez: Yes, these symptoms don't normally occur when we're babies in the Natural State; they start arising after the Wound and the identification with Personality. But because, for the most part, the tribe of man doesn't question that identification, the sickness that's an outcome of it is accepted as being normal.

Physically, these psychological problems manifest in the body in any number of ways, because stresses in the mind translate to stresses and blocks in the body. As I said when we talked about health,* a healthy body is a body in flow; all these symptoms are caused by a lack of flow – by tension, stress and stagnation. This is how disease arising from Personality starts.

Matthew: But these symptoms, both physical and mental, can change; some people have therapy and it helps them.

Jez: Yes, psychotherapy attempts to rearrange and modify the Personality in order to reduce these symptoms. For example, an alcoholic may go to Alcoholics Anonymous and give up drinking, but the addiction hasn't disappeared. This is proved by the fact that ex-alcoholics have to stay away from alcohol in case they start drinking again. So the Personality gets rearranged into a less damaging formation, but that's not Healing in the sense I'm using it. Healing (with a capital 'H') is the *ending* of those patterns of sickness, both physical and mental, and the cessation of the creation of new patterns. Healing can only happen through addressing the root of the problem.

Matthew: Which is identification with Personality?

Jez: Yes, that's where the sickness begins. So without the Shift, real Healing can't even begin. With the Personality in control, the 'natural process by which healing happens' isn't allowed to take place because identification with Personality not only causes the sickness but also blocks Healing from happening.

Matthew: Why is that?

Jez: Because Healing involves opening up to the Residue – everything that's repressed and hidden in the Shadow: the beliefs, addictions, pain, anger, grief etcetera. This is something the Personality doesn't want to do. The reason it repressed those Emotions in the first place was so they wouldn't have to be felt. But all that repression has consequences: The Emotion just wants to be heard. When it isn't heard, it comes out in any way it can; it manifests as physical and psychological illnesses. So now the bodymind is trying to get your attention with these symptoms; it's yelling: 'Something's wrong, you need to feel this, not lock it away.' And what do we do?

---

* *The Story of 'You'* – Chapter 29

Matthew: We go to the Doctor.

Jez: And the Doctor gives us drugs that *repress* the symptoms. So a problem that's caused by repression is dealt with by the application of *more* repression. Symptoms may temporarily abate, but the original problem is just pushed further into the bodymind. And now, on top of that, the body has to deal with the side effects of the drugs it's been medicated with.

Matthew: So, you're saying that after the Shift, Healing of the Residue – the patterns and Emotions from the Personality – becomes possible?

Jez: Yes.

Matthew: In our discussion on Stillness you said that, after the Shift, one realises there's nothing to be done. How does that fit with the idea that Healing needs to happen?

Jez: Good question! Your use of the word 'need' is significant. When identified with Personality, the internal dialogue comments on your life trying to change it, to make it happier, more pleasurable. After the Shift, changes can still happen in psychology and the bodymind system, but there's no voice telling you those changes need to happen. The belief that 'When I get this I'll be happy' no longer governs your actions.

What I'm describing here has nothing to do with therapy or growth. We're not talking about reshaping parts of the Personality in order to create more happiness or peace. This Healing is simply something that happens in non-Doing when Personality is unhooked from.

Matthew: So you're saying it's just a natural process.

Jez: Yes. It appears that the bodymind system wants to cleanse itself of Residue from the years when you were identified as Personality. I see it as a beautiful manifestation in the Relative Level; life has a momentum, it wants to keep flowing and evolving and this move towards Healing is how that momentum manifests in a human being after the Shift.

Matthew: We've talked about how, in the breakdown of the Personality

before the Shift, anything that's buried in the Shadow can d...
seen by Choice-less Awareness. What's the difference between t...
what happens after the Shift?

Jez: If there's some Choice-less Awareness it's possible that some of the Emotions and beliefs buried deep in the Shadow can be released and Healed. However, until the Shift, identification with Personality will always come back in. This means Personality Awareness will return and start practicing its selective view on what it becomes aware of.

After the Shift, things are different. The Personality has lost its control; it's no longer holding everything together, pushing down feelings it doesn't want to feel. So there can be quite a rollercoaster ride as the repressed Emotions, beliefs, patterns and all the detritus of your Personality's Story are gradually released. Healing of all this is possible because the Residue arises within an unchanging environment of Choice-less Awareness.

Matthew: Can you give me an example of what you mean so I can understand it in practice?

Jez: Sure, let's take Emotions as an example of part of the Residue. In Personality there are basically two different relationships to Emotions: The first, which we've already touched on, is based around repression. If we repress Emotions in an attempt to escape them, we only succeed in compounding our stress, because the more Emotions are repressed, the stronger they become and the more they want to be released.

The other relationship to Emotion is what we see in Personalities that become fixed around a certain Emotion, for example an angry Personality. In these cases the Emotion of anger isn't repressed, it's engaged with; it's acted out and dramatised.

Matthew: I know what you mean by dramatising the anger; I wouldn't say I have an angry Personality but sometimes I really enjoy feeling righteously angry.

Jez: It can feel great to be really angry: The energy passes through the body and there's a sense of relief, because the root of that energy has been tied up in the body for so long. But these Emotional releases

:harges; the Emotion from which it arose is
it's not diminished in any way.

.matisation of Emotion is all part of the theatre
are a kind of participation in it. Acting out an
g it are two sides of the same coin; both are
Choice-less Awareness, your relationship to
because your participation with anything that
nality goes. There's no longer any possibility of
repressing or dramatising Emotion.

Let me give you an illustration of what I mean. Every school has a bully, a child who's driven by anger, resentment and a need to hurt others. What a bully wants from those around them is a reaction: They want you to play a part in their drama, to participate in their bullying by being a victim of it. Or, if you're an authority figure like a teacher or parent, they want you to chastise them and make them wrong. They want you to either be afraid of them or to confront them. That's the deal, that's how bullying works: The Emotion that's at the root of the bullying wants to be heard. Getting a reaction from someone gives the bully a sense of release as some of that hurtful, angry energy is discharged. However, this doesn't stop the bully bullying again, because by terrorising others the Emotion is not being finished with, it's simply being exercised. For the bully, the act of bullying is an addiction: They do it, they get high on the attention and the release of anger, then they want to do it some more because it feels good.

Imagine if that bully comes up against someone who can't be manipulated into giving them the response they want, someone who's tougher than them or who can see right through them and consequently can't be pulled into any form of participation in their game. By not reacting, what happens to the dynamic? The bully is robbed of their power; they lose their control.

This is what I mean by having a different relationship to the Emotion, belief, addiction or whatever's appears in the Residue; Choice-less Awareness sees it but there's no participation in it.

Matthew: So if there's no repression or dramatisation of the Emotion, what does happen? I presume you still feel it?

Jez: Oh yes. Before the Shift, when there's pain, (whether physical or psychological) there's usually a pulling back from fully experiencing it. After the Shift, when that instinctive flinch has gone, you're in full-feeling engagement with life. Without the Personality editing your experience, without the Contraction, there's no resistance to feeling.

Matthew: So after the Shift, anything could be felt as part of the Residue? Even, say, depression?

Jez: Why not? Let's say someone has suffered some depression in their life before the Shift; with Choice-less Awareness there's no voice saying: 'I shouldn't be feeling this,' or 'I won't feel this.' That sort of filter has gone.

Matthew: It seems crazy, counterintuitive, to open to pain.

Jez: Yes, but remember, *you're* not doing anything. You're not consciously choosing to let go into it; letting go just happens.

Matthew: But however you get to it, depression still feels awful.

Jez: Yes. Sometimes life does feel awful – who said that this experience called life doesn't involve feeling awful sometimes?

Matthew: So, to be clear, you're saying that Waking Up doesn't protect you from having painful feelings?

Jez: No, that's all part of being human. To consciousness, which perceives those feelings in the Relative Level, it may be very painful. But after the Shift, this experience of depression is also perceived from the perspective of Consciousness. The light of Choice-less Awareness is falling on those painful feelings; it's not judging, repressing or dramatising them, it's simply observing them. Consciousness is always bigger than the trauma; Consciousness is the ground in which the trauma is arising. So this perspective gives a certain detachment to whatever is arising from the Personality's history. Without identification or ownership, it no longer seems like 'your' Story any more.

Matthew: Talking about having a 'full-feeling' relationship to life at the same time as having detachment seems contradictory to me.

Jez: Detachment, as I mentioned before, is often seen as a detachment from feeling. Here we're talking about a detachment from identification with Personality, which actually results in an openness to feeling. The point is, because of that lack of identification, there's the ability to feel it without getting emotionally involved in what's being felt.

Matthew: I don't follow you.

Jez: Let me put it this way: If a hypochondriac gets a fever, he has a strong participation in it. All of his neurosis, fear and beliefs about illness are activated and projected onto the fever. 'What does it mean?' he thinks, 'What disease have I got?' 'How long will it last?' So now on top of dealing with the fever, he's also dealing with how his Personality is reacting to it.

All of that neurosis and fear, which of course is a sickness in itself, then interferes with the natural process of the body being ill and healing itself. As well as dealing with the fever, the body is now also burdened with worry and stress and this compounds the original sickness.

When a non-hypochondriac gets ill, they're just ill. It's just a physical thing; nothing mental is projected onto it. They let the sickness be: They feel lousy but they allow the body to just get on with expelling the fever so the healing can happen. In the same way, after the Shift, when the Residue comes up – if Emotions arise, for example – detachment allows you to feel the Emotion fully with no resistance. Then, by going fully into the Emotion, you reach its root.

Matthew: I know we've talked about this when we discussed Emotion;* can you remind me what you mean by 'the root of it'?

Jez: Let's have a recap. Emotions are feelings that have been buried. After the Wound, we learned that feelings are not safe, because they lead to us being hurt. This is why we Contracted: to avoid those painful feelings. The Personality said: 'These feelings are so awful, if you feel them it will be too painful, so I'll protect you from them. I'll lock them away and keep you safe from them.'

Matthew: And those painful feelings that are repressed stagnate and

---

* *The Story of 'You'* – Chapter 17

become Emotions...

Jez: Yes. Emotions are not threatening to the Personality because as long as you're engaged and caught up in the Emotion, you're not feeling the core feeling on which it's built.

Matthew: So, you're talking about contacting that original feeling?

Jez: Exactly, that's the root of the Emotion. Contacting that original feeling is how Healing happens. There's no longer any Contraction or repression to stop that happening... You just feel it.

Matthew: You say: 'You just feel it', but I imagine that the original feelings, which have been the root of so much pain in one's life, must be horrific.

Jez: You're demonstrating what your Personality has always told you to dissuade you from going into those feelings. In reality, one finds that contacting those original feelings might be a painful experience but it can also be a massive relief.

Matthew: I don't understand; how can that be?

Jez: All that original feeling wanted was to be heard, so finally listening to it brings tremendous relief, resolution and peace to the whole bodymind system. Even if the feeling is very painful, it's not nearly as painful as the Contraction, the blocked energy, the deadness, depression or whatever it grew into. If the Residue of your Personality holds pain, then there is pain – but then the Healing happens.

Matthew: How does the Healing actually happen?

Jez: When the feeling at the root of the Emotion is felt, it is released. That whole cycle, from repressed feeling to Emotion, is completed; the energy returns back to its source...

Matthew: Which is?

Jez: Love. Ultimately, all Healing is about the return to Love.

(Pause.)

Matthew: We've talked about Emotion, what about other forms of Residue from the Personality, like addiction?

Jez: Before the Shift, you were identified as Personality. The addiction arose from the Wound; it was an attempt to replace that loss of Love. If you have the Love, the addiction becomes defunct; you no longer need it as a coping mechanism.

Matthew: Does this sort of Healing happen gradually after the Shift?

Jez: In my experience, yes, but I've heard of some cases where people with severe drink and drug habits experience an instantaneous Healing after an Opening where the addiction suddenly leaves. But remember, that doesn't mean the whole Residue of the Personality has been cleared out. The physical addiction is just one aspect of the Residue; there are many aspects of the Personality, such as Emotions and belief patterns, that can still be in there.

Matthew: Tell me about belief.

Jez: Belief is like the software, the programming in the mind. These thought loops are laid down in childhood and usually run for the rest of your life.

Matthew: Unless you Wake Up?

Jez: Yes, then they can leave the system but, once again, this isn't necessarily immediate. Just because the Shift has happened, old beliefs don't suddenly disappear; the programming can still be running. But now, after the Shift, there's a dissonance between those thoughts and the Being that is your experience. For example, some Personalities have low self-esteem patterns built on the belief that they're unloveable, they're not good enough. These beliefs limit Joy: the ability to take in life, to share, to Love. This is obviously incompatible with Being, so after the Shift such beliefs would be shown up and eventually they'd dissolve like frost in the morning sun. The energy that was tied up in them would be released back into Love.

TEACHING

24

TRUTH

Is there such a thing as objective truth?

'Just as the great ocean has one taste,
The taste of salt,
So also this teaching and discipline has one taste,
The taste of liberation.'
– Buddha

Matthew: From the point of view beyond Personality, is there such a thing as truth? I mean an objective truth?

Jez: To go into this let's be clear on what the word 'objective' means.

Matthew: The dictionary says: 'Not influenced by personal feelings or opinions in considering and representing facts.'

Jez: When asking: 'Is there such a thing as objective truth?' we have to consider the context. For example, science is based on the principle of objective truth; the point of scientific experiments is to find out what is true objectively. To do that, the person conducting the experiment must have no personal stake in the results and no influence on them.

So, in areas of scientific study such as chemistry, biology and physics we can say that there *is* such a thing as objective truth. But as soon as you enter areas where human psychology becomes a factor, the answer's not so clear. For example, in the world of modern art, what one person judges to be a work of genius another may consider to be a waste of paint. And as soon as you enter the area of religion, the subject of belief appears, which means there's an endless variety of opinions on what is true. You can see that in many areas, other than science, the idea of what is true becomes subjective rather than objective. How does the dictionary define 'truth'?

Matthew: 'A fact or belief that is accepted as true.'

Jez: That definition is very telling: It points to subjective truth because it suggests that the 'true-ness' of something is defined by the person believing it to be true. As I said, when it comes to science and physical laws of nature, this clearly isn't the case. Someone high on LSD may believe they can fly but objective reality – in the form of gravity and the hard ground – can easily prove that they can't. However, in the world of religion and beliefs, where truth is subjective, this definition – a fact or belief that is accepted as true – becomes more apposite.

Matthew: Some people say that all teachings and religions are true in the sense that they're true for the people believing them.

Jez: You mean, just by the fact that a religion appears true for some people – that it is *their* truth – it has validity and meaning? I think that's half correct: By believing something it becomes true for you, within your psychology, in your worldview. So it has validity for *you* – it's your subjective truth – but I don't think anyone would say it has objective truth if they really thought it through.

You could call what we're talking about here 'Personal Truth'. It might sound open minded and inclusive to assign objective validity to all religions and beliefs, but the inaccuracy of this viewpoint can be exposed simply by raising the subject of any dangerous cult, such as Jim Jones's People's Temple. He's the guy who set up a community in Guyana in the late seventies and induced his followers to mass suicide. I'm old enough to remember tragic photos of the poisoned victims on the front pages of newspapers: a stark warning against the dangers of taking on other people's beliefs!

My point is, if you take on the belief that all religions are expressing their own truth and, in that sense, they're all valid then you'd have to include extreme examples such as this. I don't think even the most open-minded person would hold up Jim Jones's religion as being an example of the truth.

Matthew: Of course not; he was obviously deluded.

Jez: It was a playing out of the 'saviour story': Jones was the saviour, the only one who was pure and able to lead his followers to salvation. His followers believed this to be true, but it wasn't *objectively* true; it was the belief system of a deluded Personality which they had taken  on. What part of them took it on? Was it the Character? No, it was their Personalities that took it on and made it into their 'Personal Truth'. It was their insecurities, fears, naivety and lack of self-love that made them susceptible to Jim Jones's subjective truth, his saviour story.

Matthew: So what you're saying is, the Personality's not usually engaged in seeing objective truth – apart from in the field of science.

Jez: Yes, and in the place of that objective truth it creates its own world of Personal Truth. Why is this? Because the Personality is loaded with its own agendas. It wants to be Distracted from Suffering, it wants to feel hope, it wants parent figures to make it feel safe, and so

me - ethical personality

on. Every Personality has its own particular patterns and agendas that lead it to take on its particular Personal Truths and beliefs.

Matthew: Isn't what you're talking about another way of describing Personality Awareness?

Jez: Yes, exactly. Personality edits its experience and creates its own Personal Truth out of what it chooses to see. So the followers of Jim Jones chose to see a saviour and looked away from all the obvious signs – such as the manipulation, sexual abuse, and even murder – that might have suggested he was in fact a narcissistic sociopath.

So, informed by its patterns, beliefs and agendas, Personality looks out at the world through the filter of Personality Awareness, and creates its own subjective, Personal Truth.

Matthew: So when it comes to this metaphysical Enquiry, do you think there is such a thing as objective truth?

Jez: That question begs another question: 'Is it possible to perceive what is true without going through the filter of Personality and all its agendas?' Or, to put it another way: 'Is it possible for a human being to see *beyond* the Personality?'

Matthew: Your answer will obviously be 'Yes' – that's what all these talks have been about.

Jez: Correct. When identification with Personality falls away, the subjective perspective that was part of it disappears with it. Then Consciousness perceives the world through Choice-less Awareness and what is Seen is objective truth – meaning it's not altered or edited by Personality and its agendas.

Matthew: I suppose that's what happened to me in my Opening on the village green?

Jez: Exactly. For as long as it lasted, you viewed life from beyond the viewpoint of the beliefs, opinions, agendas and patterns of your Personality. In order to See from that viewpoint, you had to momentarily See through the most basic, primal Personal Truth, one that we are all brainwashed into believing as children: the belief that we are our Personality.

Matthew: I've never thought of it like that. Can you give me a moment?

(Pause.)

Jez: When it comes to this Enquiry, this is the core Personal Truth that's exposed. That belief is the root of everything: As long as you believe it's true, then you open the door to all the Suffering, madness, neuroses and wars of humankind.

   Once this core personal belief is seen through, you perceive the world without the filter of Personality. So when we talk about truth in this area of metaphysics, this is what I'm talking about. Releasing that core belief allows you to see the objective truth of how we operate as humans: What Being is, what the Natural State is and how we lost it. That truth isn't something the mind makes up; it's simply what is Seen beyond the viewpoint of Personality. This is the meaning of the quote from Buddha:

> *Just as the great ocean has one taste,*
> *The taste of salt,*
> *So also this teaching and discipline has one taste,*
> *The taste of liberation.*

Matthew: So these talks, and everything we've discussed here, isn't just 'your' truth?

Jez: It's not my truth in the sense that it's not a subjective truth that my Personality believes in; it's an objective truth. By that I mean that it exists before and beyond my Personality.

*Matthew: That's the first time I've heard you say, '**my** Personality'.*

Jez: As you can see, language becomes difficult with this subject. I'm talking about there being no identification, no one to claim anything and then – in order to maintain a natural flow of English – I have to use words like 'you', 'my' or 'mine', which conflict with the very point I'm making. So we have to be conscious of this limitation of language when discussing this.

Matthew: I see what you mean but, just to be clear – although the Personality isn't 'yours', you're suggesting that there is still a Personality there?

Jez: As I mentioned in our discussion on the Residue, a Personality with its own Story can occasionally arise, but there's no identification with it.

Matthew: So, beliefs and agendas could arise?

Jez: Yes, anything could arise from the Story... But my point is, after identification has fallen away, you no longer believe what the Personality says. The whole show has been seen through.

Let me give you an illustration to show you what I mean: A young boy watching a puppet show believes that the puppet on stage is a real living being because it can apparently move its body and talk. When the boy runs up to the stage and looks behind the curtain he finds out that the puppet isn't real: Its voice and movements – which make it appear real – are actually provided by the puppeteer.

When the boy returns to his seat in the theatre his experience of the puppet show is totally different. He knows that when the puppet appears to speak, what he is hearing is the voice of the puppeteer. The illusion has been broken; the puppet is no longer taken to be real. The boy sees the objective truth of that.

This is what happens after the Shift: the Personality is no longer taken to be real and so its voice and its viewpoint are no longer believed in.

Matthew: You're saying that whatever you express here doesn't come from that Residue of 'your' Personality?

Jez: Correct. Of course, normally when you converse with people that is what happens; you're mostly getting the opinions and beliefs of their Personality. After the Shift that can't happen; the illusion of the puppet show has been seen through.

This is not a sharing of 'my truth' – i.e. a subjective truth that my Personality believes in. It's a sharing of what is Seen from the perspective beyond Personality. It's also not my truth in the sense that there's no one here claiming or owning it.

Matthew: But it's said in a way that is particular to you.

Jez: Yes, indeed. It's '*my*' expression of what is true about these matters expressed through the Character, but not the Personality. So it's said in a certain way, with 'my' particular emphasis and wording, but there's no spin on it from Personality. There's no Doing in it, nothing to prove by it, no Shadow influencing or informing it.

Matthew: Can you remind me of the difference between Personality and Character?

Jez: You must have a pretty clear idea of what I mean by Personality by now: It's the idea, the construct of you that grew in response to the Wound. By Character I mean your essential nature: your quirks, talents and idiosyncrasies. None of that came from the Wound and its Suffering; rather it's an expression of the Joy of Being that you came with, that existed in you before the Wound. It's part of the diversity and wonder of manifestation – we all have different Characters just as all snow crystals have different patterns of configuration.

So I'd argue that the truth of what is being said via this Character is universal, but the *form* of it is personal to this particular Character. That is, it comes from a particular angle, with a particular expression and emphasis.

25

ENERGETIC SOURCE

Everything carries an imprint of its source

'I'm looking for the face I had before the world was made.'
– W.B. Yeats

Matthew: You say there's one basic, objective truth when it comes to metaphysics: We are not our Personality. But there are so many different types of teaching out there, it's very confusing. It's hard to know which I can trust, which have this objective truth in them.

Jez: To help clarify things, in the next few talks we're going to discuss three main categories of teaching: Personal Growth, Pseudo-Spiritual Teaching and Spiritual Teaching. I'll explain in detail what I mean by each category as we come to them but, in general terms, what distinguishes these categories from each other is their 'energetic source'. Knowing their energetic source can help illuminate whether they have any objective truth in them or not. In other words: Do they point beyond Personality?

Matthew: I understand the phrase 'energetic source' – meaning the source of something's energy – but can you describe what you mean by it in this context?

Jez: In the Sixties people started talking about things having 'good vibes' or 'bad vibes'. This was one of those instances when a deeper truth leaked into the group consciousness. The root of this phrase is the Understanding that everything has an energetic source that shows in the vibrations it's emitting.

Matthew: A sceptic would say that's just New Age psycho-babble.

Jez: Actually, it's quite obvious; no weird beliefs are required. Imagine that you're shopping in a busy supermarket: You're walking through the aisles, bumping into people and their trolleys, trying to find the item you're looking for on the shelves.

Matthew: OK.

Jez: Now you leave the supermarket, walk into a cathedral, and sit on a pew for half an hour in silence. These are two very different energetic experiences. The first is frenetic, possibly even stressful and the second is calm and peaceful. The different experiences are a reflection of the energetic source of the two locations: The energetic source of the supermarket is consumerism while the energetic source of the cathedral is one of worship, contemplation and Stillness.

Everything has a different vibration. If you can understand the energetic source, you can understand the reason for that difference in vibration. You can apply this principle to physical objects, for example: If I pick up this quartz crystal in my left hand and take my wicker waste paper basket in the other I experience two very different feelings. It's not just a difference of texture, of smooth and rough; they feel different because they have a different vibration, or energy. This is because their energetic source is different; the crystal comes from deep within underground rock and the cane used to make the wicker is grown in soil on the earth's surface.

Even objects of the same generic material can have different vibrations: A lump of granite feels different from a lump of limestone; a piece of oak wood feels different from a piece of pine. The vibration of any object varies depending on its energetic source: where it has grown, where it has formed or, if it's living, the seed from which it has grown.

But this doesn't just apply to objects or environments: Everything has an energetic source. We touched on this in *The Story of 'You'* when we talked about Group Personalities.* What would you say was the energetic source of a political party?

Matthew: I assume it would be their core values, their principles.

Jez: Yes, and the energetic source of a religious sect would be its beliefs; in nations it's often their history.

This energetic source can be found in anything produced by humans because everything carries an imprint of the motivation, the intent, the beliefs or the psychology of the person or persons who produce it. The area of music gives some good examples of this: If I asked you to describe what Punk music is, what would you say?

Matthew: I'd say that it's a form of music that's loud, crude, confrontational and ugly.

Jez: Yes, and all of that is reflection of its energetic source, which is anger and teenage rebellion. By contrast, classical music is refined, nuanced, and technical; it comes from a more mature, refined, even intellectual sensibility. The Energetic Source of Country music is often a place of heartbreak, yearning and sentimentalised love,

* *The Story of 'You'* – Chapter 7

while Blues – with its history rooted in enslavement – comes from a place of sorrow, pain and social injustice.

When you listen to each type of music, you're tuning into the vibration of its energetic source. So, the music you're attracted to is a reflection of who you are. For example, it would be rare to find a middle-aged intellectual type listening to Punk music, unless they'd been into it in their youth.

Matthew: It's the same with comedy, isn't it? What makes one person laugh means nothing to someone else.

Jez: Exactly. There are many different types of comedy: sophisticated, satirical, silly, surreal or even angry. What you're drawn to, or offended by, is a reflection of who you are.

Matthew: When I was growing up, jokes based on crude stereotypes about all sorts of minorities were common and widely accepted; I never felt they were funny. It wasn't conscious but I sensed there was cruelty in them.

Jez: Now the mainstream Group Personality has moved on and deemed those sorts of jokes politically incorrect. Their energetic source is intolerance and hatred, so they give an instant insight into whoever finds them funny, and who doesn't.

Matthew: It's not just cruel comedy that I dislike; I've noticed that sometimes I try watching stand-up comedy on TV and I take an instant dislike to it, even before I've really thought about it.

Jez: I know the feeling. For example, some comedians use a self-deprecating trait in their act; the punch line might be how they can't find a date, how they're too fat or always screw up etcetera. I just can't relate to that sort of comedy. I don't find it funny because I don't resonate with where it's coming from, which is a lack of self-love. This is not about being pretentious or judgemental; my response is simply a reflection of how well I resonate with the source of the comedy.

If you're sensitive, you can perceive the energetic source from which anything is arising: You might read a news report and find that it has a left- or right-wing bias behind it. You could look at a painting – like Edvard Munch's The Scream for example – and feel the fear and angst that the artist felt when he painted it. You can hear a love song and feel the joy of the composer being expressed through the lyrics and the melody.

After the Shift, another perspective becomes obvious to you when observing the world. On a meta-level you can perceive whether art, film, comedy or whatever is coming from the energetic source of Personality or not.

Matthew: But, unless whoever creates the art, film or comedy had Woken Up, wouldn't you say that it all comes from Personality?

Jez: Not necessarily; it could be an expression of the Character. I'll give you an example of what I mean: Last week I watched a programme in a series about people who've gone off to start a new life in remote locations. Although each programme follows the same format, every episode has a very different feel, which is all down to the person the episode is focussing on.

The previous episode that I'd watched told the story of a guy who used to be a research scientist; he'd left that life behind to go and live on a remote island off New Zealand. He explained his disillusionment with the politics of academia and how this had caused him to leave; it was obvious that he was still harbouring some resentment. The scientist's air of distrust also showed in the fact that he didn't go out of his way to hang out with the few indigenous locals with whom he shared the island. The genial, well-travelled host of the programme is used to getting on with all sorts of Personalities but it was obvious that he wasn't exactly bonding with the scientist. This made the programme slightly uncomfortable to watch.

By comparison, last week's episode focussed on a guy who was trying to set up a trekkers' lodge on a remote mountain in Guatemala. He'd worked hard to bond with the locals and, even though they'd been slightly hostile at the start, he'd eventually formed a mutual trust with them and treated them like family. He was not running away from his past life; he was opening up to a new life in a beautiful place he wanted to share with fellow trekkers. The programme's host obviously liked and respected this man, and the programme had a lightness, openness and Love in it that was a reflection of his Character.

Neither of the two subjects of those programmes had Woken Up, but the scientist in New Zealand was coming from a sense of repressed resentment and Contraction in his Personality, while the Guatemalan guy seemed to be coming from Joy and Love.

My point is that, although motivations of the Personality are often the main governing force in human life, they're not the *only* force. All the attributes we've discussed as being outcomes of Waking Up can appear before Waking Up because we all originally come from the Natural State. So of course, there can be Love, Joy, Stillness and non-Doing before Waking Up; it's just that the appearance of those attributes can be restricted by the governing force and the motivations of Personality.

Matthew: I can relate to that; as long as the internal dialogue of self-judgement is going on in my mind, I'm not really experiencing Stillness.

Jez: Yes, as long as there's neurosis, Emotion, or a need to be Distracted, the experience of Stillness is elusive. If there's violence or self-hatred, then Love is diminished; where there's Suffering and unhappiness, obviously Joy is restricted. But the point is, those attributes are restricted in their appearance but not wiped out; they can break through into the life that's mostly governed by Personality.

Matthew: Like the Opening I had broke through into my life?

Jez: Yes, but I'm not just talking about Openings breaking through the stranglehold of the Personality's Contraction; Being can also manifest in inspiration and creativity for example. Personalities who are really difficult and messed up can produce great art – we mentioned Van Gogh in an earlier talk. If you look at the lives of great artists, most of them had quite screwed up Personalities - many were addicted, abusive and misogynistic – but that didn't stop them having moments of tremendous inspiration in which masterpieces were produced that can touch us all.

Matthew: And that's because we respond to the energetic imprint of where those works of art are coming from?

Jez: Yes. I'd say that all great art comes from an energetic source beyond Personality. It all depends on the artist's mental state, on their psychology at the time when the art was created. Inspiration can take you beyond the influence and constraints of Personality.

26

PERSONAL GROWTH TEACHINGS

Self-Help, Therapy & Human Potential

'My one regret in life is that I'm not somebody else.'
– Woody Allen

Jez: I started the last discussion by saying that each category of teaching, whether it be Personal Growth, Pseudo-Spiritual or Spiritual Teaching, is defined by its energetic source. Now we're going to take each category in turn and look into what its energetic source is.

The first category we're going to discuss is Personal Growth teachings. I've broken down the subject of Personal Growth into three sub-categories: Psychotherapy, Self-Help and Personal Development. So, the question is: What is the energetic source of these teachings? What do you think?

Matthew: Well, I presume they grew out of different people's understandings about human behaviour.

Jez: Yes, that's true... but I have to clarify something here. In an earlier talk, I used 'Understanding' with a capital 'U' to describe what can happen in an Opening. I said that an Understanding is an insight which is informed by the knowledge that we're not our Personalities. So for example, what I share with you in these talks is all based on Understandings, whether they're about Unconditional Love, Choice-less Awareness or purpose. Although Understandings obviously arise in the mind, they're from a viewpoint beyond Personality; they relate to what is beyond Personality.

When you said that Personal Growth teachings 'grew out of different people's understandings about human behaviour', you weren't referring to 'Understandings' with a capital 'U'. They don't come from beyond Personality; they are understandings that anyone with intelligence and perception could have about the world of people, psychology and energy. It's those understandings that are the energetic source of Personal Growth teachings.

Knowing this helps one comprehend where these teachings are 'coming from', what their function and purpose is. They're not informed by what lies beyond Personality – they deal with what lies within it. They comment on, and illuminate, appearances in the Relative Level such as Emotions, neuroses, unhappiness, success and failure, but they don't address the Absolute Level.

Modern psychoanalysis began with the understandings of Sigmund Freud, but he drew on earlier understandings about the unconscious. The German philosopher Schelling coined that term in the 18th Century, but in turn he was building on writings by Paracelsus in the 16th Century. I've done a bit of research on this – apparently, references to the unconscious can even be found in the Vedas, the Hindu texts that predate Christ.

Just as with scientific discoveries, each breakthrough builds on the understandings of pioneers who went before. So Freud was a link in a chain, who in turn inspired students such as Jung, Adler and Wilhelm Reich to make further discoveries. Through these understandings, the mind of man breaks through and expands to a deeper knowledge of its own nature.

Matthew: And these understandings help to relieve psychological Suffering?

Jez: To a degree. Psychotherapy doesn't address the root cause of Suffering, which is identification with Personality; it addresses the outcome of that identification. Most people engage in therapy to decrease mental Suffering; by rearranging the furniture of the Personality, it's possible to make living as it a bit more comfortable. Psychotherapy can lessen the Suffering a little, but it's not concerned with *transcending* it.

Matthew: Isn't it helpful at all when it comes to this Enquiry?

Jez: Yes, it can be. Whilst its intent is not to go beyond Personality, with someone who has Yearning and Readiness, it can be a powerful step in the right direction. Psychotherapy is about bringing about some level of awareness of the workings of Personality; this is definitely something that can contribute to Seeing *beyond* Personality. Most people come to spiritual life because of the Suffering of the Personality, so awareness of that system – of how it arises and functions – is part of the journey, but only if it's used as a springboard to go further.

I watched a documentary recently about a therapy programme in a maximum-security prison in America. It was amazing to see these hardened men – thieves, rapists and murderers – gaining some awareness of their Personalities. Many of them realised they'd become trapped in a version of manhood in which toughness and violence are valued while openness to feelings is seen as a weakness. To make any sort of progress in this therapy programme these men had to go *beyond* this stereotype and find a deeper, more holistic definition of manhood. For example, at one point a prisoner broke down in tears. When he hung his head in shame to hide them, another prisoner said: 'Lift your head up. In this group we cry like men.' The therapy programme had taken the belief that 'Real men don't cry' and replaced it with 'Real men own their tears'. They all knew about being violent criminals, cut off in their macho Personalities; real bravery for them was found in going beyond that comfort zone and daring to feel their vulnerability.

This comes back to the loss of the original state of Being; full-feeling engagement with life is what we lose touch with after the Wound. The prisoners shared stories of how their trust in their fathers was lost and how they took on a twisted, narrow version of manhood which arose from their fathers' own Wounds. This is how that template gets passed on from generation to generation, and of course some of the inmates had sons themselves so they were in danger of continuing the cyclic pattern.

Matthew: But they were aware of that?

Jez: Yes, they had enough Choice-less Awareness to cut through their programming, to realise the turn their lives had taken, to see what had gone wrong. It was obvious that some of the inmates had powerful breakthroughs on an Emotional, psychological level: releasing dammed up tears, pain and even some Joy. So therapy can be a marvellous tool that can help relieve some Suffering, but it's not at all concerned with looking beyond Personality for answers. That's not its objective at all, that's not where it's coming from.

Matthew: And you'd say this is true for the other two sub-categories: Self-Help and Personal Development?

Jez: Yes. In *The Story of 'You'* we talked about Personal Development.* I'm using this name to refer the kind of courses which promise to make you a better, more fulfilled, more efficient person. This category of teaching grew out of the counterculture of the 1960s and formed around the concept of cultivating 'creative potential'. This was something that its founders believed existed, mostly untapped, in all people. It's like taking the techniques of therapy and

* *The Story of 'You'* – Chapter 34

using them, not just to resolve normal suffering, but to realise and fulfil that creative potential. Personal development isn't about just being OK; it's about being extraordinary.

As we've discussed, this is all very positive work; seminars and encounter groups can be powerful places to break through psychological barriers and expand your potential. However, just like psychotherapy, the goal of this work is polishing and adapting the Personality, not Seeing beyond it.

Personal Development began in the Sixties; it was underpinned by the optimism and openness of the 'Age of Aquarius', which meant it was all about sharing knowledge for the good of your personal freedom and, ultimately, for the benefit of society. As hippy culture died out, this sort of idealism gave way to consumerism; some people realised that Personal Development courses offered a good business opportunity. They're easy to monetise: The number of courses offered can be endless because there's always 'higher levels' of development to achieve.

I'm not saying there's anything wrong with making money out of therapeutic growth work, but you can see that if the intent behind it shifts to primarily making money, its energetic roots are firmly in the Relative Level – not the Absolute Level, in which one learns about life beyond Personality.

Matthew: What about Self-Help teachings? These have also been commercialised.

Jez: Yes, let's use the 'Law of Attraction' as an example of Self-Help teaching because many Self-Help practices arise from this law. It's based on an understanding that our beliefs create our reality: For example, if you think poor you'll be poor, if you think rich you'll attract money. We'll never know when this understanding first entered human consciousness, but it's been around for quite a while – I have a book about it that was written in the 1920s.

An understanding, like the Law of Attraction, opens like a flower in someone's consciousness: The 'aliveness' of the understanding, and the truth it holds, produce a certain charge. It can have enough power to transform some aspects of people's lives on the Relative Level. So someone who has the understanding of the Law of Attraction might use it to become rich, and their wealth becomes a physical demonstration of the power of that understanding. This can then attract people who want to know what happened: How did they transform their life in this way? They want to know the secret.

If someone has some charisma, and they teach that understanding well, it's quite likely that their teaching will also have power because it's fed by the energy of their understanding. If someone hears or reads about this teaching, its power can be transmitted; the same understanding can open in them.

Matthew: I suppose you could say that Self-Help is like a more commercial and more accessible version of Personal Development teachings.

Jez: Yes, it's like Personal Development, but in a form that's easily digestible for the masses. You don't have to attend intensive courses; your only commitment is to read a book. Self-Help doesn't even require much introspection: Just repeat the affirmations and your whole life could change!

*Matthew: But, it **can** work, it can make your life easier...*

Jez: Yes, to an extent. For example, creating more wealth can make your life easier; you could be less stressed, perhaps a bit more self-confident. All this is definitely better for your mental health than having self-doubt; so it can work on that level, but it doesn't always.

Matthew: Why not? If the understanding behind it is true, then why doesn't it always work?

Jez: The law itself may be true – beliefs and intent have a big input into creating our reality – but that doesn't take into account the beliefs of the Personality that are already there, hidden in the Shadow. So your conscious mind might start affirming all the riches it wants to attract, but the subconscious could easily override those affirmations by saying: 'You don't deserve riches.' It will only get a chance to work by getting free of the underlying negative beliefs, and that involves exposing those beliefs that are hidden in the Shadow of the Personality.

Understandings like the Law of Attraction can point to the nature of man and belief, but that doesn't mean that, in themselves, they help deliver you beyond Personality. That would require you to enquire a little bit beyond your desires and ask: '*Who* wants to change their reality? *Who's* holding the belief of poverty?' Without taking it a step further, this powerful understanding just becomes a tool with which the Personality can strengthen itself.

In many cases Self-Help teaching becomes a servant of Personality. Think about it, the Law of Attraction plays into everything the Personality is about: desire for something – usually money or success – and the idea that, when the universe delivers it, happiness will follow. It's not about being happy or Joyful now, it's about gratification and fulfilment in the future. It's based on the belief and hope that 'When I get more powerful/assertive/thin/ wealthy/healthy, then I'll be happy.'

You don't have to have had any deep spiritual Openings to understand or to teach these principles. You can pick them up from a book, which is why Self-Help publishing is so successful; it sells principles that anyone can adopt and have some measure of success with. It's based on the idea that by rearranging and modifying your Personality you can create a happier life. It could work; it could make you more affluent in your Dream, but this has nothing to do with Waking Up from the Dream of your Personality.

So, in summary, I'm not implying there's anything wrong with this form of teaching, I'm simply pointing out that the energetic source from which Self-Help, Personal Development and Psychotherapy arise is Personality. This means that the Personality's seat of power is not challenged or threatened in any fundamental way. On the contrary, in many cases – through the encouragement of desire, hope, belief and the building of a stronger identity – it's strengthened.

Matthew: Some Self-Help teachings do have more spiritual content; Mindfulness is a current example.

Jez: I would put Mindfulness in the next category of 'Pseudo-Spiritual teaching'.

27

Pseudo-Spiritual TEACHING

How the genuinely Spiritual is neutralised

'Life always bursts the boundaries of formulas.'
– Antoine de Saint-Exupéry

Jez: To explain what I mean by the term 'Pseudo-Spiritual', we need to remind ourselves of the definition of the word 'Spiritual' we used in *The Story of 'You'*.

Matthew: *It was: 'A broad concept with room for many perspectives but, in general, it includes a connection to something bigger than ourselves.'*

Jez: I take 'bigger than ourselves' to mean a connection beyond Personality. So for example, we could definitely define your Opening on the village green as a Spiritual experience because you were momentarily operating from beyond the perspective of your Personality.

In the last discussion you noted that some areas of Self-Help have a more Spiritual content and gave Mindfulness as an example. So the question arises: Is Mindfulness a practice of Self-Help – is it serving the Personality – or is it a practice pointing beyond Personality? Mindfulness is quite a modern word; how does the dictionary define it?

Matthew: *'A mental state achieved by focusing one's awareness on the present moment, while calmly acknowledging and accepting one's feelings, thoughts and bodily sensations, used as a therapeutic technique.'*

Jez: This takes us back to our discussion about meditation and Spiritual practices* in *The Story of' 'You'*. I think it's fair to say that Mindfulness is a form of meditation. Can you look up the definition of 'meditation' that we found?

Matthew: *'Meditation is a practice where an individual operates, trains the mind or induces a mode of consciousness, either to realise some benefit or for the mind to simply acknowledge its content without becoming identified with that content.'*

Jez: There are two parts to that, two very different interpretations of the word. The last part illustrates the fact that meditation has an original root that *is* Spiritual. 'To simply acknowledge the mind's content without becoming identified with that content' – that's basically a description of Choice-less Awareness.

Matthew: *Which, by our definition, is definitely Spiritual because it's*

* *The Story of 'You'* – Chapter 35

238

Awareness that comes from beyond Personality.

Jez: Right. The first part of the definition: '...a practice where an individual operates, trains the mind or induces a mode of consciousness... to realise some benefit...' is definitely not originating from beyond Personality.

Matthew: You mean because there's Doing in it?

Jez: Exactly: The words 'operates', 'trains' and 'inducing' give it away; it's all Doing. Who is doing this 'training'? Who is trying to 'induce a mode of consciousness to realise some benefit'?

Matthew: The Personality?

Jez: Yes. So meditation – in this use of the word – is not coming from beyond Personality, it's coming *from* it. So it is, by our definition, not Spiritual.

Matthew: But it appears to be Spiritual: When we hear of people training their mind to become more aware, it's generally thought of as 'being spiritual'.

Jez: Yes, because it wears the clothes of Spirituality; but it's just a costume, just an appearance. This is what the Group Personality of man does: It takes the Spiritual – meaning 'that which is beyond Personality' – and turns it into the Pseudo-Spiritual* – meaning 'that which appears to be beyond Personality, but actually is arising from it'.

The definition of Mindfulness included the phrase: 'Focusing one's awareness on the present moment.' Another phrase we hear all the time now is: 'Be in the moment.' It's an odd phrase because, strictly speaking, you can only ever be in the moment; where else can you be? But, allowing for the limitations of language when it comes to metaphysics, I'd say that originally this phrase was a way of describing our Natural State. Think of babies before the Wound: They're 'being in the moment'. There's no Personality yet to distract or obscure them from full-feeling engagement with whatever is arising in each moment.

So the phrase 'be in the moment' may have originally pointed

---

* Up until now I've used 'spiritual' and 'Spiritual' to point to the different usages of this word; adding 'Pseudo' makes the distinction clearer.

beyond Personality, but the way it's used in popular culture has no relation to the timelessness of the Absolute Level that's experienced when the Personality is seen beyond. In the Group Personality it's devolved into a cosy maxim in which the Personality tries to be 'in the moment' as a panacea for the busyness and stress of modern life. It's just meaningless jargon, because the one trying to 'be in the moment' – Personality – is the one who is actually *stopping* you 'being in the moment'. How? By obscuring the experience of Being with Emotion, neurosis and incessant thought. The idea of 'being in the moment' is just one more of those thoughts that Personality uses to Distract you from Suffering.

Matthew: So to summarise, you're saying the Group Personality takes what originally pointed beyond Personality and kind of neutralises or disarms it.

Jez: Yes.

Matthew: Because anything that points beyond Personality is a threat to Personality, right?

Jez: Exactly. So it needs to neutralise the threat of that which is beyond itself; it does this by turning it into something safe. Another example of this phenomenon can be seen in the current craze for Yoga; will you look up a definition for me?

Matthew: 'Yoga is a practice of Spiritual development to train the body and mind to self-observe and become aware of one's own nature.'

Jez: You can see that the definition is similar to that definition of meditation in that it has two distinct parts. It contains the Spiritual element – 'to become aware of one's own nature' – and the Pseudo-Spiritual part – 'to train the body and mind to self-observe'.

'Becoming aware of one's own nature' is a good way of summarising what Waking Up is all about; it's another way of saying 'return to Being'. The word 'Yoga' is derived from a Sanskrit root meaning union, to join, to become one. So originally, Yoga was about Non-Duality, about Oneness. However, what Yoga has become about is summed up by the second part of the definition: 'To train the body and mind to self-observe'. That sounds good doesn't it? If we take the word 'observing' as a synonym for awareness, it's talking about becoming self-aware or, in other words, to become aware of Personality.

Matthew: Which, you've said, is a major part of the way out.

Jez: Yes, Waking Up from Personality permanently usually involves knowing what Personality is, how it works, and how it keeps you identified with it. So what it seems like they're talking about is Choice-less Awareness.

Matthew: But it's not?

Jez: No, because Choice-less Awareness is not something you can adopt or train yourself in. It's not an action of Personality, because Choice-less Awareness is the opposite of Personality Awareness. It arises spontaneously from beyond Personality.

The practice of Yoga that you often see in popular culture is not interested in self-awareness. Personality has taken Yoga and turned it into a Pseudo-Spiritual pursuit. It's focussed on one of the natural outcomes of the true root of Yoga – health – and built a business around it. It's taken this ancient teaching and reduced it to a series of physical exercises that are adopted simply to lose weight, stay healthy and, in some cases, fulfil the needs of Personality to look good, wear the right yoga clothes and be in with the 'in' crowd.

I'm not criticising Yoga itself, I'm just pointing out what sometimes happens to it in the modern world. Yoga that's sold and practiced in this way can still have some benefit to the body and mind but it's not Spiritual by the definition we're using; it doesn't point beyond Personality. A lot of teaching out there sounds Spiritual, it sounds like it's coming from beyond Personality, but in fact it isn't.

Pseudo-Spiritual teachings arise originally from genuinely Spiritual sources that have been taken over and neutralised by the Personality. Like Self-Help, Pseudo-Spirituality serves the Personality by helping it feel safer, stronger, more in control and powerful. The difference is, Self-Help is more honest – it doesn't pretend to be Spiritual. Although both these categories of teaching might make you feel temporarily better, they have nothing to do with rediscovering your original state of Being. They're not about Waking Up from the Dream; they're about making you feel more comfortable within it.

AWAKENING TEACHINGS

28

EMPTINESS & FULLNESS

Manifestations of the Absolute appearing in the Relative Level

'Love says, "I am everything."
Wisdom says, "I am nothing."
Between the two, my life flows.'
– Nisargadatta Maharaj

Jez: Having covered Personal Development, we now come to a whole new category of teaching: That which *is* Spiritual.

Matthew: According to our definition, that means this teaching is coming from beyond Personality.

Jez: Correct. Personality is a manifestation in the Relative Level, Awakenings are direct experiences of what lies beyond Personality, which is the Absolute Level. So the energetic source of these teachings is the Absolute Level.

There are two subcategories to Spiritual Teaching: The first is 'Awakening teaching' – which comes from someone who's had an Awakening; the second is 'Shift teaching' – which originates from someone who's had the Shift.

Matthew: Just to recap: An Awakening is an experience beyond Personality. The Shift is when identification with Personality falls away for good.

Jez: That's right. Here we'll be focussing on Awakening teaching. When we talked about Personal Growth teachings I said they can be very powerful because they're charged with the understanding from which they arose. For example, the Law of Attraction has a power to instigate changes in a person's life because it's based on a truth about how energy and intent works in the Relative Level of human psychology.

Awakening teaching is also very powerful, but in a different way from teaching that come from understandings. Because its energetic source is the Absolute Level it has the power to change someone's fundamental relationship to the Absolute. Awakening teaching is not about physical laws and human behaviour; it's about Being.

Matthew: There's something I've often wondered about teachers of Awakening: If they've all had the experience of Awakening, why is it they emphasise different things? Some talk about God, Love and Spiritual practice, while others – like the Non-Dualists, seem to shun all that and talk in a very clinical, almost cerebral, manner about Oneness.

Jez: Basically, there are two different expressions of an Awakening depending on the person it happens to and the environment in which it happens. I'll talk about the environment first. If the Awakening happens in an ashram under the influence of a guru and some kind of spiritual practice, then the lineage of the guru, and the tradition from which they come – usually Indian – is adopted and the aspects of Love and devotion are usually emphasised in the teaching.

Others, whose Awakening happens spontaneously and outside of any Spiritual practice or tradition often adopt a more impersonal, Non-Dual standpoint without all the Indian terminology and devotion.

*Matthew: Is this another example of two apparently opposite things being true at the same time?**

Jez: Yes, very much so. They are interpretations of Awakening from different perspectives; both have truth in them with regards to life beyond Personality. In the devotional perspective, one experiences life beyond Personality primarily through fullness; in the Non-Dual approach it's through emptiness. They are two sides of the same coin; both are aspects of Oneness. Other phrases are sometimes used to point to these aspects of fullness and emptiness, such as 'form and formlessness' or 'everything and nothingness'. The focus, or the interpretation, comes from the person having the Awakening and the environment in which it happens.

Matthew: Why did you pull a face while you say that?

Jez: Because that phrase – 'the person having the Awakening' – isn't quite right. I've used it a few times now and it grates a little. It's pointing to something that appears to be true from the Relative Level, but it's not true from the Absolute Level.

Matthew: Can you explain that?

Jez: From the Absolute Level, to say: 'the person having the Awakening' is incorrect, because no person is having an Awakening. An Awakening is what happens when that person, or Personality, is seen through. Having said that, we're discussing the context in which the Awakening happens, meaning the life in which it appears. From that Relative Level perspective, there appears to be a person who has an Awakening. In one sense you can say that an Awakening

---

* *The Story of 'You'* – page 44

is the meeting point of the Absolute Level and the Relative Level, because the Awakening (Absolute Level) is experienced 'in' the form of a human being (Relative Level).

So you can look at an Awakening from two different angles: From the Absolute Level you can say 'there's no one having an Awakening'. From the Relative Level, in which we have the phenomenon of the appearance of a separate person, it feels natural to talk about 'a person who has an Awakening'.

To try and cover all these intricacies of meaning every time we talk about Awakening experiences would be laborious; the words would start fighting with each other, the sentences would get clogged up and we'd lose our flow. So if I use the phrase 'a person having an Awakening', be aware of these caveats: It's just language rather clumsily pointing to something beyond its scope.

Having clarified that, we now need to dig deeper and look into what I mean when I talk about an Awakening experienced by a human being. How is it experienced? Who is experiencing it?

Matthew: It's not the Personality, because you said an Awakening is what happens when that Personality is seen beyond.

Jez: Right.

Matthew: But something is experiencing it, otherwise how would we know about it?

Jez: Exactly – if there's no experiencing of it, then who is reporting it? Who's able to label it an 'Awakening' and talk about the fullness or the Love? Ironically, this is true of emptiness too. If a guru is talking about emptiness, then some point of view must have perceived that emptiness.

Matthew: So what is it that perceived it? What is it that can report on it?

Jez: Those are actually two different questions, with two different answers.

Matthew: OK, so first of all: What is it that perceives an Awakening? I presume you'd say that it's Consciousness...

Jez: Yes, or more specifically, Choice-less Awareness.

Matthew: Right, but it doesn't report on it?

Jez: No. Choice-less Awareness is a function that arises in Being. It observes without any judgement, interpretation or comment on what is seen. It's passive rather than active; it doesn't do anything with what is observed. So Choice-less Awareness perceives the Awakening, but Choice-less Awareness doesn't translate it into human feeling and it doesn't try to express it in language. This comes from the self, specifically the Character.

So you could say the Awakening has a journey into the life of a human being: First it's perceived by Choice-less Awareness then, as it penetrates deeper into the Relative Level, it becomes a sensory experience in the body and mind of the person. Next, the Character of the person feels it and, if asked to describe it, translates it into concepts. This explains why different teachers can present different views of Awakening: The interpretation comes from the influence of the environment in which the Awakening happens, and the Character of the person experiencing it.

To illustrate what I mean, think about the phenomenon of light passing through a prism. The light represents the Absolute Level of formlessness; the prism represents the Relative Level where there is manifestation and form. What happens to the white light as it hits the prism?

Matthew: It separates into its component colours; it's called 'dispersion'.

Jez: Right. When an Awakening 'happens to a person', there's also a kind of dispersion. The light of the Awakening appears to the Character of the person in its different component colours, such as emptiness and fullness. Each is a manifestation of the Absolute appearing in the Relative Level of a human life and each can be focussed on as a description of what that Absolute Level is.

So the Non-Dual description of Awakening focuses more on the emptiness while the devotional approach focuses on the fullness: Both are simply different emphases appearing in the person in whom the Awakening opens. A more complete perception would include both perspectives: the Indian teacher Nisargadatta Maharaj expressed it like this:

> *Love says, "I am everything."*
> *Wisdom says, "I am nothing."*
> *Between the two, my life flows.*

This means there is balance; all aspects of the Absolute manifesting in the Relative Level of human life are embraced.

Matthew: Are you suggesting that this doesn't always happen?

Jez: Yes. Without this inclusive embrace, one or other of the aspects can be focussed on and can become predominant. It's as if the 'form' of the Awakening, the way in which it appears to the person, is focused on rather than the Awakening itself. It's like looking at the orange light coming through the prism and saying that it's more important than all the other colours. Then balance is lost and problems can arise because the complete picture of Awakening is not represented.

Focussing solely on either fullness or emptiness brings potential limitations to a teaching; we'll discuss those of the fullness, or devotional, way first.

29

DEVOTIONAL TEACHINGS

The way of the heart

'Love is the bridge between you and everything.'
– Rumi

Jez: Devotion is a manifestation of the fullness aspect of Awakening. It's a very human response to the beauty, mystery, and ultimately the Love that's seen and felt in life. Awakening opens our eyes to the fullness of life and in response it calls forth the fullness of the human heart. In other words, perceiving the Love that manifests as the world pulls forth the Love in us.

In the Personality our perception of the world is limited, our field of vision is narrow. A 'separate person' sees separate objects in a world that is 'out there', outside of us. In an Awakening the idea of being separate dissolves: The individual disappears and the narrowness of that individual view is transcended. The vision becomes wide, all encompassing. The differentiation between outside and inside falls away. All that's left is the fullness, the Love in all things.

Matthew: I recognise that feeling from my Opening on the village green, but it only lasted about half hour before it went away.

Jez: Did it have any lasting effects in your life after it passed?

Matthew: If I'm honest, not really; I got pulled back into my usual way of being. I can see now that that perception was packed away in the subconscious.

Jez: This is what happens; it's because the gravitational pull back to Personality is so strong. The identification with it has been challenged, but only for a short while. Like a TV temporarily losing reception; normal service is quickly resumed!

Openings and Awakenings are temporary phenomena – when they pass there's a return to the Relative perspective – but Awakenings last much longer. Imagine that Absolute perception you experienced on the village green going on for many hours, days or even weeks and you'll understand the power that an Awakening has to transform the life in which it appears.

Matthew: So how does an Awakening manifest in day-to-day life?

Jez: In the devotional way, that perception of fullness, of Love, is brought back into the Relative Level and is often projected onto the form of a guru or a deity. These become personifications of divinity, icons of sacredness. It's like a translation of the width of vision of the Awakening into a narrower, more relatable view. The formless is given a form.

I'm not suggesting there's anything wrong with this; devotion is simply a human response in the Relative Level to what's been perceived in the Awakening. There's no Doing in it, no intent to gain anything; it doesn't come from the mind, it arises spontaneously from the heart. Although devotion has no goal, no objective, it has a very practical, beneficial function. I'll tell you what that is, but first let me give you some context.

An Awakening gives a life-changing experience of the Absolute perception. When it ends, the Relative comes back in all its manifestations – including the Suffering and delusions of Personality. This presents a challenge: to keep steadfast to the viewpoint that's been Seen in the Awakening. As you found after your Opening on the village green, it's very easy to get pulled back into identification with Personality. As soon as Choice-less Awareness is replaced by Personality Awareness, the Personality is in charge again and the old life is returned to. It's like waking up from a dream then going back to sleep and continuing with the same dream.

Matthew: You said that the devotional path can be helpful; how does that work?

Jez: Surrender to, and love for, the guru keeps the focus on the Absolute. This is the true function of the guru: They act as embodiments or icons of the Awakened state. The light of their 'enlightenment' illuminates the path and stops the disciple getting lost in the shadows of the Relative Level.

Matthew: This sounds very logical...

Jez: Yes, but as I mentioned in the last talk, there are potential problems with the way of the heart just as there are with the way of emptiness. When I say problems, I mean anything that can act as a block that impedes movement towards the Shift.

Problems can come from two directions: from the guru's side of the relationship or from the devotee's side. The guru's side of the relationship is a big subject that we'll cover when we talk about cults; here we'll discuss the problem that can arise from the devotee's side. Basically, the problem comes from conflicted motivations which arise in the devotee:

On one hand, their hunger for the truth draws them closer to the guru like a moth to a flame. As I said, this person represents and embodies the fulfilment of their own spiritual search, so this pull to surrender to the guru comes from their own Yearning to Wake Up.

But there is another motivation, one that arises from the Personality. Do you remember what I said the primary motivation of Personality is?

Matthew: Self-preservation.

Jez: Yes, the Personality wants to survive at all costs, and here it's being confronted with its own dissolution. The closer the disciple gets to the genuinely Awakened guru, the more the threat builds. I don't just mean physically closer, I mean in terms of surrender to what the guru represents.

Matthew: The death of that identification with Personality?

Jez: Yes, that's the function of the guru: to burn away that identification in the fire of truth. So as much as the Yearning to return home to Being pulls the devotee closer to the flame, whatever's left of the Personality at this stage in their Spiritual journey has a different agenda: survival. It wants to protect itself; it wants to go in the opposite direction of surrender. So there's a pull in two different directions: The Yearning wants to surrender, the Personality wants to escape.

Matthew: So it's a question of which motivational force wins?

Jez: Unless the person has come to the point of Readiness, to the jumping off point, the Personality wins.

Matthew: Why do you say that?

Jez: Because otherwise all these Spiritual groups in their ashrams would produce many Shifted beings, who would have outgrown the role of disciple and the need for the group, and left. The world would be flooded with Awakened people.

Matthew: It's a lovely idea.

Jez: Maybe, but I think it's obvious that this isn't the reality. In the world of man, the phenomenon of Awakening is mostly unknown in mainstream society.

Matthew: You say the Personality usually wins but, if that were the case, wouldn't these groups lose most of their members as they escaped the intensity and threat of the 'fire'? That's not what happens, is it?

Jez: No, the Personality wins. It escapes the 'fire', not by leaving, but by hiding in plain sight.

Matthew: What do you mean?

Jez: From the outside the Personality gives the appearance of being the perfect, surrendered disciple. It chants the mantras, does the practices and listens to the lectures. This is simply the Personality adapting, shape shifting, hanging on in any way it can to survive. If it has to wear orange robes and have an Indian name, so be it. The identity of a devotee is still an identity, and as long as there's identification with it, the Personality is still in charge. And now it has the chance to strengthen its identity – by becoming the most pious, surrendered and unattached devotee.

Being engaged in that role is a perfect way for the Personality to hide. As long as the right image is presented, no one knows. It's easy to hide in a group; everyone is going about their business, they're focussed on their own spiritual development, their own relationship to the guru. Who has the time, energy or insight to see that you're playing a convincing role, wearing a disguise so as not to be Seen?

Matthew: The guru?

Jez: Yes; if they are really Awake then their interest is in you and your Waking Up. Small, intimate groups around such people are the most powerful contexts for transformation because there's nowhere to hide. The insight and Choice-less Awareness of the guru sees everything; the actions of Personality can be pointed out and exposed. But in large ashrams, where the sheer number of devotees makes intimate contact with the guru impossible, hiding in plain sight is easy.

This kind of hiding is common in devotees who haven't had an Awakening experience, but it can still arise in those who have. After Awakening the Personality has all the more to fight for, because it has stared in the face of its own dissolution.

The best way I can describe this phenomenon is with an analogy. Imagine you've lived within the confines of a house all your life: You feel trapped, you yearn to have fresh air, to be out in nature but you've never found a way out of the walls which imprison you. Then one day, behind a curtain, you discover a door and you realise that this door will finally lead you out of the house for good. What happens?

Matthew: You open the door and get the hell out of there?

Jez: Yes, this is what happens if you're so thoroughly sick of that imprisoned life that you're ready to get out. But if you're not ready, you might grab hold of the door handle, and think: 'Hang on a minute; I don't know what's on the other side of this door – it could be dangerous out there. This house has always been my home; I've grown used to the walls and the ceilings. I might be trapped here, but at least I know I'm safe.'

So you have conflicted motivations – one part of you screams: 'Get out of there,' while another says: 'Stay where you are.' Trapped in this dilemma, your focus starts to turn from what's on the other side of the door, to the door itself. The door offers the promise of what's on the other side, but without the danger of actually experiencing it. So you sit by the door; you admire its colour, its shape. You decorate it with garlands, you bring it offerings; you might even peer through the letterbox once in a while, but you stay this side of the door.

Matthew: There's one thing I don't get: Why would someone do that? Why would they waste their time?

Jez: You have to understand, Personality Awareness means that they're not conscious of what they're doing. This is not a conscious plan they're carrying out. If you asked them if they were fully committed to their search for enlightenment most of them would say: 'Of course I am – look how surrendered I am to the guru.'

Even when the role of a devotee is not used as a way to hide there can still be drawbacks to the guru-devotee relationship. The devotional way can begin with the perception of fullness – of Love – in an Opening, which is then projected onto the guru. But this can become a block if one gets stuck at the level of relationship.

Matthew: What do you mean: 'stuck at the level of relationship'?

Jez: As long as there is this exclusive focus on the other, there's a kind of stuckness in Duality. Oneness is continually turned into the experience of twoness. The formlessness of what is seen in an Opening or Awakening is reduced to the specific form of the guru. The guru is turned into a sort of parent figure, which keeps the devotee in a childlike role and prevents them growing into their own ongoing perception of fullness and emptiness.

This explains why you have people who've followed a guru for years, even decades, without having Woken Up. After all that close proximity to the 'doorway', there's no Shift, no deliverance to the other side. The door can become the block.

A commune surrounding an Awakened being can be a very seductive energy field; you can get high on it. But in the end, you're riding on someone else's experiences, on their Awakenings. The author Wei Wu Wei called it: 'Worshipping the teapot instead of drinking the tea.' If you fall into the trap of thinking that the guru is more divine than you, that's a subtle denial of your own divinity.

After the Shift, it's realised that everything is divine; it has no name, no lineage, no religion. This experience of the fullness aspect of Oneness, which is at the heart of the path of devotion, only becomes a limitation when it isn't balanced by the aspect of emptiness. If that balance is present, it is Understood that, ultimately, Oneness is beyond all form, all approaches and names.

30

ABSOLUTIST TEACHINGS

When emptiness is focussed on more than fullness

'A narrow-minded scholar cannot discuss the Tao,
Because he is constrained by his teachings.'
– Chuang Tzu

Matthew: We've discussed the potential traps of identifying with the fullness aspect of Oneness; what about the problems associated with the Emptiness aspect?

Jez: In the trap of what I call the Absolutist approach, emptiness is emphasised as if it's the only true, complete expression of the Absolute. This perspective of emptiness is often expressed in negating phrases such as: 'There's no one there', 'There's no Story' and, 'There's no teaching'. Devotion is looked down upon as being dualistic: How can there be a relationship between the guru and the disciple if there is only Oneness? Manifestations of the Relative Level – such as the appearance of separation, relationships, the Story of Personality, and feelings – are apparently seen as things that are somehow lesser than the Absolute view.

Teaching that comes from this perspective seems to be based on the erroneous idea that, by not recognising or addressing the Story of Personality, it will just go away and you'll be free of it and its Suffering. Teachers who adopt this approach can become like evangelical preachers who are unyielding in their one-sided message, as if the more the Relative is ignored, the more 'Absolutely true', radical and pure they believe their message to be.

I recently watched an interview with one of these Absolutists who wouldn't even say the words 'me' or 'I'; she referred to herself as 'this bodymind system'. I get the intention – to represent the Understanding that you're not the Personality by not referencing it – but avoiding the appearance of the Relative like this starts to sound like mental illness after a while.

Matthew: Because it's not the complete picture?

Jez: That's right. Teaching from this lopsided viewpoint becomes limiting because only one experience of the Seeker is acknowledged: the Yearning for the Absolute and the experience of Oneness. But the Seeker's reality – of being identified as Personality – is usually ignored and, as baffled or irritated members of the some of these teachers' audiences find out, simply ignoring the Personality doesn't make it go away. Ignoring traits of Personality in this way is nothing more than a kind of spiritually sanctioned repression. Emphasising nothingness without fullness can be an approach that supports the repression and avoidance of difficult feelings. It's a very cold, detached position in which safety is found in a castle built of an intellectual interpretation of emptiness. This is the polar opposite of the heart-based, more feeling approach of the devotional path.

People who are attracted to this Absolutist approach can become narrow in their outlook, parroting the same mantras as their teachers: 'There is no one there', 'Who is asking the question?' etcetera. Without the ability to discuss the whole range of human experience in the Relative Level, the teachings can become stiff, dry and heartless.

Matthew: So an Absolutist would not agree with much of what you say in these talks?

Jez: Oh no, definitely not – especially what I've told you about the Residue and the Healing: That would be dismissed before you could even start a discussion. If there's no real recognition of the Relative Level, then there's no time, no karma, no process, no Healing. The idea seems to be that Awakening is some fixed point of arrival, after which everything in the human experience stops.

Matthew: What form, or interpretation of Awakening did you adopt?

Jez: I adopted this emptiness approach because it seemed to best represent my experience of Awakening, which happened outside of any spiritual group or tradition. It gave a lexicon of phrases and concepts in which what I'd experienced could be expressed and understood. I knew someone who has since gone on to become one of the main teachers of this Absolutist version of Non–Duality, so I was somewhat influenced by him. It was the best interpretation I had at the time.

Matthew: But you obviously stopped seeing things that way?

Jez: Not totally, because the description of the emptiness side of the equation was sometimes quite accurate and helpful; but after a while, certain aspects of it bothered me. The description of Awakening seemed too narrow. Although it felt true on the Absolute Level, it started to sound facile to keep coming back with phrases such as 'There's no one there' to every question that referenced the appearance of a separate self. I knew something was missing.

I remember trying to discuss my misgivings about that narrowness with the teacher I knew. I told him: 'When you teach, it's like you're describing an elephant to a blind man. All you keep saying is "It's big," over and over again. The words are ultimately true, the elephant *is* big, but the elephant is so much more than that as well: It's rough skinned, wrinkly, hairy, smelly; it has tusks, a trunk etcetera. To reduce the wonder and majesty of an elephant to the description "It's big" is inadequate and inaccurate.' This is how I felt about the Absolutists – I realised that what they were teaching was a partial truth; it had limitations.

Matthew: One teaching that Absolutists seem to put out is that 'There's nothing to get. All you have to do is accept how you are, to realise that you're already perfect as you are.'

Jez: The root of this statement is true. Remember how I told you that before the Awakening there was a letting go into the Suffering of the breakdown, an acceptance of it? In a poem about Awakening, I wrote:

> *Beyond the drama of Personality,*
> *This moment, and everything it contains,*
> *Good, bad, happy or sad,*
> *Is perfect just as it is.*

Matthew: So that is a truth that's realised in an Awakening?

Jez: Yes, on the Absolute Level, it *is* true. The one who watches *is* absolutely perfect; there's no Suffering in that Choice-less Awareness. And from there it's seen that even the breakdown I suffered is psychological trauma being perfectly expressed.

So the energetic root of this teaching that 'There's nothing to get' is what's recognised in Awakening, and the fact that it's true means that it has the potential to be a powerful tool in the teaching of Non-Duality. If the internal dialogue of your Personality is self-critical, it's possible that this radical message of acceptance can trip it up. Suddenly problems seem to disappear; everything is all right and it's so simple: All you have to do is take away the judgement on yourself that you're not OK and accept everything. The release it can bring can be phenomenal; it works almost like a magic trick. The problem is, ultimately its ability to deliver someone permanently beyond Personality, and Suffering, is limited.

Matthew: I'm reminded of a period earlier this year when I was depressed. One of my Personal Growth courses is big on what they call 'not resisting'. I tried to accept that I was feeling down and didn't have the energy to do things; then I became more depressed because I was angry with myself for not fulfilling the goals I'd set for myself.

Jez: You see that self-critical internal judgement just wants to continue; it's not interested in your Self-Help techniques. Unless someone is really Ready to break through the Dream, the relief this approach gives from Suffering doesn't last long. The momentum of Personality is so strong, it stops this message penetrating deep. As long as the architecture of the Personality is still in place, Suffering follows like a shadow. Acceptance doesn't stop it, because this acceptance has just become a technique. It's just more Doing.

Matthew: What do you mean when you say this acceptance is just a technique?

Jez: There's a difference between an Understanding being revealed to someone in an Awakening and that Understanding being passed on to others as a technique. One is active: It's fed by the event of the Awakening. The other is passive: It's just an idea related in words, a truth reduced to a technique, a practice. This is why techniques don't work – unless the person applying them happens to be Ready; if that's the case, almost anything could crack them open.

The reduction of the Awakening into an Absolutist form of teaching – such as 'Everything is perfect as it is' – can limit the teaching's ability to reach the student. Let me demonstrate what I mean with another example. What would you say to an Absolutist teacher who proclaims: 'There's nothing to learn?'

Matthew: I'd say: 'If there's nothing to learn, then why are you adopting the role of a teacher?'

Jez: It's a fair point. From the teacher's side it seems disingenuous: Either be a teacher and accept and fulfil that role or admit you have nothing to teach and go and do something else. From the student's side, following such a teacher is like wanting to eat a cake, going into a cake shop, then just hanging around sniffing the air and waiting while the owner keeps saying: 'There are no cakes here.' That would be illogical, wouldn't it?

Absolutists teachers who say: 'There's nothing to teach,' base their message on one aspect of their Awakening. I pointed to this aspect in my own poem about Awakening:

> *Now there is nothing to fight for,*
> *Nothing to escape,*
> *Nowhere to go.*

In the Absolute perspective that's experienced in an Awakening, all of this is true. However, to someone who's Suffering with their Personality, it makes no sense at all. From that Relative perspective, there is something to fight for, there is something to escape and a place to get to that is free of the Suffering.

So when it comes to teaching, this Absolute truth is not necessarily useful because it's not addressing the student where they are. I say 'not necessarily useful' because in certain cases it can cause a spontaneous loosening of the grip of Personality, but Openings like this are temporary. You can have experiences beyond Personality, but to stay in that revelation, you have to finish with its domination. That doesn't happen by ignoring the Personality; it comes by Seeing it so completely that it can no longer trick you into identifying with it.

*Matthew: So let me get this straight, you're saying that there **is** something to get?*

Jez: Yes – at least from where you're standing. There's something you don't know yet, otherwise we wouldn't be having this conversation – there'd be no need for it. What you don't know yet, apart from on a conceptual level, is that you're not who you think you are – you're not the Personality. If that Understanding was there, *then* there would be nothing to get. That is a huge difference. So it would be more accurate to say that, until you realise for yourself that there's nothing to get, then there *is* something to get.

A teacher who simply repeat phrases like: 'There's nothing to get, just accept things as they are,' is ultimately not helping their students. They haven't understood – or are at least not representing – the full picture.

Matthew: Because they're not addressing the appearance of the Relative Level?

Jez: Exactly. The role of the teacher is to address the student according to where they are in their Understanding. If the teacher can only throw one teaching at the student without leading them to the bigger picture – exposing the Personality itself – then that's a testament to the narrowness and limitation of their Understanding.

Consider this: The Absolute Level manifests as the Relative Level; so to not acknowledge that manifestation in all its appearances is to not acknowledge the Absolute. While Absolutists purport to be sharing the ultimate, highest teaching, what they're actually teaching is incomplete.

Most people only focus on the Relative Level and are mostly unaware of the Absolute Level. They have to reject its existence in order to maintain the illusion of the sovereignty of the Personality with which they are identified. Conversely Absolutists – who obviously know about the Relative Level – focus mostly on the Absolute that the Awakening has revealed to them. They've become the mirror image of most of the world: the other pole of it. Ironically, focussing so much on the Absolute and effectively rejecting the Relative is a dualistic activity in itself. Of course, Absolutist teachers would deny any of this.

Matthew: Why do they deny it? That's what I don't understand. It's obvious that seekers' questions aren't being met. Don't these teachers see their audiences' confused response?

Jez: Their audiences' confusion, or even shock or anger, is often taken as confirmation that their teaching is radical, powerful and true. Personality Awareness sees only what it wants to see to confirm its position, its beliefs and its perspective.

Matthew: So you're saying there's Personality behind Absolutist teaching?

Jez: Yes. Perceiving the fullness or emptiness aspect of the Absolute is how humans experience an Awakening, but getting stuck in either aspect is something else. As soon as you start emphasising one aspect over another, the balance is lost, something is missing – the teaching is no longer representing the full picture. Then a teaching system is built up with an angle, a spin to it: There's the need to defend it, to say that this is the only true way. Where does all that come from? What is it that chooses to look at and expound one aspect but looks away from another? Is that Choice-less Awareness? No, it's Personality Awareness that sees what it wants to see.

Matthew: So why would Personality come in and reject one aspect of an Awakening, whether it's fullness or emptiness?

Jez: The same reason that Personality Awareness rejects anything: Because it is, in some way, threatening to the position of the Personality. That authority, that viewpoint has to be defended, so whatever challenges it is ignored. The devotee who gets stuck in devotion doesn't want to see beyond the guru or the deity because the role of devotee has become a safe place. The Absolutist who only stresses the aspect of emptiness doesn't want to acknowledge the Relative world of relationship because that viewpoint has become a safe haven for a variety of possible reasons.

Matthew: Like what?

Jez: In the world of psychology they use the word 'disassociation'. It refers to a kind of entrenched detachment from feeling; another term for it would be 'the Contraction'. The Personality can use anything to hide behind, to protect itself, even Openings and Awakenings.

Matthew: I presume these teachers can only be presenting an incomplete picture of Awakening because they haven't been through the Shift?

Jez: Yes, but you don't have to have had the Shift to see beyond this incomplete picture. Recently there have been a few teachers who, having originally adopted this hard-line Absolutist position after an Awakening, now reject that stance as incomplete. This means that Choice-less Awareness has been strong enough to break through the position that was being held onto. Also, many devotees have broken through long-term cultish attachments to gurus.

The potential problems and traps that can arise from being stuck in either a fullness or emptiness perspective can be transcended, but in many cases this isn't what happens. Earlier we discussed what can go wrong in the disciple's side of a relationship to a guru. Next we're going to discuss what can go wrong from the teacher's side when they haven't gone through the Shift.

31

SPIRITUAL PERSONALITIES

How Personalities can rebuild themselves
around an Awakening experience

'Leading yet not dominating,
This is the primal virtue.'
– Lao Tzu

Matthew: What I don't understand is: If someone has had an Awakening, how can they teach a partial truth? How can they get stuck in the traps of Absolutism or the Devotional path?

Jez: This all comes back to one very basic misconception about Awakening: the belief that it wipes out identification with the Personality for good. As I've said, an Awakening reveals the viewpoint beyond the Personality, but only for the duration of the experience. When the Awakening passes, the Relative perspective is returned to, and that includes the re-arising of Personality.

What is experienced in Awakening is a challenge to that Personality because, on a fundamental level, it doesn't fit with it. The Awakening is a direct experience of Oneness, connectedness and Love. The Personality is built on the disconnection from Love.

Matthew: You mean what happened in the Wound?

Jez: Yes, and the results of that disconnection from Love, the Suffering of the Personality, can actually be shown up by that temporary reconnection to Love. In order for what's experienced in the Awakening to be lived and not lost, the operating system of the bodymind has to change – otherwise it can't hold it, it can't contain and sustain what's been experienced.

There are two possible responses: In the first, the person is Ready to receive and use the Awakening; it's like a seed falling on fertile ground. The seed might take some time before it germinates but it's not rejected; it has the right soil in which it can come to fruition.

Matthew: So you're talking about Choice-less Awareness increasing?

Jez: Yes. If there's Readiness, the effect the Awakening has on the operating system of the bodymind is allowed to happen. The Personality is exposed; Choice-less Awareness watches what is shown up and doesn't try to repress it. In this way the Awakening is synthesised into the operating system. Eventually Identification with Personality drops away.

Matthew: I presume this is this what happened in your case – you had that Readiness?

Jez: Yes. When the Awakening happened, this system had been primed by quite a few Openings and also undermined by the breakdown. Imagine the Personality as a castle, a fortress built to survive attack. The breakdown I had was like an earthquake erupting underneath it, shaking its foundations and causing them to crumble. This attack on the stability of the 'fortress of Personality' happens in the Relative Level, via the breaking down of psychology.

An Awakening is an attack on the stability of that fortress too, but it comes from the Absolute Level. The Personality loses its power, not because it has broken down, but because it is seen through and beyond. It temporarily becomes irrelevant. This is the most serious threat to its authority that it's encountered.

In my case, the combination of the two affronts to the Personality – from the breakdown in the Relative Level and the Awakening in the Absolute Level – meant that identification with it was severely undermined. Try as it did to withstand the shocks, they were so powerful that the foundations were irreparably damaged. After the breakdown it was as if I had very little solid 'castle' to return to.

Matthew: So the Personality wasn't totally wiped out?

Jez: No, it struggled on in a weakened state, trying to come back in and continue as if nothing had happened, but the identification with it was too thin for it to recover. However, it took a few years before identification with it finally fell away in the Shift.

Matthew: So Readiness is the first possible response to an Awakening; tell me about the second.

Jez: Just like Openings, Awakenings are threats to the sovereignty of Personality, but Awakenings are much more powerful, so any life in which they appear is deeply affected. Unlike Openings, Awakenings can't be confined to the subconscious; their force is too strong. The Personality can't defend itself from the threat by pretending it never happened, so it finds another way of protecting itself: It incorporates the Awakening into its system.

Matthew: What does that mean?

Jez: In order to survive, the Personality has to keep your identification with it intact; otherwise it starts to lose control. It sees that it can't repress the Awakening so instead, it cleverly rebuilds itself around the experience.

In the Shift, the Absolute Level is synthesised into the Relative Level; here, the Relative (Personality) just adapts itself around that experience of the Absolute and uses it to make itself stronger. You could say that the Personality acts like a parasite, feeding off the Awakening.

So ironically, after an experience beyond Personality, the Personality returns and simply takes on a new form: It becomes a 'Spiritual Personality'. A new Story is built around the Awakening, which kind of anaesthetises the threat of it. It turns it into a 'thing', an event that's been experienced.

Matthew: Which it isn't.

Jez: No, it's a break in the continuity of Personality. But the Personality brings this experience of Oneness into Duality and claims it in order for it to feel safe and in control.

Matthew: And then, I presume, on the back of that new Spiritual identity they become Spiritual teachers?

Jez: Yes, but because these teachers haven't progressed to the Shift, they're limited in their scope in two ways. First, you can only teach as far as you yourself have gone, so they can't guide anyone towards the Shift because they've not experienced it themselves.

Second, because they've not gone through the Shift, they're teaching through the filter of whatever's left of their Personality, and this has an effect on the purity of what is being taught. What I mean by purity in this context is teaching that's untouched by Personality.

Matthew: So you're saying that Awakening Teachings might not be totally pure, in this sense?

Jez: Yes. But remember, this doesn't mean that parts of them can't be true and powerful. Their energetic source is the Awakening and that can still be drawn upon in the teaching. However, as long as there's a Personality that's still being identified with, then its functions and attributes will inevitably start creeping into the teaching. There are all sorts of consequences to this: Some are negative, while others are relatively benign.

At one end of the scale it can simply be the need to be 'right'. Hence you get dogmatic Absolutists or devotional types who hold tightly to their narrow interpretations. There's nothing particularly negative in this: Teachers of any subject can become a little dogmatic and arrogant in displaying their knowledge. This doesn't mean Spiritual teachers who have this trait can't teach well in some areas.

At the other end of the scale you get Personalities who have a stronger, almost pathological need to prove themselves, to be superior. There's a quote from T.S. Eliot on this:

> *Most of the trouble in the world*
> *is caused by people wanting to be important.*

What better way to strengthen the new Spiritual Personality than by having people start to adore and look up to it, to recognise this Awakening it has 'achieved'? The Awakening has been turned into a business and the teacher's personal take on the 'event' is the product that's being sold. In the minds of these spiritual Personalities, they are the highest authority on this spiritual journey.

Matthew: But surely any guru role, by its nature, is a position of authority?

Jez: Yes that's true, but after the Shift the relationship to that authority is totally different. There's nothing to prove by that authority; there is an acceptance of that role but there's no Doing in it. It's simply the sharing of what is known without the influence of Personality and its needs.

In a Personality with issues of narcissism and grandiosity, the authority that comes with the role of guru can be used in the service of that underlying psychological trait.

Matthew: You mean through the attention and adoration they receive from the followers?

Jez: Yes, and with a narcissist, all the traits we talked about with Personality – like purpose, beliefs and a sense of identity – are picked up again and even amplified.

Matthew: Can you give me some examples?

Jez: The role of being a guru can give a new sense of purpose with new beliefs attached – "I am the chosen one", "I am special" – which in turn can induce them to spread their teaching and 'save the planet'. They may have new desires (to be the most famous guru, to have the most followers, to pull in more money etcetera) and new distractions (the opportunity to control and dominate followers, and to spend all the money that's rolling in.)

Of course, the image that's projected is just of a teacher with authority and integrity. The teaching is often performed in the name of service. The trouble is, in these cases it's mostly in the service of the teacher's Personality. It's a perfect symbiotic system: The followers want an icon of enlightenment and the teacher wants followers to affirm his or her 'enlightenment'.

Matthew: You're talking about when a cult forms around a Spiritual Personality?

Jez: Yes, this is the subject for our next discussion.

32

CULTS

When Spiritual Personalities create a tribe

'*The measure of a man is what he does with power.*'
– *Plato*

Jez: Before we talk about cults it will be useful to look at the subject of spiritual teaching and indeed, teaching in general. Teaching requires two things of the teacher: One, to be well versed in a subject, and two, to be able to impart that knowledge to students with skill and passion. Did you have any good teachers at school?

Matthew: There was one I particularly liked – he seemed to enjoy teaching us as much as we enjoyed learning from him.

Jez: That's an archetype of a good schoolteacher, isn't it? They want nothing but for the child to learn their lessons well, to nurture their understanding of the subject they're teaching. It's a beautiful thing, an example of interconnectedness, of Love being shared.

Matthew: I presume it's the same principle with Spiritual teachers?

Jez: Ideally, yes. The teacher has Woken Up, and in the fullness and Joy of that revelation he or she is moved to share it. But with Spiritual teachers there's a big difference: What's being taught is existential. What's being communicated is not a series of facts; it's a way of Being. Not even a way, it is Being. Basically, the Spiritual teacher's role is to show up your Personality and, in so doing, point to that which exists beyond it. That's no small thing; a lot is at stake.

When you're engaged in learning about a practical subject, let's say Physics, nothing much is at stake. What you learn isn't going to affect you in your daily life; if you don't understand the lessons and you drop out of the class it won't *really* matter. There's no great cost to you personally because learning about physics has no bearing on the experience of living your life. What I mean is: You'll continue living identified as Personality – and experience the outcome of that – whether you learn about physics not.

When you engage in this Enquiry the stakes are high. If you have the Yearning for liberation in your bones, you know that nothing else can satisfy you. You've come to realise that, if you don't find what you are looking for, you'll remain in the Suffering that you're desperate to leave behind.

A Spiritual teacher is, ideally, the bridge between you and the freedom that you long for. If you have the Yearning and you meet a person who is Awake, something wonderful can happen. What can be more sacred than someone who has travelled this path before helping a brother or sister to find their own way? This can be a very beautiful thing; it's a different kind of relationship from that which is usually found in the world. First, because it requires the student's Readiness, and second, because it requires absolute trust to follow the teaching despite the resistance of their Personality. This Enquiry is not always easy; as well as releasing enormous Joy it can release great fear and pain from the Personality's Story. Not normal pain – like you feel after losing money on an investment or the break-up of a relationship – but existential pain which comes from your core. So allowing someone to guide you on this journey, through the pain, fear and resistance that can surface, involves an incredible amount of trust and surrender.

In placing this trust in the teacher, the student becomes vulnerable. Why? Because that trust can be abused; the sanctity of the relationship can be violated. This is what we often see happening in cults. I think we need a definition of that word.

Matthew: Here's one: 'A social group defined by its religious, spiritual or philosophical beliefs or its common interest in a particular personality. A system of religious veneration and devotion directed towards a particular figure or object.'

Jez: It's good that this definition uses the phrase 'interest in a particular Personality' because this highlights where things go wrong: The figurehead at the centre of the cult is often still identified as a Personality. If the teacher had Shifted *beyond* Personality then such a community could be a positive environment in which the knowledge of Being is shared by a teacher to a group of students. However, the word 'cult' has negative associations because we hear so many accounts where this isn't the case, where influences and motivations from the teacher's Personality come in to play.

Matthew: You might think that people would only be attracted to teachers who had Shifted...

Jez: It's generally not difficult for Spiritual Personalities to find followers. As long as they have extreme confidence – which is often a characteristic of the new Spiritual identity – and an ability to communicate well, it's easy for a Seeker to be impressed by them. All it takes is for the teacher to have a bit more knowledge of Spiritual matters than those who are looking for guidance. If I'm a layperson who's interested in biology and I speak to someone who's passed a basic exam in it, they'll know more than me about the subject. They may only understand a *little* more than me but, for all *I* know, they might be a professor of biology.

Matthew: In the land of the blind, the one-eyed man is king...

Jez: Exactly. If a Spiritual teacher talks about their Awakening with great certainty to a student who's not had such an experience, the student can be impressed by their superior knowledge. In their ignorance of the subject of life beyond Personality they might assume that the teacher has Woken Up. They may take on the belief that the teacher is fully free of identification with their Personality and their teachings are absolutely free of its influence. It's as if they're so in awe of the teacher, they set aside their normal critical faculties.

Matthew: I know some people in religious groups that are considered to be cults and they're highly intelligent and normally quite sceptical.

Jez: Yes, cults attract all sorts of people. Some are highly motivated, intelligent Seekers who've had success in the world but want to find out why they're not fulfilled on a deeper level. Usually they've had some spiritual experiences that have shown them there's something more to life but they don't know what it is or how to find it. Such Seekers want guidance and, as I said, their openness makes them vulnerable.

Matthew: But still, I do wonder how this can happen to smart people. When troubling signs start to show up, why do you think intelligent people like my friends don't see through what's going on and walk away?

Jez: It's partly because the indoctrination usually starts in a very benign way. They hear about some teacher and are seduced by the sales pitch: the Awakening story, the promise of liberation, the atmosphere around the group and the testimonies of the followers. In the lectures and meetings their own Spiritual experience seems to be validated and this helps draw them in.

Euphoria about these feelings of acceptance can produce

further Openings and experiences which seem to confirm that what they're engaged in is the 'real thing'. These experiences are then linked with being connected to that guru and their community, as if the guru has produced them in the student. In time all these feelings add up and they're corroborated by all the other followers who seem to be experiencing similar breakthroughs.

Matthew: So it's self-generating: People who come validate it, which then causes more people to come.

Jez: Yes, and at the same time the teacher's Spiritual Personality is being validated too, so it's a perfect circle: a reciprocal arrangement in which a story of liberation is believed and kept alive from both sides.

Matthew: But you're saying the energetic source is not liberation?

Jez: Remember, here we're discussing cultic situations in which the person at the centre of it *hasn't* Woken Up. They haven't lost their identification with Personality – but they've probably had Awakening experiences. I wouldn't call an Awakening experience 'liberation' because without the Shift there isn't permanent deliverance from the Personality; but presumably the teacher believes they *are* liberated from Personality. The followers take on this belief and the whole set up consolidates into a Group Personality in which that shared belief becomes stronger because it's magnified and intensified by the force of numbers.

In the early stages of its life the Group Personality can look the same as it would had the teacher been fully free of his or her Personality, so why wouldn't someone who's searching for answers be pulled in? It's a powerful vortex of energy that's easy to get sucked into if you have little experience of life beyond Personality.

Things start to get problematic when the guru at the centre of all this has a narcissistic Personality with a need to dominate. In the protected arena of the spiritual community, free from the scrutiny of more mainstream culture, the Shadow side of the teacher's Personality can start to show itself. Narcissistic patterns of behaviour can be hidden from the followers for a while, but in the end, life has a way of exposing them. As they start to appear publicly, a mismatch arises between the image of enlightenment that's being sold and the reality of the Personality that's selling it. The teacher's carefully cultivated image of purity may be betrayed by an increasingly obvious desire for fame and wealth, by revelations of clandestine sexual activity or rumours of alcohol or drug addiction.

There have been many reports of respected, famous teachers being accused of bullying and physical abuse of students. There are also many reported cases of sex abuse; often the guru advocates celibacy as a practice and then is found to be using his position of power to be having sex with disciples. All this is clear evidence of the lie at the heart of the cult.

Matthew: Which is?

Jez: The lie that the teacher at the centre of the cult has Shifted beyond Personality.

Matthew: I've seen a few websites and books dedicated to exposing that lie about certain teachers.

Jez: Yes, but it can take a few years to get to that stage. Narcissistic type gurus usually surround themselves with yes-sayers to reinforce their absolute authority. Any questioning by followers of the teacher's conduct is put down as resistance, or 'an inability to surrender'. But people can only look the other way for so long; in the end some brave disciple goes beyond the brainwashing and dares to question what's going on. Once one person challenges the teacher's integrity, the questioning can spread and doubts that had previously been repressed emerge from the subconscious of the Group Personality.

At this potential crisis point the guru has two possible directions to take. If the Yearning to Wake Up is still there, then they'll use this grand drama they've created as a mirror to learn a valuable lesson. Choice-less Awareness will see that, despite their Awakening experiences, Personality is still playing itself out. Before the emergence of the cult, that playing out happened in a life that was unknown publicly; now it's happening on a public stage and it is being exposed.

Matthew: Do you think any of these teachers and gurus actually learn from their mistakes?

Jez: I don't know of any actual cases, but then people who really see through their Spiritual Personality would probably give up the guru role and disappear from public life.

Matthew: I've heard of some cases where such teachers display contrition but, I must admit, I don't trust them.

Jez: The Personality is very tricky; it can shape-shift and adapt around most situations that threaten to undermine its authority, even when it's been caught red-handed with some misdemeanour! A new story is created in which the teacher was naive about the role of being a guru, mistakes were made but they have nothing to do with the purity of the teaching. The Personality is so slippery it will keep throwing out smokescreens, half-truths and evasions in order to retain its position. As you say, it might even wear the mask of contrition for a while, but unless the situation has been used to see through the whole game of Personality, these are just more strategies which enable the Personality to continue.

Remember, the main function of Personality is self-preservation; it will do anything to survive. A Spiritual Personality that's been looked up to, even worshipped by many people becomes even stronger than it was before it had this Spiritual role to play out and pump itself up with. It has a belief in its own specialness and it's not going to relinquish that just because some people have dared question it.

Matthew: Do you think these teachers who put on a display of contrition and then carry on as before know what they're doing?

Jez: You mean, do they have Choice-less Awareness? If they had enough Choice-less Awareness to really observe and become conscious of what they're doing then why would they go on doing it? There's no reason to continue upholding that Spiritual Personality, there's no gain, no pay off. All it does is create the continuance of Suffering, which for the shamed teacher now comes laced with the loss of respect of some their followers. If these gurus really knew what they were doing, the whole game would collapse. Instead, the stakes just get higher: There's more to defend, more denial and ridiculous justifications.

When they've been caught out having sex with devotees they

claim that intercourse with the master is a great blessing which will further their victim's Spiritual development. Talk about Personality Awareness! You wonder if they're trying to fool the devotees or themselves with this line! I'd have more respect for them if they just admitted that they had carnal desires like everyone else.

The same sort of trickiness occurs in cases of mental abuse where devotees – who'll do anything to gain their teacher's favour and acceptance – are humiliated and ridiculed. In the world outside the cult, in cases of psychological bullying and torture like this – such as domestic abuse involving children, partners and servants – the perpetrator is locked away and given psychological help. When it happens in an ashram different rules apply: The wily Personality gives a spin to this scenario that would never be acceptable in the outside world. In ashrams you may find that the abuser is not considered responsible for the abuse!

Matthew: You mean they blame the victim?

Jez: Yes. The justification is that the student is being abused because they're lagging behind in their Spiritual development! The idea is that the abuse is for their own good; the humiliation is actually a method to break down the defences of the devotee's Personality. They rationalise it as the ends justifying the means. So the teacher's Personality is justifying its behaviour by saying it's abusing the devotee *with compassion*. Welcome to the madness and trickiness of Personality!

*Matthew: Just to put the other side, do you think there **could** be any truth to that claim? After all, you've said that one side of Waking Up is the exposure of Personality. Isn't that what Zen masters are attempting to do when they hit a student with a Zen stick?*

Jez: Yes, the Personality has to be exposed, and there's a kind of contract between teacher and devotee to do this. Just being around someone who's Awake is a mirror to your Personality; whenever the truth is talked about, the Personality is exposed.

Matthew: So you could argue that in an ashram situation, there are methods that are engineered to expose the masks and games of Personality so that... presumably, surrender can happen and it can be dropped.

Jez: First of all, you can't force surrender to happen. Surrender is a natural, spontaneous letting go; it's not something that happens under pressure in an atmosphere of psychological or physical violence. All the breakthroughs I had which led to the Shift came about through surrender, but that surrender didn't arise through trying or in an environment of outside pressure. All of that is Doing; it's the opposite of surrender.

You don't have to organise or control life to show up your Personality; you might have noticed life does a very good job of showing it up at any opportunity! If you're willing to look, you can't *not* be confronted with your Personality. But, for the sake of argument, let's say there are some situations in which resistance in people could be worn down by some sort of a regime of control administered by the teacher. Even then, it would be all about where the teacher was coming from. If the energetic source was Love and compassion then that's one thing, but if there's any intent to humiliate, to put people down, that can only come from the Shadow side of Personality.

Matthew: Some teachers who've been caught out physically or mentally abusing their disciples don't even bother to fake contrition. They justify their actions by their so-called Enlightenment, as if it's a licence to act out any kind of morally questionable behaviour.

Jez: These teachers claim that their enlightenment means they operate on a different level to other people, a level where normal rules of morality don't apply. They argue that there's no link between Waking Up and behaviour. I'd suggest that anyone saying this is still identified as a Personality because, if they were Awake, they'd know that behaviour is definitely affected by Waking Up.

Matthew: It sounds obvious to me, but can you tell me exactly why that's so?

Jez: If you've Woken Up you're no longer governed by the desires, Distractions, hopes, beliefs and thought patterns of Personality; without all this activity your behaviour changes in many ways. One of the main changes comes from the fact that you're not acting out the Shadow side of your Personality any more; this means there are no subconscious motivations which could wilfully hurt or abuse others. All violence that doesn't come from the survival instinct comes from Personality. So whatever grand Spiritual, enlightened story is being told, any abuse or brainwashing is a form of violence that betrays the actions of Personality.

Matthew: If you're not governed by Personality any more, what are you governed by?

Jez: You're governed by Love. I know that sounds like a big fancy statement but, apart from being true, it's actually totally logical. If all is made of Love, and the only thing that keeps you from the ongoing perception of that Love is identification with Personality, then Waking Up delivers you to that perception. You're not motivated by gaining anything, only by the living of that Love. There's a quote from Carl Jung on this:

> *Where love rules, there is no will to power,*
> *and where power predominates, love is lacking.*
> *The one is the shadow of the other.*

Most morality comes from the mind. It's necessary because people exist identified as Personalities whose Shadows contain all sorts of repressed Emotions and subconscious motivations which can be violent in nature. If these Emotions, desires and impulses were all acted upon there'd be chaos, so we have rules in society to keep that in check. Whether driven by religion, philosophy or ethics, Group Personalities agree on a code of behaviour. We try to be 'good', we try to do the right thing, we try to be loving in order to have more harmonious, safe societies.

Where there is Love, a moral code of behaviour isn't needed to keep behaviour in check. If you think about human life in its original form – the Natural State – there's no violence there; even serial killers once existed in that state in which wilfully hurting another being was impossible.

Of course, as adults we're not like babies. We have highly developed minds, we have Emotional histories and we have the ability, both mentally and physically, to act out our Shadows and be violent to other beings. However, if you're unhooked from the

Personality, then that history no longer controls your behaviour.

Personalities operate from the mind; in Waking Up there's a relocation from the mind to the heart centre. Although you live in the Relative Level as an apparently separate being, you're orientated to Oneness and Love. This means there's a respect for other beings which arises from the recognition of that Oneness in all of us. Love cannot wilfully hurt, dominate or shame another, so if you see any signs of this in a teacher you know you're dealing with a teaching that's informed by Personality and not Love.

So you can see the limitation of Awakening Teachings which come from Spiritual Personalities. The teacher is supposed to be leading you out of the Dream of Personality, but they themselves are still in it. The cult created around them is part of that Dream and followers become bit players within it.

SHIFT TEACHING

33

SHARING

The motivation behind Shift Teaching

'Thousands of candles can be lit from a single candle,
And the life of that candle will not be shortened.
Happiness never decreases by being shared.'
– Buddha

Jez: When someone Wakes Up from the Dream of Personality, that radical Shift is experienced as the attributes of Being: Stillness, Joy, Choice-less Awareness and full-feeling engagement with life. But the Shift can take other more active forms too, because often there's a natural move towards expressing and sharing what's been revealed in Awakening. There's no Doing in this sharing, no ulterior motives of Distraction or self-aggrandisement – it's simply the overflowing of energy, of Love. Exactly what form this expression takes depends on the person's Character and their talents: A painter will express it in paintings, a musician in music and so on.

Some people who Wake Up to this perspective have abilities that lead them to a more direct way of expressing it. For example, because I'm a writer and storyteller, it's natural for me share this in this particular form – a kind of tapestry of themed discussions. Some people are charismatic and gifted at public speaking and so sharing this in public lectures is a natural step. It's this latter category – people who have both Woken Up and have a creative talent with language – who can become Shift teachers.

Matthew: So, just to be clear, not everyone who has the Shift teaches?

Jez: No. Teaching requires two things: First, your Character has to be creatively inclined to share in that way and second, in order to do that there has to be a certain level of Adaptation to the Shift on a cerebral level. You see, losing identification with Personality doesn't necessarily mean you've made what's happened to you, and the ramifications of it, conscious.

Matthew: You're going to have to explain that.

Jez: In *The Story of 'You'* I used our character Lucy wanting to go to Timbuktu as a metaphor for her Yearning to Wake Up.* Now imagine this scenario: Lucy is going about her life in her familiar surroundings when suddenly she finds herself actually *in* Timbuktu. She's never been there before, so at first she doesn't understand anything about this new location: its geography, climate, people or its laws. This new location isn't anything like the country she's come from; much of what she took for granted in her previous life doesn't apply any more.

* *The Story of 'You'* – Page 296

So although Lucy is physically located in Timbuktu, she doesn't actually know anything about it. There has to be a period of living and finding out about Timbuktu to discover what its nature is. To some extent this will happen automatically: If she wants to know where to get water, she'll walk around until she finds it. In this way, she starts to become conscious of her new surroundings.

Matthew: Isn't what you're talking about the Adaptation?

Jez: Yes, a particular part of Adaptation: Physically she's just getting used to where things are and how they work; this is necessary just to function in a new place so it happens for everyone. But there's also a mental, intellectual acclimatisation that may or may not occur as part of Adaptation. For example, Lucy might want to find out about Timbuktu's history, or its geography, how it relates to other places. It's as if she's making conscious where she is: the location, the parameters, the context. She doesn't *need* to do this to live in Timbuktu – she's already living there, breathing the air, walking the land – but if she wants to be able to discuss in detail what Timbuktu is like with anyone who doesn't live there, then it becomes necessary.

Matthew: So not everyone who Wakes Up takes on this more cerebral perception of where they are, of what's happened?

Jez: Correct. They've Woken from the Dream of Personality – but they've not translated it, or at least all of it, into a mental framework. In the Relative Level, where there's the appearance of a person with a mind, they've not turned that experience into mental constructs such as thoughts and concepts.

Let me give you a more practical example of this to help you understand what I mean: Imagine a student in an academy of music playing some classical piece on his guitar. Because he's studied musical theory, he understands exactly what he's doing; he knows what notes he's playing, the scales they come from and the chords they collectively add up to.

Outside the academy sits another guitarist, a busker, playing for the passers-by. He has no knowledge of musical theory whatsoever but possesses an innate musical talent. He plays equally well as the student in the academy, perhaps even with more feeling, but he has no technical understanding of what he's playing.

If you have the inclination to teach anyone else about the perspective beyond Personality, you have to be like the student of music – you have to make that perspective conscious. Then you can you 'draw your own map' of that perspective, which basically means you express it in your Character's unique way. This is what all teachers through the years have done. If they hadn't made their Awakening conscious, they wouldn't have been able to share it – and with no record of their teachings, we wouldn't have heard of them.

Matthew: So to be a Shift teacher, it's not enough that you live in Timbuktu; you have to become a kind of an expert on it?

Jez: Yes. In our metaphor, 'Timbuktu' represents Being, so anyone who 'Wakes Up in Timbuktu' realises that they've been there before, not as an adult but as a baby in the Natural State. Everyone starts out in Timbuktu but, when it's re-discovered as an adult, you possess a developed mind that's able to think about it. You already have a physical and sensual engagement with it; applying the mind to life beyond Personality can give access to a conceptual Understanding of it.

I should point out that this Understanding is always limited; we understand only as much as our human viewpoint allows. Our perspective on the Absolute will always fall short because our perceptions and descriptions arise in the Relative Level. How can the Relative fully perceive the Absolute? It's impossible. The Great Mystery itself can never be understood, but we can understand a human perspective on it. For example, we can comprehend how we lose our connection to it in the Wound; we can describe its attributes when it is re-found. This limited, human Understanding of the Absolute can be of use to fellow human beings because they share that same Relative viewpoint.

So if there's the inclination to gain this Understanding, Choiceless Awareness falls on this perspective beyond Personality; it observes and becomes conscious of how it affects the life that is lived. As you say, this is all part of the Adaptation; it happens through simply living – and interacting – in and from Timbuktu.

Matthew: You mean like talking to me, for example?

Jez: Yes. All those years of self-examination spent writing journals gave me quite an extensive understanding of the landscape of Timbuktu, but your interest and our discussions became a catalyst for me to make even more of it conscious. To explain Timbuktu and answer your probing questions about it, I've had to understand and make conscious things that otherwise I might not have even thought about.

Matthew: Why you wouldn't have looked at them anyway?

Jez: We all come to this from our own angle; there may be subjects in this Enquiry that are really important to your Character and your path but of no particular relevance or interest to me. This happened when you asked me where the Yearning comes from: I was aware I'd always had this Yearning – it was what drove me to find this – but the question of where it came from had never occurred to me. I'd never considered it because it wasn't relevant to me; but to answer your question I had to consider it.

To go back to the metaphor, it's like you asking me something about Timbuktu – if I haven't asked that question myself then I have to look around to fetch the answer. Then I have to translate it into concepts and words which relate to where *you are* in order for my descriptions to make any sense to you. Thanks to your questions and our discussions I've looked around Timbuktu more thoroughly and gained a wider conceptual understanding of it. Through the process of teaching, the teacher also learns.

This is obviously very different to how teaching works in non-Spiritual subjects. People who teach usually have one specialist subject; they study and learn its history and then become holders, and to some degree interpreters, of that knowledge. But at its root it's basically about taking on other people's knowledge from the past; it's learned knowledge.

This teaching is alive; the answers aren't learnt, they aren't just known in the mind, they're known existentially. The teacher's role is to activate that existential knowledge in the student. To do this the teacher has to translate the experience of Waking Up into a series of concepts, each one adding to a collective representation of life beyond Personality.

That's my side of the equation; from your side – the student's side – there's the question of what happens to all these concepts and thought forms that I put to you. There are three possible responses from someone hearing a teaching of life beyond Personality; each is dictated by the Readiness of the person.

The first response is actually a *lack* of response: The person has no Readiness at all. There's no interest in this subject so communication of it is impossible because the teaching falls on deaf ears.

The second response looks more promising: The person seems interested, they engage with the concepts but only on an intellectual level. The student relates to it in the same way as they would a non-Spiritual subject: The concepts are learnt and understood intellectually.

When it comes to actually discovering life beyond Personality, intellectual learning can't take you very far. Why? Because you can entertain all sorts of concepts about how life is and how it works, but they're just thoughts sitting around in your mind. Unless there's Readiness to open to what the concepts are pointing to, they're not in any way challenging to the Personality.

Matthew: What about the third response?

Jez: I gave you an example of the third response in our discussion about Openings. Remember I told you how, when I was younger, I'd be browsing in a Spiritual bookshop and a quote from Buddha or Lao Tzu would really hit me? Whatever the quote was pointing to would open up in me and my mind would suddenly become still. This happened because there was a Readiness for the quote to be heard, to be received. I'm not saying I fully understood it, but the truth it pointed to resonated in me and worked on me. It penetrated beyond my Personality.

The third response comes, at least in part, from the energetic source of Readiness. I say 'in part' because there are degrees of Readiness depending on how broken down the Personality is and in what areas there's still resistance. Like an old tyre, some areas of the Personality might be wearing really thin while others can still be robust because they retain much of their original structure. So a person's Readiness informs how they relate to the concepts.

Concepts are like doorways that can lead the student to experiences of this revelation; they are entry points or portals. When confronted with these doorways a person having the first response of indifference will simply walk away. The person having the second response of staying safe on an intellectual level will hang around the doorway; they'll study it and talk about it but will never actually go through it.

If a person approaches the doorway with the Readiness of the third response, it's possible that it could open and let the person in. Then the concept has done its job of communicating something of what it's pointing to. There's a lovely poem from Chuang Tzu that illustrates what happens next:

> *The purpose of a rabbit snare is to catch rabbits.*
> *When the rabbits are caught,*
> *The snare is forgotten.*
> *The purpose of words is to convey ideas.*
> *When the ideas are grasped,*
> *The words are forgotten.*

So the concepts that Spiritual Teachings use are linguistic devices operating on the Relative Level to point to the Absolute Level. Once the concept has done its job, there's no need for it any more. In my everyday life I don't continually translate my experience into these concepts I'm sharing with you. I'm not going round all day thinking: 'All is made of Love' or 'There is no Personality'. That would be like a fish in the sea constantly thinking: 'I am in water; there's water all around me.' The fish doesn't do that – the fish just swims.

So when I talk to you about this perspective and use a lot of concepts, I'm simply presenting doorways to you. Some of them have opened; they tripped up your Personality just like those quotes used to do to me.

Matthew: I know what you mean: Sometimes they catapult me beyond my normal busy mind and I feel more Stillness.

Jez: You return to an experience of Being. But not all of the concepts that I talk about 'land' like that. Some of them stay on an intellectual level; others hit up against resistance in you and bring up Emotion: fear, frustration or anger. I don't know which doors will be the ones that open for you; every Personality has its own unique construction and its own places where its defences are thin.

The range of subjects covered in these talks mean that it's likely that some concepts could get through at least some of the Personality's defences. But as I say, it's all dependent on a person's Readiness. I've written a short story to illustrate this:

A very religious man called Jason becomes a disciple of a guru who is considered to be full of wisdom. Jason becomes convinced that, if he can just understand this guru's teachings, he'll finally find the peace and happiness he's looking for. However, before Jason has a chance to spend any time with the guru, he hears the devastating news that the great teacher has passed away.

Jason doesn't give up his search for happiness; he buys a book of the guru's teachings and settles down every evening to study and try to memorise the words of wisdom. He feels certain that if he can just apply his mind and understand the teachings, it will deliver the peace he craves.

During the day, when Jason is working at his job in a pet shop, he recites what he's learnt the previous night. As he sweeps the floor and feeds the rodents, snakes and birds, he repeats his guru's teachings over and over again and tries to understand them.

*

One day the bell on the door rings and a lady shuffles into the pet shop. Her face is pale, her shoulders slump; she has a look of sadness in her eyes. In a slow, low voice the lady explains to Jason that she's lonely and she's looking for a pet to keep her company.

'What you need is a parrot,' says Jason. 'Parrots are excellent company. I have a beautiful red one here; the woman I bought him from said he was very clever; she called him Chit-Chat because every evening, after the sun goes down, he starts talking. He'll definitely keep you company.'

The lady peers into the cage; Chit-Chat looks back at her and squawks: 'Hell-oo.' The lady is so charmed that she decides to buy the red parrot on the spot. 'Come on Chit-Chat,' she says, 'You're coming home with me.'

*

A couple of weeks later, Jason is sitting behind the counter studying his guru's book when the bell on the door rings and the lady strides into the shop. Jason is struck by how different she looks: She stands upright, her face is bright and smiling.

'I'd like some bird seed for Chit-Chat,' she says in a strong voice. 'The very best that you've got.'

'Certainly,' says Jason, placing a pack of his finest birdseed onto the counter. 'I hope you don't mind me asking, but... What happened to you? You look so different!'

'It's Chit-Chat,' says the lady, hardly able to contain her joy. 'That parrot has changed my life.'

Jason smiles as he takes the money: 'I told you he'd keep you company,' he says.

'He's more than just good company,' the lady replies. 'Chit-Chat is so wise – he's like a little guru. Every evening he starts giving these lectures; he teaches me all these wonderful things. All I did was listen, and something changed in me – I found the peace and happiness that I've always looked for.'

34

WHO WANTS TO SAVE THE PLANET?

What is compassion?

'Yesterday I was clever, so I wanted to change the world.
Today I am wise, so I am changing myself.'
– Rumi

Matthew: What would you say to someone who suggests that this Enquiry is all just self-indulgence? What I mean is, rather than 'selfishly' focussing inwards on yourself, you could be out in the world doing useful work. If this is about Love, why aren't you doing something practical to help others?

Jez: It's a good question. From the world's point of view this Enquiry can look like a totally selfish pursuit because in order to Wake Up there's necessarily a turning inwards, away from the world. To See *beyond* Personality, not just in Openings and Awakenings but permanently, you have to be able to See Personality – to become aware of its form, its beliefs and its functioning.

Personality patterns are easy to observe in others; earlier you mentioned that you became aware of your friend's habit of complaining and passing on his negativity to those around him. However, it would be hard for him to See this about himself because his Personality has a vested interest in *not* Seeing it. Patterns like that serve the Personality by keeping it safe. They are ways of dealing with Suffering: with stress, pain and difficult Emotions. If you take them away, those Emotions will have to be felt. The Personality doesn't want that to happen; its job is to keep everything intact, to keep operating as this Contracted idea of who you are. And part of that is maintaining its structure, keeping it safe from Emotions that could threaten its stability.

So Personality has a vested interest in maintaining those patterns. If they're pointed out, Personality Awareness will reject that information in order to protect its structure and keep it intact.

Matthew: But I don't have that vested interest; that's why I could see the pattern in my friend clearly...

Jez: Yes. It's easier to have this objective viewpoint about others because we don't have as much bias or inclination *not* to see what's going on. But to Wake Up, this objective viewpoint has to be applied, not just out there in the world, but also to our own Personalities. The attention has to turn inwards so that Personality is Seen. It's this turning inwards which, on the whole, the world sees as self-indulgent.

Matthew: Why do you think that is?

Jez: Because the world doesn't want anything to do with this. When we say 'the world', we're speaking figuratively to mean 'most people'. Another way to put this would be to say: 'The Tribe – or Group Personality – of mankind'. We've talked about Group Personality in many different forms – political parties, genders, nationalities – but here I'm using the term in its meta form to apply to mankind as a whole.

Matthew: So why use the term 'Group Personality of mankind' rather than just 'mankind' or 'the world'?

Jez: Because it points to the specific orientation of that mass of people. In other words, most people live identified as Personality, with all the outcomes that involves. One of those outcomes is Personality Awareness, and this is what's behind this rejection of looking inwards.

All Personalities have the same goal of survival. One way in which Personality ensures its survival is to prevent itself being exposed. So naturally, the Group Personality of mankind will be against introspection, and one way to register that objection is to make the very act of self-enquiry unacceptable by labelling it 'selfish'.

Matthew: So the Group Personality of mankind sees it as self-indulgent; but you seem to be saying it's actually beneficial to the world.

Jez: Yes, I'm saying that if you want to 'help the world', self-enquiry is the best thing you can do. Ramana Maharshi put it like this:

> *Our own self-realisation is the greatest gift*
> *we can render the world.*

The majority of people don't turn their attention to the question: 'Who am I?' Has that strategy helped the world? Has it made mankind more peaceful? Look at any news report and the answer's obviously no: Nations are fighting nations, religious factions are fighting religion factions and neighbours are fighting neighbours. We're born with a default setting of Love, Joy and Stillness; this is our Natural State as babies. By contrast, the world as run by adults seems infected by a form of madness. We could call this 'the madness of Personality'.

There are many levels and forms of this madness: At one extreme we have dictators who impose their egomania, control and violence on millions of people who happen to be born into the same nation. (It doesn't stop there; any other nation that threatens the power and dominance of the dictator can become victims of that madness too.)

Then there's the Personality madness of the gurus who, in the name of Spiritual development, manipulate and control thousands of people who become their followers. As we've discussed, in some cases this control can develop into sexual or psychological abuse.

Finally we have Personalities in which the madness and its effect is on a much smaller scale, such as your friend who spreads his negativity by complaining to those in his social group. So the effect can be global or local, it can be powerful or mild, but the root of it all – the madness of Personality – is the same.

If someone Wakes Up, the very least you can say is they're not contributing to that madness out there. Waking Up is the best thing you can do for the world because there's one less Personality walking the planet inflicting its Emotions, Suffering and madness on others.

A Shift beyond Personality transforms the life of a person, but it also affects anyone who comes into that person's sphere of influence. The extent of the effect varies according to the person. For example, if Stalin had Woken Up there would have been enormous life-altering changes in the populations of whole nations. If your friend Woke Up, it would only affect the people he meets: Instead of spreading his stress and negative moods to them, he'd be sharing Stillness and presence.

So you have an effect on 'your world', on the people you come into contact with, just by Waking Up. This can be passive, in the sense that you're no longer spreading the stress or Emotion of your Personality, or it can be more active. If you're moved to share what you've found, you might become a teacher.

Matthew: If the Natural State is everyone's potential, doesn't someone who's found this have a responsibility to share it, to help others find it?

Jez: A responsibility to whom, or what? You're making the mistake of thinking of this like it's a religion with altruistic goals. There's no mission here to convert people, no belief system or goal   the planet'.

Matthew: But some teachers of Non-Duality do speak of having a divine purpose: to 'raise the consciousness of the planet' and help it evolve.

Jez: When teachers claim their teaching has some higher purpose of saving the planet, I'd suggest that has the distinct scent of Personality about it. Do you think the wave can change the ocean? Who's claiming to raise the consciousness and save the planet? It's often just the Spiritual Personality pumping itself up with a divine purpose to make it feel more important.

Matthew: It's odd because on the surface, it looks like these teachers are altruistic. I always thought, whether you buy into their teachings or not, at least they're giving something back. But what you're suggesting casts them in a very different light: You're basically saying that they're deluded!

Jez: They are deluded! Anyone who's not Awake is deluded because believing you're the Personality is a delusion. It's the biggest delusion of all and the Group Personality of mankind suffers from it, so it's a mass delusion! (Laughs.)

    Perhaps some of these teachers are well intentioned; maybe they think they're giving something back. But in this realisation the idea that you can save the planet becomes ridiculous. This Enquiry asks: 'Who is the one that feels the need to save the planet or believes that they can?'

Matthew: But some people do have a lasting, positive effect on the planet – people like Marie Curie or Nelson Mandela.

Jez: I'm not saying that some individuals aren't agents of positive change in the world; I'm saying that, if those individuals had been Awake, they would know that, in the end, they could not claim their great work as their own – they were simply living out the talents and qualities of their Characters. This goes back to our discussions on choice, purpose and Doing.

    By changing yourself – i.e. by realising you are not the Personality – you become wise to the fact that change can happen, ponsible for it. You're not even responsible for

r all this 'we have no choice' argument, but I can't
t that some people will never experience anything
d want everyone to have it?

Jez: ~~~~ eeling – it's born out of compassion for your fellow man. It's a very human, loving response in the Relative Level of human relationships. However, the Absolute Level raises a different perspective on this. It asks: 'What business is it of yours who does or doesn't experience this?'

Matthew: You've basically just applied to me what you applied to those teachers who want to save the planet.

Jez: Yes, because it's the same mistake being made: the belief that there is a doer who can choose to change other people's lives.

Matthew: But you've helped me. I'd go so far as to say that, in some ways, you've changed my life. Isn't that compassion? And, if it is, doesn't that contradict what you're saying?

Jez: No. You can be compassionate while knowing that there's no doer. True compassion comes when there's no Personality behind your actions.

The subject of compassion comes up a lot in Spiritual circles, and there's a lot of confusion about what it actually is. For example, in Buddhist teachings, a Bodhisattva is the personification of perfect compassion, a great being who aspires to help all sentient beings be free of Suffering before entering the bliss of Buddhahood. I'm all for compassion, but this legend – along with its enlightenment myth of the 'bliss of Buddhahood' – has no relation to the point of view beyond Personality.

Matthew: Why not?

Jez: We might feel to help those who, like you, have asked for guidance, but to try to help those who don't ask would be totally inappropriate. If someone doesn't have any interest in this, then what business is it of yours? What is it in someone that wants to change other people's lives and has the audacity to tell them what's good for them? That motivation can only come from Personality.

How others live their lives is nothing to do with us. All we have to do is be what we are and live the life we've been given. If that life includes a Yearning in your heart for a return to your original state of Being, then that's beautiful. If it doesn't, that's also beautiful, but in that case these discussions will be of no interest to you.

Matthew: I can't help feeling that you're talking about this from the Absolute Level, and when it comes to helping others, you're missing some human response from the Relative Level.

Jez: I feel compassion, so there is feeling, but at the same time I know I have no choice about what I or anyone else does. My response is being informed by the view beyond Personality.

Everyone has the opportunity to look at themselves, their Personality and their Suffering. If one has the Yearning, and this opportunity is used, it can lead to the Personality and its Suffering being transcended. If there's no questioning of who it is that's living, of who is Suffering, then a life is lived in which the Personality is identified with and believed to be who one is. When it comes to Spiritual life these are the two possibilities: You're either born with the Yearning to Wake Up, or you're not. How does that have anything to do with you? How other people are is up to life; it has nothing to do with you. If you try to change others beyond their will, you're simply acting out the madness of Personality because that's an act of violence.

This Enquiry is a sacred journey. No matter how much Love or compassion you have for others, you can't make the journey for them. The only way to Wake Up is through making this journey yourself.

Matthew: You talk about needing to make the journey oneself, and yet you're teaching: You're teaching me now.

Jez: Yes, teaching happens, compassion happens; I'm not talking against any of these things. As I said in our last talk, after Waking Up you might be moved to do anything: You might teach, you might carry out some grand charitable project. All that would be beautiful, but it wouldn't come from a need to prove anything. There'd be no claim to be saving the planet; it would come from pure altruism.

ıt this in our discussion on non-Doing. Charitable d out for all sorts of reasons, many of them ıe Personality. All of that is Doing. Non-Doing is rom Stillness; it has no ulterior motives behind it. ing shared. So the root of altruism is Love.

35

LIFE IS THE TEACHER

You can learn from any experience

'Search, no matter what situation you are in.
O thirsty one, search for water constantly.
Finally, the time will come when you will reach the spring.'
– Rumi

Matthew: What do you mean when you use the phrase: 'Life is the teacher?'

Jez: Life brings you experiences of many kinds. They may be painful, joyous, frightening, annoying – whatever their nature, you can basically have one of two responses: You can either learn from them or not. If you're willing to learn from your experiences, you come to realise that life is a teacher that never stops giving you the opportunity to learn. That opportunity may come in small, seemingly insignificant moments, like observing a bamboo bending in the wind. It could be in hurtful moments like being rejected by a loved one, or it may be through events that are really powerful, like an Opening or a breakdown.

Matthew: To say that you can learn from any event seems pretty obvious, so can you be more specific? What does it mean in relation to this Enquiry?

Jez: Everything experienced 'out there' in your life reflects back on the one 'in here', the one who's experiencing it. Life is a mirror in which you can see yourself. Of course this only works if Choice-less Awareness is doing the observing. If there's only Personality Awareness then, as the name indicates, Personality is in control and observation is selective. This means that awareness is turned off when any event threatens its security, such as when something emotionally painful occurs and we Contract. The senses are shut down and the potential lesson which the event contains is missed.

The same can happen in a less dramatic way when we're confronted with a view that's contrary to our own belief system. We shut down from even considering that viewpoint in order to keep our own beliefs intact. Life is no longer able to reach you with its lessons; the Personality is limiting what's experienced and so the potential lessons go unlearnt. In this way the Personality is not threatened; it stays safe within its own world, its own parameters. A good example of this is what happened when you tried to tell your parents about your Opening and they weren't interested; they missed out on learning something from your experience.

If there is some Choice-less Awareness, the possibility of learning opens up because awareness is not selective; it's not editing experience in the same way. Life becomes a playground of learning because all experience is allowed to reflect back on the experiencer.

The first level of what is Seen is the Personality and all its characteristics. As I've said, this happens whether the event is 'positive' or 'negative'. For example, let's say you get a promotion that you've been hoping to get for many months: You watch how it makes you feel more happy, more secure and perhaps even more powerful.

Now imagine a scenario in which a colleague gets the promotion that you so badly wanted: You feel sad, less powerful and more insecure. You feel angry at the boss who didn't choose to promote you and maybe some resentment for your colleague.

You can see how one event like this acts like a mirror reflecting back the whole world of Personality: its Emotions, desires, Contraction, hope etcetera. If there's Choice-less Awareness then, rather than just be in the middle of that storm of reaction, there'll be one part that's witnessing it happening, a part that's not caught up in it. Choice-less Awareness acts like an island from which the storm can be observed.

Matthew: But this isn't detachment you're talking about, is it? You are feeling those Emotions as well.

Jez: Yes, Choice-less Awareness isn't used to detach from feeling. In fact, if you Contract from feeling, how are you going to become aware of it, because you won't be experiencing it fully? Whatever happens, you're engaged with it, feeling it fully. If you remember, full-feeling engagement with life is part of Being – this includes feelings that are less enjoyable.

Matthew: But presumably you'd rather have enjoyable experiences?

Jez Of course. Having Choice-less Awareness doesn't preclude having preferences; it doesn't mean you wouldn't have liked to have won that promotion at work – that's all part of being human. Choice-less Awareness operates beyond that psychological level, which means that those preferences and responses will be observed just as Emotions or any other responses are observed.

When it comes to learning from life, your preferences are beside the point. In this Enquiry the point is not the nature of the experience, but whether you learn from it. Why is that? Because whatever happens reflects back the Personality, its structure, its history – and once you can See Personality clearly, you're naturally led to Seeing and experiencing what lies beyond it.

Matthew: You mean Stillness and Joy…

Jez: Yes. It's interesting that we've already mentioned the other two attributes of Being – Choice-less Awareness and full-feeling engagement with life – because these are what lead us back to the experience of Stillness and Joy.

Matthew: I can see that happening when things go well, but can you still experience Joy or Stillness when they don't?

Jez: This question leads us to an important point. These attributes of Stillness and Joy exist *before* experience. They're part of Being; that is, they're part of who you are before interaction with human life – before relationships, love affairs, promotions etcetera.

Think of a baby laying in a cot, staring at the ceiling. There's Joy from engagement with life: The bodymind system is breathing, looking, feeling the silence, energy is moving in and outside the body. There's Stillness; the mind's disengaged. This Stillness and Joy isn't caused by any particular event; it's simply part of the Original Relationship to Life.

When the baby's father enters the room, there's a different sort of engagement that comes through relationship. She hears the deep tones of her father's voice as he speaks to her, she feels the warmth of his arms as he cradles her. Through all these sensations she feels the Joy of interacting with life in the form of her father; but before this, she already felt Joy from interacting with life in the form of everything else that was in her experience.

Matthew: But what if the father doesn't come and the baby is hungry or neglected?

Jez: Then the baby may feel stress and this might be expressed in crying to gain the attention she needs.* So this all happens in her experience in the physical world. On the circumference she can feel stress, but at her centre, there's Stillness; that comes from Being.

Matthew: But that's not the case with adults, is it?

---

* Discussed in *The Story of 'You'* – page 67

Jez: Yes and no. The Stillness is always there, but most people have lost access to it. This happens after the Wound, which is the foundation on which the Personality is built. The baby in the original state of Being has access to that Stillness, because it has no Personality to block it. Identification with Personality is what lies between 'you' and that Stillness. That's why Seeing Personality is so vital to this Enquiry, because in Seeing it, identification with it is undermined. When that happens, access to Being – which is who you really are – begins to open up.

Matthew: Are you saying that, even in great pain, you can experience that Stillness at the centre?

Jez: Yes. You might even say 'especially in great pain', because when pain is acute it can focus and sharpen your awareness. The greatest psychological pain I've felt in my life was in the breakdown. I've never been one to have suicidal thoughts, but the psychological trauma was so horrendous that I had the thought: 'If this is going to be my experience of life I don't want to live.' But however bad it became, there was always some part of me observing the fact that: 'This is really bad', and that part was outside of the Suffering. So although my experience in the Relative Level was almost unbearable, on the Absolute Level – at the centre – there was a Still point observing that painful experience. This is a good example of how, if you have Readiness, any situation in life becomes your teacher. What I learned from that experience was that Consciousness is always bigger than the trauma.

I'm not saying that Choice-less Awareness gives you some free pass to avoid suffering – that can still be there, and it's felt. But like any experience, suffering comes with the invitation to become aware, to witness what is happening. In witnessing it, you are already aligning with the centre, rather than the circumference.

Matthew: The centre is Being?

Jez: Yes, in the form of Choice-less Awareness.

Matthew: Does this watching of Personality still happen after the Shift?

Jez: Yes, although it's different then. You've learnt the 'big lesson':

that you're not your Personality. That's what the Shift means: You've Woken Up out of the Dream of Personality. But Waking up isn't the end; it's a beginning: Life keeps unfolding, but it unfolds without the perspective which comes from identification with Personality. That means there's no projection into the future of a 'better' state of happiness. There's the realisation that whatever's happening is perfect, simply by the fact that it's happening. In Being, you just watch it. Lao Tzu put it like this:

> *Empty yourself of everything.*
> *Let the mind rest at peace.*
> *The ten thousand things rise and fall*
> *While the Self watches their return.*
> *They grow and flourish and then return to the source.*
> *Returning to the source is stillness,*
> *Which is the way of nature.*
> *The way of nature is unchanging.*

Matthew: So it's another one of those paradoxes where two different things are true at the same time: Stillness and change?

Jez: Exactly. You know that on the Absolute Level there's just Oneness but in the Relative Level there's evolution. Everything is watched; Choice-less Awareness is like a light that can't be turned off. Personality patterns, beliefs and Suffering can still arise, but they lose their intensity and focus: It falls into the background. As I said in our discussion on Healing, after the Shift, the relationship to it is different. Without identification with Personality, all of its drama is not Emotionally engaged with – it's simply observed just as everything is observed.

Matthew: OK, so life is the teacher, but what about human teachers? I'd like to talk about that.

Jez: One of the ways life can teach you is more directly in the form of a human teacher; this is what's happening now with you and me.

Matthew: Did you have a human teacher or a guru to help you find this?

Jez: My way of finding this has not been through one specific teacher, but I've learned from many teachers along the journey. If you're interested in a subject, that's what you do, isn't it? You go to people who profess to be experts on the subject to learn what they've found out about it. The teachers I've checked out, both Absolutist and devotional, have all given me valuable lessons.

Going to a teacher is a more direct form of learning; when you're learning from life in general, you yourself are extracting knowledge from your experiences. Also, the source of the learning is passive; events that come your way don't have any intention of teaching you anything, they're just incidents happening around you. It's your approach to them that extracts the lessons.

Yesterday I observed a neighbour's marmalade cat on our back terrace. It was lying on its back, legs in the air, gently twisting from side to side. This beautiful animal was in its own world, just enjoying its body, feeling the warm wooden decking on its back. This is one experience of the Joy of the Original Relationship to Life: The body wants to take in air, the muscles want to stretch; it feels good. I felt a kinship with this cat because it was reflecting back my own experience of the Joy of being in a body.

But the cat did something else which demonstrates the point I'm making about learning from life: When it spotted me watching her, I thought it would scamper away, but instead it got on its feet and calmly walked towards me. Then it just stared at me; there was no fear in those green eyes at all, just pure observation.

Matthew: Choice-less Awareness?

Jez: Yes, exactly. This is how your approach to life has to be: Even if there is fear, the awareness and intent to find out what is going on has to be bigger than that fear. That beautiful shaggy cat reflected that back to me.

Matthew: It became your teacher.

Jez: Yes, but only because I was willing and open to receive that lesson – that interpretation came from my side. The cat was just hanging out, doing its thing; it doesn't care about my insights. So this is what I mean when I say when life is your teacher, the source of the lesson is passive; it's our approach to it that extracts the lesson.

When you learn from a human teacher, it's an active relationship from their side; I mean there's an intent from them that you learn something. To facilitate this, the lesson is formulated so as to make it useful to the student. For example, I'm laying out this lesson in a form that hopefully makes it digestible to you, so that you can absorb it. It's like a mother bird giving its baby pre-digested food. There's a stage where this is necessary: The teacher presents the concepts and, eventually, this gets the student to a place where they can experience life beyond Personality themselves. This can be a thrilling, energising process which opens up the student, but there are potential drawbacks to it.

Matthew: You mean, as we've talked about, the teacher might be untrustworthy and abusive?

Jez: Yes, but let's suppose that the teacher isn't abusive. If the teaching is pure, even then there are potential problems from the student's side. We touched on this when we talked about devotional teachings: The student can hide in the shadow of a teacher and stagnate. Rather than helping, the teacher then becomes a block to the student finding their own path to this. You must have heard the Zen phrase: 'If you meet Buddha on the path, kill him.' It means: Don't let anyone get in the way of your own finding of this, not even the Buddha himself.

However much the teacher knows, they can't just magically give it to the student. You have to live your own life and gain your own Understanding of that knowledge. Anyone who's Woken Up knows this is the way it works: The mother bird knows that she can't go on feeding her baby forever – in the end the baby has to learn how to go out into the world to find its own food. That's the mother's job: to help the bird leave the nest so they can feed directly from life. Nietzsche put it like this:

> *No one can construct for you the bridge*
> *Upon which precisely you must cross the stream of life,*
> *No one but you yourself alone.*

Matthew: I presume this problem, of hiding in the shadow of a teacher, wouldn't occur with a teacher who had Shifted?

Jez: It could, but it wouldn't come from the teacher's side of the relationship. A teacher who has Shifted knows that they're just a link, a tiny part of the whole. They know that whatever they teach a student is just nudging them in the direction of them having a direct experience of it from life. This is why they know that one day, the student has to leave.

Spiritual Personalities who become teachers often take themselves and their role very seriously; they think they possess the truth and they're the only true source of it. If a student decides to leave their community they meet with resistance. Why? Because their leaving suggests that there must be something lacking in the teachings. Their leaving works against the whole image of the teacher; it's a challenge to their power, their omniscience.

Matthew: I've heard many stories of how some gurus make it very difficult for disciples to leave the community.

Jez: As we know, Personalities are very tricky; they'll twist things around to protect their own dominance and sense of control. They'll make the person who wants to leave wrong; they'll say that they're not Ready, not Spiritual enough or that they're weak.

Led by the guru's example, the Group Personality of the cult rises up against anyone who wants to break free. It tries to pressurise them not to leave by shaming and ridiculing them in all sorts of ways. You see, one person leaving is a threat to the security of everyone who stays. It raises the question: 'What if that person's right and the guru *is* a fake? I've given up so much to be here, I've invested so much in this, what if I'm wasting my time and the whole thing's been a huge mistake?' That possibility is often too much to bear, so Personality Awareness looks the other way and everyone agrees to make the leaver the one who's wrong.

This is a huge pressure for the person who wants to leave: It's a test of their strength, of their Yearning to be free. Are they willing to go through this ordeal to find the truth for themselves? You see what I mean when I say that the most difficult situations are often the ones that give you the biggest lessons?

Matthew: It's a common situation; there are quite a few websites and books exposing abuse in cults, written by people who've left them.

Jez: Yes. So the Group Personality of the cult becomes threatened, defensive and even violent; it tries to discredit the authors and their message. I've even heard of cases where people have been physically attacked. What does all this have to do with Waking Up? Nothing at all; it's simply the theatre of Personality. If you ever see any of this behaviour in a cult, you know there's a Spiritual Personality at the centre of it.

A teacher who has Shifted has nothing to protect because they know they don't own anything. The teaching is not theirs – what's shared is shared in absolute freedom. When the time comes for the student to move on, the teacher will recognise that 'the bird' is leaving 'the nest' and that this is a beautiful thing; this is the Tao. Who comes and who goes has nothing to do with the teacher.

Matthew: It must be preferable to have a teacher who's Shifted, who won't be playing out that Personality drama?

Jez: It all depends on the lessons you need to learn. Perhaps you need to have a personal experience of an abusive or controlling guru to get a sharp lesson in what a Spiritual Personality is. If you've invested a lot in the guru and have then been disabused of that trust, the experience will be strong and that may be the best way for you to receive that lesson.

As I say, you can learn from anything – even abusive gurus – because by defining what this Understanding isn't, they help define what it *is*. A lot depends on what you specifically need to learn and where the best place is for you to learn it. Life has a way of giving you what you need; if you're willing to learn, any situation can teach you.

Having said that, once you're further along the path, yes, a Shifted teacher will be a whole different learning experience. Why? Because you'll be able to trust them. Things still may be difficult or painful depending on what you're holding on to – where your Personality's resistance is – but at least you'll know the teacher is leading you in the right direction. That trust is invaluable, because the more you trust, the more you'll be able to let go. Then you'll be able to start experiencing for yourself what the teacher is speaking about.

36

THE INFINITE JOURNEY

Before and after Seeking

'You are not a drop in the ocean.
You are the entire ocean in a drop.'
– Rumi

Matthew: When I asked you what I could do to discover life beyond Personality* you advised me to ask myself the question 'Who am I?' Now I'm asking you: Who is Jez?

Jez: Someone put this question to me recently, but they phrased it differently. Instead of asking 'Who is Jez?' they asked: 'Where is Jez?', meaning in what aspect, in what part of what appears to be 'me', is Jez found? It amounts to the same question.

 The first answer that came into my head was: 'There is no Jez'. This sounds a little glib on its own; I'm going to have to give it some context, which will mean picking up on many of the themes we've covered.

Matthew: As we come to the end of these discussions, an overview of the whole Enquiry seems like a good way to wrap things up.

Jez: I think you're right. The way I see it, Consciousness – or we could use the words 'Love' or 'Being' – appears in the form of human beings. This manifests in each individual as their unique Character. As young children, this Character becomes the nucleus of our sense of self and this self, this 'I' is what we become identified with.

Matthew: Just to be clear, you're not saying there's anything 'wrong' in that?

Jez: (Laughs.) Of course not; that would be like saying there's something wrong in the fact that we grow arms or that we have ears. The sense of self is vital; without it we wouldn't be able to function in the world.

Matthew: But then the Wound happens...

Jez: Yes. As we grow up, at some point, the self experiences separation from Love. In response to this, over time, it becomes overlaid with Emotions, beliefs, desires etcetera. Then our sense of who we are migrates from the self to what the self becomes: the Personality.

 This identification with Personality is just something that happens in the Relative Level so, once again, there's nothing 'wrong' with that. But there are major consequences to that identification, which arise in the life of the person. These can be summarised by

* *The Story of 'You'* – Chapter 39

the statement that our connection to the Nat~~~ previously enjoyed, is lost.

Matthew: And then the Suffering comes in...

Jez: Yes. But it's possible to discover that being identifie~~ Personality isn't the only way for a human being to exist. In~ experience beyond Personality – such as an Opening or Awakeni~~ – it's realised that you are not the Personality. Not just that, but the sense of self, the essence on which the Personality is built, is also an illusion. When we were born we didn't have any sense of being a 'me' or an 'I'; it's just a practical device that develops as we grow, to enable us to function in the world. That sense of self is the embodiment of the appearance of being separate. When the identification with it falls away, it's realised that, on the Absolute Level, there is no 'me' or 'I'.

*Matthew: But there is **something** there.*

Jez: Yes. There's a life arising, and there's a witness to that life. Something *is* aware of the appearance of an apparent separate being, of an 'I'. After the Shift, something is *also* aware of the fact that, beyond that construct, there is no one.

Matthew: I presume you'd call that something 'Consciousness'?

Jez: Yes. Consciousness appears in physical form as human beings, and part of that appearance is the awareness that human beings have.

Matthew: So Consciousness, through the appearance of an individual, realises that... there is no individual?

Jez: I couldn't have put it better myself.

Matthew: It's mind-boggling, isn't it?

Jez: Yes. It's the play of life, the Great Mystery.

Matthew: So, your answer to my original question – 'Who is living the Great Mystery?' – is Consciousness?

Jez: Yes. After the realisation that, on the Absolute Level, there is

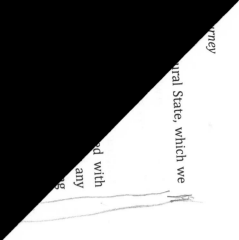

hat remains – i.e. Consciousness /
ou' are. That's why you hear gurus
am Consciousness' or 'I am that.'

cation isn't it?

ot with Personality, but with the
v of Personality arises.

away from identification.

ns are built; we operate in the
we have awareness and consciousness which can
say 'I am this.' So as long as you're alive, there's always going to be
this sense of being something, even if that something is just the
awareness that observes and is able to say: 'I am Consciousness.'

After the Shift, there's no denial of the arising of the personal
self, but there is the ongoing perception that it's just an appearance
in the Relative Level. This means that there's no longer any
identification with it, which in turn means that there's no buying
into the idea that we have any personal volition. From the Relative
perspective, it looks like I am coming up with these words; they
are the product of this brain in this head. But, if that very sense of
'me' and 'my' brain is a construct, then who's coming up with these
words? It all belongs to life.

So when you ask: 'Who is Jez?' My answer – of course it's not
really *my* answer – is that there *is* no Jez, but there is the appearance of
him, and that appearance of him would say that he is Consciousness.

*Matthew: When you say, 'I am Consciousness,' I can see, from everything
we've discussed about the Absolute Level, that it's a logical statement.
But to lots of people, it could sound extremely egotistical.*

Jez: Could it?

*Matthew: Some people's word for Consciousness is 'God', so you could
be accused of claiming to be God!*

Jez: (Laughs.) The statement 'I am Consciousness' only becomes
controversial or egotistical when the Personality gets involved
and starts overlaying it with an idea of specialness or superiority –

which totally contradicts the original meaning.

Matthew: I'm reminded of a friend of mine who had some kind of a manic breakdown and, for a while, took on the belief that he was God.

Jez: 'God' is a word I don't really relate to, but if you believe in some higher creator figure, then to say you are 'the Creator' is surely the most egotistical claim any Personality could make. Many Personalities have a bit of superiority or arrogance about them, but to think that you're God is really taking it to the limit. If you're going to be egotistical, you might as well do it properly!

(They Laugh.)

Matthew: The amazing thing is, this sort of delusion isn't that rare – when I visited my friend in hospital a nurse told me there were at least two other people on the ward who believed they were Jesus.

Jez: That's going to be an interesting group therapy session! This kind of delusion doesn't just happen in mental hospitals; there are many Spiritual Personalities, gurus and teachers, who believe they are the saviour, the Christ or God himself! Even Spiritual Understanding can be taken by the Personality and used as raw material to spin such stories.

Matthew: You're talking about Spiritual Personalities?

Jez: Yes. When there's Readiness, the realisation 'I am Consciousness' can be the final blow to identification with Personality. However, without Readiness, the Personality can fight this threat to its sovereignty by using it to make the identification stronger. Taking on the belief that you are God is a good way to do that. The Personality will use anything to avoid confrontation with its own dissolution. It's all just the madness, the theatre of Personality. Isn't the play of life amazing?

Matthew: It is, but this subject – 'Who am I?' – is also quite confusing and complicated.

Jez: It sounds complicated when you try to put it into words, because the question 'Who am I?' points in the direction of the Absolute. Of course, when you asked me that question, I could have answered it much more superficially. I could have given you my Story: my place of birth, my upbringing, details of my professional life etcetera. That answer wouldn't have been complicated, it would've been logical, and language would have easily been able to convey the facts of it to you. Even if I'd gone a bit deeper and delved into the area of my psychology, there'd wouldn't be much of a problem in communicating it all to you. This is because my Story – what I did, where I did it, who I did it with and what I felt – arises in the Relative Level.

But you weren't asking about my Story. When you asked: 'Who is Jez?' you meant 'Who are *you*?' on an existential level. So I had to talk about 'Jez' in relation to the Absolute. As we keep coming back to, this is when language starts to become inadequate. It's difficult for the Relative to reflect back on the Absolute, for the 'something' to describe the 'everything'. It's like two people speaking different languages trying to communicate with each other.

Matthew: But ultimately, they're really the same language, the same thing...

Jez: Yes, you can say the Relative arises in the Absolute – but ultimately, they're the same thing. In the end there's only Oneness.

Matthew: I always think of the wave analogy when we come to this point; it helps me grasp it.

Jez: It's a really useful analogy: The wave thinks it's separate, but really it's just one tiny part of the ocean.

*Matthew: But you're saying that it's possible for the wave to see beyond its particular form and come to realise **consciously** that it's just a part of the greater ocean?*

Jez: Yes. Having lost that perception of Oneness in childhood, one can go on this Infinite Journey and discover it again. But, describing this perception with language is almost impossible; it's like trying to paint an image of a rainbow using only black paint. You can suggest the overall curved shape, but without colour, the painting will always be fundamentally inaccurate.

So, as we've talked about, teachers use concepts, stories and analogies to point in the direction of the Absolute viewpoint. That's the best that language can do, and it serves a vital purpose for the Seeker, because it allows you to engage with this Enquiry.

I engaged with the teaching concepts and asked the question: 'Who is Jez?' for most of my adult life. It started after those Openings I had as a teenager and ended after the Shift over four decades later. I observed this Personality called Jez; I became familiar with its particular shape and form, its Emotional history, patterns, Suffering and Distractions. The asking of all those questions is, in most cases, a necessary stage to finding this. That's why I call it 'the Enquiry'. The Enquiry takes us on an infinite journey; it's infinite because it never ends.

Matthew: Even after the Shift?

Jez: The Shift is definitely a huge turning point. It's the end of identification with Personality, but it's not the end of the infinite journey. You could say it's when the journey really gets going! After the Shift immersion in the Great Mystery is even greater, because there's no Personality, no beliefs, no Contraction or Distraction to keep it at bay. So the journey into the Great Mystery, and the experiencing of it, never ends because the Mystery itself is limitless.

Matthew: But you're saying that, before the Shift, there's Seeking and after... there is an end to that.

Jez: Yes, Seeking ends at the turning point of the Shift. The infinite journey – which continues afterwards – is not fuelled by Seeking. There's nothing being sought, there's only immersion in the journey.

Matthew: But before the Shift, there's a whole journey towards that turning point...

Jez: Yes. We start our lives as babies in the Natural State. We are One but we don't know this consciously because we haven't yet developed a mind. We don't need to know it; like animals, we just live it.

Then our minds develop and we identify as a self which eventually becomes the Personality... That's when all the Suffering begins. The Suffering is a symptom of the fact that we've lost the

Natural State; it's a by-product of identifying as this separate self. When you take away all the details, this is the Story of every life: We're born in 'It', we lose It, we suffer.

But some people have the inborn Yearning to return to It. If they follow that Yearning, they start asking: 'Who am I?' and eventually the identification with Personality is broken, and with it goes its Suffering.

Matthew: I can't help asking why? Why do we lose it? And why do some people have the impulse to return to it?

Jez: That's impossible to answer; this is a mystery that can't be solved. It's like a hall of mirrors; the more you look into it, the more reflections you see.

You can understand the mechanics of *how* Personality works because it operates in the Relative Level where logic applies. What's *beyond* Personality, the Absolute, is a different matter. After the Shift you stop trying to work it all out; you come to a point where the 'Why?' drops away and you're left with the 'is.' All we can do is live the Mystery, enjoy the show. This is why I love the phrase: 'This is it.' We're going to finish by talking about what that means.

37

THIS IS IT

The highest teaching

'I and this mystery, here we stand.'
– Walt Whitman

Jez: We're going to start by talking about death. I think it's fair to say that most people are scared of death; why do you think that is?

Matthew: This seems pretty obvious – because it's the end of our lives.

Jez: But what in particular bothers us about that? Is it because this body will no longer be functioning? Or because we're scared that death will be painful? Is it because we won't be around to see what happens in the future? Those reasons give part of the answer, but I'd say the main reason is this: We have this identity – this Personality – that we think is who we are, and when death ends the life of this body, it also ends the life of the Personality. So, if you're identified with Personality, this is the worst thing about death: It extinguishes our sense of identity, the sense of 'I' disappears.

This is the main reason most people don't want to talk about death, but when it comes to this Enquiry, excluding it in this way is missing an opportunity. Life is the teacher, but so is death. In fact, when it comes to the subject of life beyond Personality, death can give the strongest, most powerful and direct lessons.

How did you feel just now when I told you we were going to discuss this subject?

Matthew: To be honest, I wasn't overjoyed; I'd rather focus on something positive, like Waking Up...

Jez: There you go – your response says it all: Life is 'positive' and death is 'negative'. I suspect most people would agree with you. When you remember all the attributes of Personality we've discussed* it's totally logical that we hold this viewpoint. Personality's function is to create this identity and then protect it, keep it safe and intact. The subject of death continually points to the fact that the Personality is ephemeral, that it's not going to survive. This is the last thing it wants to face up to. Personality wants to maintain the illusion that it's invincible.

So when it comes to death, the Personality does everything it can to try to regain control. It does this by exercising Personality Awareness and 'looking the other way'. We all know logically that death is there, but as we go about our lives, Personality tries to maintain the illusion that it isn't. It does this by either ignoring it or compartmentalising it.

* *The Story of 'You'* – Chapters 19-27

Matthew: What do you mean by 'compartmentalising it'?

Jez: If we read in the paper about someone dying it's not such a direct threat – death is one step removed because it happened to someone we don't know. It's as if Personality has you believe that 'Other people can die, but I will never die.' I'm not saying we aren't aware of death, but Personality has this way of keeping it at a safe distance, of consigning ongoing awareness of it to the subconscious.

Matthew: I know what you mean, but that's not always possible – for example, when someone close to you dies.

Jez: That's a problem for the Personality because it's forced to confront death and the fact of its own eventual demise. But in many people, the Personality has a final trick up its sleeve: belief. It very cleverly tries to buy dominion over death through beliefs in reincarnation or the afterlife. 'You're not going to disappear,' it says: 'You're going to continue in a different body' – or, 'You're going to live forever in something called the afterlife.'

Matthew: You often talk about not having any beliefs, that they're obstacles to seeing life as it is. How does one's attitude to death differ in this Enquiry?

Jez: In the Group Personality of mankind, Personality is running the show – it's the operating system that's in charge of people's lives. When this Enquiry begins, that dominion starts to be challenged by the arising of Choice-less Awareness – which operates beyond belief. Choice-less Awareness allows life to be the teacher; it watches everything and learns from it – and that includes anything that seems to threaten the survival of Personality.

Matthew: Such as death.

Jez: Correct. But remember, to the Personality, death doesn't just come in the form of the physical demise of the body. Death of the Personality is threatened by anything that challenges its sovereignty, its position of power.

Matthew: So you're making a distinction between physical death and 'death' of the Personality?

Jez: Yes. By 'death of the Personality' I mean that it's no longer in command of your life; it's lost its power. This obviously happens in physical death but it can also happen before that. Any situation in which identification with Personality is undermined is an opportunity for that 'death' to be brought about.

For example, sleeping is a kind of threat because the Personality's control is partly relinquished. I say partly, because the Personality still operates as a character in our dreams, just as it does in the waking state; but there is a difference between those two. In the waking state the conscious mind is in control; in sleep it relinquishes that control and the subconscious takes over. This is dangerous because the subconscious is where Personality Awareness puts everything that threatens its illusion of control; such as ridicule, failure, physical threat, confusion, fear. This creates a specific kind of dream: the one in which our fears are played out and the character of 'I' that appears in them experiences stories involving danger, being lost, falling, losing loved ones etcetera.

So in the night, during sleep, the Personality is still there as a character in our dreams but it loses some of its control. When we wake in the morning, the threat contained in those dreams has gone and the conscious mind resumes control. What happens to those dreams, those calling cards from the subconscious which for a while still exist in the memory? Usually, Personality Awareness rejects them, which keeps them locked away in the subconscious. This is how Personality regains control of the threat that those dreams pose. Once the conscious mind takes over, it gets on with living the day; before long you can't even remember what those dreams were.

Matthew: But when those sorts of fear-based dreams are very strong they can really affect you and stay with you for a while after you've woken up.

Jez: Yes, some dreams are more powerful, but even then, their power in the conscious state is not that strong. You've probably had thousands of such dreams in your life, but do you remember any of them now?

Matthew: I can't right now, no.

Jez: I rest my case. Some people have recurring dreams of a threatening nature; this means that something in the subconscious is screaming to be heard, to be recognised. But in general, once the

Personality assumes full control again in the waking state, it does a good job of packing dreams away so they don't bother us.

So sleep is not such a big threat to the Personality because it's only a temporary break in the waking state, where Personality is in full control. Aging, however, is a threat to the Personality that's harder to ignore. Everything living has a life cycle – a birth and a death; aging is a stark reminder of the death side of that equation and that our time on this planet is limited. The celebration of birthdays is often mixed with a kind of dread that we're one year older, one year closer to death.

So to the Personality, whose main goal is survival, physically aging is a big threat that must be dealt with. How? The same way it deals with any threat: by Personality Awareness, by looking the other way. This is why the Group Personality of mankind, at least in the West, has a cult of youth worship. If you look at films, magazines and online media you can see this celebration of youth everywhere.

Matthew: Do you think that's negative?

Jez: Not necessarily, youth has a lot going for it: health, energy, optimism... good skin. (Laughs.)

Matthew: So you could argue that it's a very positive thing, that it's just a celebration of life.

Jez: At a superficial glance, you could argue that; but if you take a closer look you'll see there's something missing, things are out of balance. We celebrate one pole of duality – youth – while turning away from the opposite pole – middle and old age. In effect, this culture is saying: 'We like the bud, but not the flower.'

When you think about it, this is an odd thing for society to do because old age brings experience, which can lead to wisdom – qualities that are in far shorter supply during youth. In some cultures, for example Native American, elders hold high positions of authority; they are respected because they have experience and wisdom with which to guide the tribe. In the Western Group Personality this doesn't generally happen: Old people don't have much power in society; they're not so valued and are often hidden away in care homes.

For most people, aging is viewed as a kind of enemy and any signs of it are eradicated as much as possible – hence the use of Botox and plastic surgery has become commonplace in our culture.

The third big threat to Personality's survival is mental breakdown. As I've said, apart from physical death, it's perhaps the most dangerous threat because the functioning of the identity breaks down, so the Personality loses its illusion of control. If this is watched, by Choice-less Awareness, then the whole edifice of the Personality can be exposed.

What usually happens is, through therapy and the administration of drugs, the person eventually returns to their normal functioning. Of course, there's nothing wrong with this. When the self can't function, it's a sickness – trying to regain that illusion of control is natural because we're made to live this life through the self, to function as the self. But as with all these threats to our idea of control, an opportunity to See Personality can be missed.

So, in summary, this is all about Seeing beyond Personality, therefore anything which leads in that direction is used; that includes the subject of death, which offers the most powerful opportunity to do that. This has nothing to do with having a morbid fixation. We're born with a will to live, to enjoy this life that we've been given; that Joy is part of the Original Relationship to Life. A fixation on death would be equally as screwed up as the fixation on life and youth that we see in our culture today. However, to ignore death, to turn away from it, is another matter – that's simply the activity of Personality.

In Choice-less Awareness everything is faced and seen. Once you know how death can teach you, how much it can accelerate this journey, you look *towards* it rather than away from it. Death is the most powerful teacher of the fact that what we think we are is transient; it's just an appearance.

Usually this lesson kicks in when someone is approaching death, because by then the tricks and illusions of Personality – the Distractions, hope and beliefs – start to lose their power. There comes a point near the end where the reality of death is so strong that it's unavoidable. This realisation of our own transience can affect different people in different ways; some fight, some become depressed. In others it can actually lead to the Personality losing its grip, and then Being can start to shine forth a bit more.

I've had the opportunity to observe this phenomenon fairly recently: As you know, my father died during the period of our first talks in this series. Throughout the last year of his life I visited him every week and, to some extent, I watched this relaxing of the grip of Personality happening in him…

Matthew: How did it show?

Jez: Well, for example, my dad was always quite opinionated. If you had a different view to his – which I usually did – he wasn't shy of letting you know you were wrong and he was right! But I noticed in that last year he became more accepting; he didn't fight me so much.

Matthew: And you think this is because he knew he wasn't far from death?

Jez: Yes. When you're staring in the face of the Infinite, what do your little opinions matter? It's as if the Personality starts to wear thin and lose its density. There were other signs of Personality relaxing its grip; Dad had quite a restless mind which he usually kept occupied. He was always working on a crossword puzzle, reading one of his computer magazines or listening to the news; he liked to keep mentally busy.

Towards the end I noticed this changing – there was a lot more Stillness in him. Every time I visited my dad I'd take him for short walks to give him some exercise. In the last year he couldn't walk far, maybe two hundred yards was his limit. So there we were, him on my arm, walking almost in slow motion, hardly saying a word. He showed no frustration, didn't complain or express any bitterness for his condition. It became a walking meditation that we shared in Stillness – although, of course, he wouldn't have called it that.

After the walk I'd make some tea and we'd play chess – until, in the last few months, his dementia made this impossible. I was always amazed to see how, at critical moments in the game, my dad could become really excited in a way that was quite childlike. In those moments, time and old age disappeared and I could see exactly what he'd been like as a boy. As his Personality loosened its grip a little, his Character was revealed a bit more.

I'm not saying that my dad totally lost identification with his Personality. There were times – a cutting comment to me or one of my siblings, or some impatience with a nurse – when his Personality manifested as strongly as it had ever done during his life. But overall, those traits that had defined his Personality definitely relaxed a little.

So this is a phenomenon that can happen when death is approaching: Life is stripped back to its essentials, social niceties become less important. You don't pretend to feel things that you don't feel; you don't have time to see people you don't want to see. When your life is soon going to be taken away, investment in your identity and its past can lessen. Who cares what you did ten years ago, or last week? What relevance does that have now? Similarly, faced with extinction, the future and the hope we invest in become irrelevant. Why would you care about goals for the future when you're not going to be around to fulfil them?

This is a kind of revelation or Opening that can be prompted by being close to one's death, but the point is: Why wait?

Matthew: What do you mean?

Jez: If you have the Yearning and the Readiness, then this Opening can happen right now. 'Death is the teacher', but you don't have to wait until your physical death to learn its lessons. Why not learn them now? Then you have the rest of your life to reap their benefits – those lessons aren't any use to you when you've gone!

So you could say that, in this Enquiry, the subject of death is reframed: Rather than being seen as 'life negative' it's seen as 'Waking Up positive'.

Matthew: It sounds like you're prescribing a practice to help people Wake Up; isn't that just more Doing?

Jez: Good question. I'd say I'm describing what happened for me; what others do with it is up to them. What *you* do with it is up to you. Personality would never adopt this approach because it's threatening to its survival, but I'm talking to that one in you who wants to Wake Up, the one who wants to come home. If you have the Yearning, then what I'm saying might be spontaneously adopted because you're ready to hear it and use it. If so, there'll be no choice in it. It won't be Doing; it will be non-Doing.

Matthew: And if not?

Jez: Then Personality Awareness will reject this information and consign it to your subconscious. But even then, it's still in there. Maybe there'll come a time when your Yearning is strong enough and my description of this will become relevant and useful to you, and it will be brought into conscious awareness.

*Matthew: OK, let's say that there **is** Readiness. Practically speaking, how do you use these events that threaten the Personality?*

Jez: Simply by not looking away, not withdrawing from them. For example, instead of repressing and losing access to the subconscious that's expressing itself in your sleep, you can write down your dreams when you wake and listen to the messages they hold about your Personality. As I always say, the Personality has to be seen. This might not sound like much, but it's all about reversing the habit of looking away, it's about turning Personality Awareness into Choice-less Awareness.

Any event that threatens your Personality's belief in its invincibility is an opportunity to practice this. For example: if you suffer physically with an injury or illness; when you observe the unavoidable side-effects of aging in your body; when you suffer Emotionally with rejection, confusion, fear, resentment, jealousy or grief; or when you suffer mentally with depression, worry or even a breakdown. Each event presents an opportunity to watch and learn about Personality; that's why throughout my life, whatever happened, I wrote about it to draw out those lessons.

When I was with my father on his deathbed, I confronted that momentous situation head on. Rather than contract, my awareness became sharper. I watched him lying in a room which he knew would be the last four walls he ever saw. I watched him looking through an old photo album, remembering moments from his life with a smile. I saw this Love that expressed itself in the form of his life come to its end, like a wave falling back into the ocean. Being was there, and then it was gone. I felt the heartbreak, magic and the Great Mystery of it all.

Much later, I tipped out some of his ashes – the summation of a life – into my palm, then released them beneath a tree and watched a cloud of white dust drift off on the breeze. An 'apparent person' returned to Oneness.

Matthew: But what exactly is it that you learn? When your dad dies and his ashes return to the earth... What does that leave you with? What's left?

Jez: What's left is this moment, the awareness which observes it, and the feelings which feel it.

(Pause.)

Being confronted with death takes away the Personality's ability to escape this present, to hide in the future or the past. It brings the focus to this moment. When it comes down to it, whatever's arising in this moment is a Mystery – it can't be understood – but it can be experienced. It can be felt.

(Pause.)

One day, this moment might reveal to you that the Personality isn't real; and you will Wake Up from its Dream. Waking Up is dying before you die. You know the self isn't 'real', it's just an identity, picked up each morning and played out during the day. Where you fall asleep each night, the source that you dissolve into is who you really are. So it's a question of allegiance, of identification. Before Waking Up you identify with the Dream, after – you know yourself to be the source in which the Dream arises.

But what a Dream it is! From the Absolute perspective, there's no 'I', but in the Relative viewpoint there's the appearance of an 'I' that loves, that feels the pain of separation, that feels Joy and wonder. There is Consciousness... and where does all that happen? It all happens in this moment. This is why the phrase 'This is it' is the highest teaching. It's just three little words, but they contain the whole secret.

Matthew: I've heard other people say: 'This is it,' but I don't fully get why you say it's the highest Spiritual Teaching.

Jez: We can talk about life beyond Personality with concepts and I can try to describe it and point to it but actually, the whole Mystery of it all is being revealed and experienced in this present moment. Not indirectly, through mental constructs and thoughts, but directly, through the senses.

There are no theories or concepts needed to experience this. And there is no future in it. It's not a case of: 'One day I'll experience this.' You're experiencing it right now. This moment, whatever is happening, is the focal point of the Great Mystery for you. The Infinite Journey always leads right back to this moment. That's what 'This is it' means.

This Moment is the Focal Point of the Great Mystery

The ABSOLUTE LEVEL / ONENESS

CONSCIOUSNESS / EMPTINESS / UNMANIFESTED

Time — — — (**NOW** 'This is it') — — — → Cause and Effect

('I')

Appearance of
the separate self

The RELATIVE LEVEL / DUALITY

consciousness / Fullness / Manifestation

My sharing this Understanding, and your willingness to listen, has given us a wonderful connection; it's been a great pleasure.

Matthew: For me too. I feel enormously grateful that I found myself in the right place at the right time to receive this teaching from you.

(Pause.)

I also feel a bit dizzy! (Both laugh.)

Jez: This is it.

GLOSSARY

*Words in **Bold** refer to other Glossary entries*

ABSOLUTE LEVEL – *A level of reality where energy exists in an unmanifest form (as a potential to be something). This formless ground of everything manifests as the phenomenal world – the **Relative Level** – in which time, space and form appear. From the point of view of Non-Duality there's only the Absolute Level – the **Relative Level** simply arises within it – but from the human perspective there appears to be these two Levels of reality. (See* The Story of 'You' *Chapter 3)*

ADAPTATION – *The process by which, after **The Shift**, the bodymind system adjusts to living without being under the governance of **Personality**. (See Chapter 21)*

AWAKENING – *An instantaneous, temporary **Seeing** beyond **Personality**; a direct experience of the Absolute reality. (See Chapter 8)*

AWAKENING TEACHINGS – *Teachings whose energetic source is an **Awakening**. (See **Shift Teachings** and Chapters 28-32)*

BEING – *The essential nature and essence that we come into this world as (rather than the **Personalities** we become). It has four attributes: **Joy**, **Stillness**, **Choice-less Awareness** and full-feeling engagement with life. (See* The Story of 'You' *Chapter 5)*

CHARACTER – *The qualities that make you individual: your talents, quirks etcetera. All this is with you at birth; it is your nature. By contrast, your **Personality** is the product of nurture.*

CHOICE-LESS AWARENESS – *Perception that sees with absolute clarity because there's no **Personality** involved selecting what awareness falls on. We all start our life with **Choice-less Awareness**; it is one of the four attributes of **Being**. (See Chapter 3)*

CONSCIOUSNESS *(With a small 'c')* – *The state of being conscious, of having awareness of one's own existence, one's thoughts and sensations. (See Chapter 2)*

CONSCIOUSNESS *(With a capital 'C') – The universal intelligence behind all creation. In some Eastern religions they call it the 'Self' or 'Atman'. (See Chapter 2)*

CONTRACTION *– A spontaneous reflex action of self-protection; a pulling back from full-feeling engagement with the world which originally arises in childhood to protect us from painful feelings of the* **Wound.** *(See* The Story of 'You' *Chapter 15)*

DISTRACTION *– A strategy the* **Personality** *uses to prevent us engaging with unwanted feelings. By being occupied in activities that we like, that make us happy, we temporarily escape our unhappiness. Whereas the* **Contraction** *cuts us off from painful feelings, Distraction simply turns our attention away from them. (See* The Story of 'You' *Chapter 32)*

DOING *– Any action that arises from either the need to* **Distract** *oneself from feeling or to prove oneself worthy, loveable or acceptable. (See also* **Non-Doing***)*

DUALITY *– Refers to the* **Relative Level** *in which the formlessness of* **Oneness** *becomes form. In Duality there is the appearance of separation, relationship, cause and effect. (See* The Story of 'You' *Chapter 2)*

DREAM (OF PERSONALITY) *– The building blocks of* **Personality** *– desires, beliefs, hopes and* **Emotion** *– combine to produce the particular psychological reality you inhabit. This version of life seems real to the* **Personality***, and in a sense it is real because it is being experienced. But it is subjective – no one else is experiencing that version of life – so, in that sense, it is like a Dream. (See* The Story of 'You' *Chapter 23)*

EMOTION *– In their effort to be heard, over time, repressed feelings become exaggerated, distorted and incessant; they become Emotions. (See* The Story of 'You' *Chapter 17)*

ENQUIRY (THIS) *– The sincere investigation into the question of 'Who are You?' which can lead to* **Waking Up** *from the* **Dream of Personality***.*

GREAT MYSTERY (THE) – *Knowledge can take you so far, then you're left in the Great Mystery: the inexplicable wonder of life.*

GROUP PERSONALITY – *The tribe we're born into and its collective consciousness: an amalgamation of its constituent **Personalities**. There are many levels and factors influencing Group Personality, including: species, race/nationality, gender, geography, income, politics and religion. (See* The Story of 'You' *Chapter 7)*

HEALING – *After **The Shift**, the bodymind system cleanses itself of the **Residue** from years of being identified as **Personality**. Healing is the process by which the history of **Personality** is revealed, felt and eventually cleared from the bodymind system. (See Chapter 23)*

HEART CENTRE – *The centre of **Love** in a human being. While still in the **Natural State** we are located primarily in the Heart Centre.*

JOY – *The original feeling that arises simply from the enjoyment of living what you are. A natural outcome of **Being** interacting with life in all its different forms.*

KNOWING (THE) – *The instinctive **Understanding** which can become available after **The Shift**. It can apply to knowing how something works (e.g. a pattern, a belief, a **Personality**) or knowing what to do or say. (See Chapter 18)*

LOVE – *(With a capital 'L') refers to unconditional Love that is perceived beyond the perspective of **Personality**. What the poet Rumi is referring to when he says: 'Love is the bridge between you and everything.'*

LOVE – *(With a small 'l') The **Personality**'s version of **Love**, which is what it becomes once we have lost touch with its unconditional source. Based on need, often sentimentalised and romanticised, love is conditional – meaning it can be turned on or off. (See* The Story of 'You' *Chapter 30)*

MASK (THE) – *The false face that all **Personalities**, to a greater or lesser extent, wear to hide the parts of themselves they do not want others to see. 'Persona' is the Greek word for 'mask'. (See* The Story of 'You' *Chapter 26)*

NATURAL STATE – *The experience of **Oneness** in which we enter this world. An umbrella term encompassing the **Original Relationship to Life** and **Being**. (See* The Story of 'You' *Chapters 4 & 5*)

NON-DUALITY – *While **Duality** relates to the **Relative Level** of form and separation, Non-Duality points to its opposite: the non-separate, **Oneness** of the **Absolute Level**.*

ONENESS – *Before energy manifests as something, it starts out as undivided, potential energy. A more metaphysical word for describing that potential is 'Oneness.'* (See The Story of 'You' *Chapter 1; also **Non-Duality, Absolute Level**.)*

OPENING – *A short glimpse beyond **Personality**. (See Chapter 1 and also **Awakening**, a more powerful, longer-lasting experience of life beyond **Personality**)*

ORIGINAL RELATIONSHIP TO LIFE – *Before any human relationship, our primal connection is to life itself, which fulfils and sustains us. The Original Relationship to Life is one of surrender; we are all children and life is the mother. As the Chinese sage Lao Tzu puts it: 'I am nourished by the Great Mother.' (See* The Story of 'You' *Chapter 4*)

PERSONAL TRUTH – ***Personality** edits its experience and creates its own subjective Personal Truth from what it chooses to see. When you believe something, it becomes true for you: within your psychology, in your worldview.*

PERSONALITY – *The Personality is the construct of 'you'; an identity built on the building blocks of the **Contraction**, **Emotion**, beliefs, desires and hope. The Personality has a function of self-preservation; it is programmed to maintain its sense of absolute authority. In the Personality, the mind is king and all of its thoughts, beliefs and **Emotions** – which are mostly the product of your past – are in control of your life. (See* The Story of 'You' *Chapters 19-27*)

PERSONALITY AWARENESS – *Perception that is governed by the **Personality**. Unlike **Choice-less Awareness**, it can be turned on or off – i.e. it is personal. If we don't want to feel something, we can distance ourselves from our experience by cutting off from our feelings. If we* *don't want to see something, we can look away from it. (See* The Story of 'You' *Chapter 21)*

READINESS – *When the authority of* **Personality** *starts to break down and its* **Dream** *starts to be seen through. (See Chapter 6, also* **Yearning***)*

RELATIVE LEVEL – *The level of existence where the potential energy of* **Oneness** *manifests as physical matter. In this level of reality there is the appearance of separation, relationship, and cause and effect. (See* The Story of 'You' *Chapter 3, also* **Absolute Level***.)*

RESIDUE (THE) – *The history of the* **Personality** *is encoded into the bodymind system. After* **The Shift***, when identification with* **Personality** *falls away, the bodymind has to align and adapt itself to living without that* **Story***. Part of that* **Adaptation** *concerns the* **Residue** *of* **Personality** *– thought patterns, beliefs, addictions,* **Emotions** *– being purged from the system. (See Chapter 22)*

SEEING – *The act of perceiving life beyond the viewpoint of* **Personality***. (See* **Choice-less Awareness***)*

SEEKING – *Searching for* **Spiritual** *answers to the problem of* **Suffering** *and the quest for fulfilment. Usually involves adopting some form of* **Spiritual** *practice such as meditation, mindfulness, chanting, fasting etcetera.*

SELF – *Our original sense of separateness which allows us to operate in the world. This begins as a neutral, functioning centre but, as we grow up, it becomes burdened with* **Emotion** *and beliefs and turns into the* **Personality***. (See* The Story of 'You' *Chapter 10)*

SHADOW (THE) – *The hidden side of* **Personality***; the subconscious where we consign everything we do not want to confront. What is hidden behind* **The Mask***. (See* The Story of 'You' *Chapter 27)*

SHIFT (THE) – *The moment when identification with* **Personality** *is broken forever. (See Chapters 10 & 11)*

SHIFT TEACHINGS – *Teachings whose energetic source is* **The Shift***. (See Chapters 33-37)*

SPIRITUAL – *(With a capital 'S') Connected to something bigger than ourselves; beyond Personality.*

SPIRITUAL – *(With a small 's') Refers to that which is purporting to be Spiritual but in fact is Pseudo-Spiritual – originating from Personality.*

SPIRITUAL BREAKDOWN – *A breakdown offers an opportunity to* **See** *the functioning of* **Personality***. When that opportunity is used, the breakdown becomes* **Spiritual***, because in* **Seeing Personality** *one can* **See** *beyond it. (See Chapter 7)*

Spiritual Personality – *A* **Personality** *that has re-built itself around a* **Spiritual** *experience. (See Chapter 31)*

STILLNESS – *One of the four attributes of* **Being** *with which we come into this world. Not just a lack of action but also the absence of thought. (See Chapter 15)*

STORY – *The physical and* **Emotional** *history of the* **Personality***: the hurt of a betrayal, the feeling of achievement in passing an exam, the disappointments when our plans fall apart etcetera.*

SUFFERING – *Psychological pain or ill health which originates from the loss of our* **Natural State***. The* **Personality***'s illusion (of thinking that we are separate) manifests as neurosis, worry, emotional states, depression, addiction or lack of self-love. (See* The Story of 'You' *Chapter 28)*

UNDERSTANDINGS – *Spontaneous insights into how life works that originate from beyond the viewpoint of* **Personality***. With* **Choice-less Awareness** *we* **See** *life as it is; this can manifest as* **Understandings***.*

WAKING UP – *In* **The Shift***, identification with the* **Dream of Personality** *falls away, and the* **Dream** *it creates is awoken from. After Waking Up, life beyond* **Personality** *is revealed. (See Chapters 8-13)*

WORLD of SEPARATION – *The* **Relative Level** *as seen in the manifestation of form, people and events.*

WOUND (THE) – *Having lost our* **Natural State** *we begin needing* to receive **love** from other people (such as our parents). **The Wound** is the moment when we experience that, unlike **Love**, such personal **love** can be absent. At that moment we feel, for the first time, the existential pain of being in the world yet outside of **Love**'s embrace. *(See* The Story of 'You' *Chapter 13)*

YEARNING (THE) – *A innate desire to go deeper, to find the root of your **Suffering** and return to the **Natural State** in which we begin this life. (See Chapter 4)*

46, 47, 67 50, 54, 122

CPSIA information can be obtained
at www.ICGtesting.com
Printed in the USA
LVHW111121170720
660973LV00002B/335